In the Shadow of Trees

In the Shadow of Trees

The Collected Poetry of
Abbas Kiarostami

Translated by
Iman Tavassoly and Paul Cronin

Sticking Place Books
New York

Shiva Sheybany
Sohrab Mahdavi
Stacey Knecht
and
Michael Beard
are thanked by the translators

www.stickingplacebooks.com
www.lessonswithkiarostami.com
www.filmmakertrilogy.com

Design by Ryan Bojanovic

ISBN 978-1-942782-43-8

The journey took me to distant lands,
and I remember that in the shadow
    of those great green trees
these words entered my mind:
Be limitless and solitary,
    humble and strong.

Sohrab Sepehri

عباس کیارستمی

1940 – 2016

Those with hearts awakened by love never die.
Our existence is recorded in the book of life.

Hafez

هرگز نمیرد آنکه دلش زنده شد به عشق
ثبت است بر جریده عالم دوام ما

Between 2006 and 2011, Iranian film director Abbas Kiarostami released his selections from and adaptations of four masters of Persian poetry: Nima (1895–1960), Hafez, Saadi and Rumi (all from the thirteenth and fourteenth centuries). In 2015, shortly before his death, Kiarostami published two further volumes, the thematic anthology *Night*, his selections from a variety of classical and contemporary poets. These books are in addition to his three volumes of original verse: *A Wolf on Watch* (2005), *With the Wind* (2006) and *Wind and Leaf* (2011). *In the Shadow of Trees* brings together English translations of all these books.

Kiarostami's project has been a contentious one, and in plucking fragments of poetry from longer works – an endeavour no less personal than the composition of original verse – he incurred the ire of critics in Iran. Some, whose lifelong pursuit has been the examination of the poets whose work Kiarostami presents in his volumes, regard him as something of a dilettante, an interloper who lacks the skills required to handle such precious material. In Iran, after all, poetry is treated with absolute seriousness, its authors regarded as the unveilers of vital secrets, endowed with powerful sensibilities, in effect keepers and revealers of the Persian soul. Certain books of verse are even treated as if they were holy texts, and it would not be unfair to suggest that the work of a handful of pivotal poets has profoundly influenced both the Persian language and, in turn, the daily lives of millions in modern Iran. With no professional training in Persian literature, Kiarostami, his critics claim, is unprepared for the task at hand, and some refuse to consider his work as legitimate poetry.

Still, along with criticism came praise. In publishing his straightforward selections for the general reader, it was noted that Kiarostami – whose work in any discipline attracts global attention – has opened up the world of Persian poetry to those largely unaware of this wondrous and vast body of work, especially readers beyond the borders of his homeland. "Some people, sitting at a dining table covered in fabulous food, don't know which dish to start with," says the meditative Kiarostami. These books are his way of navigating readers through that particular feast. Absorb and begin to understand these adaptations – "trailers," Kiarostami calls them – and we are, he believes, better equipped to tackle the originals in their fuller forms. There are many costly, ornate and ostentatious editions of poetry in Iran. But, says Kiarostami, such illuminated books exist "to be given as gifts, and rarely do they actually encourage reading." The opposite could be said of Kiarostami's versions: relatively inexpensive and unembellished, containing nothing but text. His self-professed and modest aim is to make an unequivocal and intimate connection between poem and reader, author and explorer.

So what precisely has Kiarostami done with the original texts? For his two *Night* volumes, he located lines of verse from an assortment of poets – venerable and present-day – each somehow relating to a single subject matter, and brought them together. ("It's worth noting," says Kiarostami, "that few of the poets write about what night actually is. Instead, the darkness and approaching dawn are used as reflections of feelings and inner conditions.") With all others, he has trimmed down poems by individual authors, pulled lines out of context and framed them piece by piece, at the same time retaining and thereby emphasising what he considers to be key concepts, characters and landscapes. Kiarostami has suggested that the unexpurgated originals are like crude oil, straight from the ground, in need of processing and refinement. By making his selections, deconstructing and breaking the metre of the original verse, cracking it open and removing the rhythm, Kiarostami has allowed specific ideas and themes to flow out in epigrammatic form. His reductionist method might be best understood by comparing a feature film, with its sweeping lines of narrative and interlocking characters, to a series of still photographs, each of which presents a single scene within a carefully constructed frame. It is as if Kiarostami has stood before a vast image, studied it carefully, isolated the elements he wants to accentuate, then affixed a frame over just one small part, so bringing to light something previously indistinct, almost unnoticeable, hitherto concealed.

Kiarostami's own poems are, more than anything, closest to Japanese Haiku, which is for the most part the form he has imposed upon his selections from the great masters. But in furnishing us with a mere three or four lines, Kiarostami – a practitioner of free verse, in both his adapted and original poetry – has striven to convey the essence, the fundamental meaning, of entire pages in the original. The result is a summary: poetry of minimalism. There is a startling compactness and simplicity to these books, with nothing extraneous, even if each page contains a discrete message and definite wisdom.

Kiarostami's process of creative condensation is uncomplicated and, to a large extent, intuitive. "In Paris one day I saw a book through a shop window," he explains. "On the cover was an enlargement of the corner of a Cezanne painting. It showed only an apple. The designer of the book cover hadn't negated the rest of the painting so much as magnified a piece of it, and by doing so asked the reader to explore this one piece of fruit. A poem is like wine, which should be enjoyed line by line, drop by drop. If you want to express love or hatred, or have been asked a question by someone, these books provide you with a great many potential responses. Younger readers will presumably appreciate their brevity, that they could be sent as graceful text messages. What's important is what the poet writes about. This is my priority, rather than how he tells it. I think more about effect than form. My duty is to transfer ideas to the audience. If this is best done in short bursts, if we are living in an age of concision, then so be it. It's important for me always to be experimenting, to re-think the kind of storytelling I involve myself with." Kiarostami explains little, instead pointing at what we should be looking at, proposing that we decipher things for ourselves. Almost every poem, however short, has more than one level of meaning and is therefore open to interpretation, although Kiarostami has suggested that the first message the reader arrives at is likely the one the poet, and Kiarostami himself, intended. At the same time, one could usefully consider Kiarostami's work on the poetry of others as aphorisms in disguise.

This is a body of work that for Kiarostami, who for decades had no intention of publishing his selections, was a long time coming. "When I took Rumi's book in hand," he explains, "I realised that I had already done much of the required work because for twenty years I have been obsessively highlighting and isolating certain poems." At a Tehran event marking the publication of his Rumi volumes, Kiarostami offered a forthright explanation for his poetry project. "I hope you forgive my foolish courage. My aim with these books was never to integrate myself into the world of literature. This endeavour I have undertaken – these selections, many of which are lesser-known verses – is not me meddling in your own work. I was consumed by literature and poetry long before I became a filmmaker."

As for Kiarostami's original verse, his poetry is equally the product of an investigative mind forever at work, and just as importantly a mode of expression that bypasses the industrial structures and technical logistics of filmmaking. For Kiarostami, poetry is a limitless world that allows a flexibility that the realm of cinema cannot offer. As he explains in his book *Lessons with Kiarostami*, which details his recognisably poetic approach to filmmaking:

My mind is like a laboratory or refinery, with ideas
as crude oil. It's as if there were a filter channelling
the assorted suggestions in different directions. An
image comes to mind and ends up imposing itself
so obsessively that I find no rest until something is
done with it, until it is somehow incorporated into
a project. This is where poetry proves itself to be so
convenient and useful for me. Some of the images
in my head are simple, like someone drinking wine
from a disposable cup, a box of wet matches in an
abandoned house, a broken stool sitting in my back
yard. But others are more complex, like a white
foal emerging and then disappearing into the fog, a
graveyard covered in snow that is melting on only
three headstones, a hundred soldiers going into their
barracks on a moonlit night, a grasshopper jumping
and sitting, flies circling a mule as it walks from one
village to the next, an autumn wind blowing leaves
into my house, a child with blackened hands sitting
surrounded by hundreds of fresh walnuts. How
much time would it take to commit those images to
film? How difficult would it be to find a subject for a
film into which those images could be incorporated?
This is why writing poetry is so rewarding. When
I work on a poem, my desire to create an image is
satisfied in only four lines. Taken together, the words
become the image. My poems are like films that don't
cost anything to produce. It's as if I have found a way
of producing something of worth every single day.
I used to take a couple of years between films, but
these days rarely an hour goes by when I feel I'm not
doing something useful.

Every one of his published volumes of verse – original
and adapted – represent deeply felt enthusiasms. As such,
consider them an essential component of Kiarostami's
oeuvre, one that includes films, photographs and

installations. Put any number of his poems alongside, for example, *The Wind Will Carry Us*, or his still images of snowy landscapes, or "Forest Without Leaves," his three-dimensional art project consisting of hollow tubes, standing floor to ceiling, covered by life-size photographs of bark, and they take on an ever greater significance. The associations between all four forms of expression, the similarities in visual motifs and concepts, the common elements, the unity between settings, characters and themes all become quickly apparent. Whether using a camera, paintbrush, pen or (at home, quietly away from public view) wood chisel, Kiarostami's innermost preoccupations reveal themselves. Whichever vehicle he uses, again and again the same images and ideas are transported into the mind of the audience.

Chapter divisions in Kiarostami's Hafez book are his own, based on the subjects of the poems. Classical Persian poetry is traditionally arranged in reference to the final letter of each line. Kiarostami's original Saadi book is presented, chapter by chapter, in this way, but our translation is not (we have discarded all chapter divisions, while keeping the poems in exactly the same order). Kiarostami himself dropped from his Rumi book the traditional arrangement based on each line's final letter. In all of Kiarostami's adaptations, his alignment of poetry on the page is very much his own (including the layout, with one poem per page). While Hafez writes in the symmetrical ghazal form, Kiarostami breaks down this structure based on his own preferences. Likewise, where Kiarostami might use three lines, we use only two. The original Persian editions of these poems contain a number of errors, so in bringing these volumes to press we aim to present the most accurate versions of Kiarostami's adapted poetry available. There is occasional overlap between Kiarostami's single-author books and *Night*, with a small number of poems appearing in both. The more idiosyncratic formatting of Kiarostami's books of selections/adaptations has been removed for this English-only edition. Readers interested in Kiarostami's placement of the original Farsi on the page are directed to the Sticking Place Books dual-language editions of all the books that follow.

As neither poets nor professional translators, we offer these fairly literal translations – something of a massive addendum to *Lessons with Kiarostami* – at the very least so they may unveil some of the mainsprings of Kiarostami's work as a master storyteller and creator of images, thereby offering insight into his work as a filmmaker.

Iman Tavassoly and Paul Cronin

Contents

A Wolf on Watch
Poems by Abbas Kiarostami

Red line on white of snow.
Injured prey,
limping.

Daybreak.
White foal
born
to black mare.

Wind will carry
cherry blossoms
into the whiteness of clouds.

Behind every tall wave,
three small waves.
Behind every three small waves,
one tall wave.

I escorted the moon
into the heart of a dark cloud.
I drank wine
and slept.

The moon turns pale
at dawn.
The star disappears
with the crowing of the rooster.

The aroma of the flower radiated
as darkness began to fall.

A bird,
unknown
even to other birds,
sings in the night.

A scarecrow with no coat.
Cold winter night.

Night.
Sea.
Winter.

First autumn moonlight
shining on the window
shook the glass.

I think about flowers.
Cold wind blows.
I stand up and close the window.

With autumn wind's first assault
a legion of leaves
took refuge in my room.

I dream
I am buried
under autumn leaves.
My body sprouts.

I lit
a cigar.
First day of autumn.

Two autumn leaves
have hidden themselves
in my shirtsleeves
on the clothesline.

With first autumn wind
a small leaf, unknown to me,
drifted into my room.

A whirl of dust
accompanies
a leaf
into Seventh Heaven.

Rainy day.
An umbrella,
destroyed by wind,
on the pavement.

I grasp my hat with two hands.
Early autumn.
Will the wind carry us?

Barefoot,
walking on hot sand
under the gaze of passersby.
I burn from head to toe.

A flowing stream
in a grassless desert
seeking
someone thirsty.

I took
three sparrow eggs
from a high mountain.
How hard
is the path back down.

I have sat
on a scale.
Weightless.
Such turmoil
all around.

My shadow accompanies me,
sometimes in front,
sometimes beside,
sometimes behind.
How wonderful
are cloudy days.

I come from the funeral.
Shoes pinch my feet.
I want to make love
to someone I do not know.

Today,
like yesterday,
a missed opportunity.
Cursing life
is all that remains.

In the desert of my loneliness
have grown
thousands of solitary trees.

Bitter taste of patience
on my tongue.
What sweetness
will remove it?

In your absence
I am with myself.
We converse
and reach agreement on everything
so very easily.

In your absence
sunshine is sunshine,
day, day
night, night.
Your presence is a moonlight mix.

In your absence
I have a conversation
with you,
and in your presence
with myself.

From my loneliness
I seek a bigger share
of you.

In your absence,
day and night
is exactly twenty-four hours.
In your presence,
sometimes less
sometimes more.

With you
I am in pain.
Alone with myself
I feel anxious.
How to be nobody?

Via express mail
I received a letter
filled with hate.

The intensity of love
makes me ill.

Hesitating,
I stand at the crossing.
The only path I know
is that of return.

I lost something
I had found.
I found something lost.

On each corner,
quietly,
quickly,
some passersby,
from one side to the other.

A broken bridge.
A traveller with unshakeable steps
en route.

I walk a dirt road
with difficulty
and no destination.

The hand of destiny
delivered to me some water
which didn't taste at all good.

Moonlight
on a dirt road
I do not want to travel.

Lantern light.
Long shadow of water bearer
on branches full of cherry blossoms.

Rice farmers
muttering about the beloved's fidelity.
Or is it backache?

After tasting a dusty cucumber from
        my neighbour's garden
I can imagine
what the fruits of Heaven are like.

My shirt
is a flag of freedom
on the clothesline,
light and liberated
from the bondage of the body.

The one I praise
I do not love.
The one I love
I do not praise.

A pity
I was not a good host
to the first snowflake
that rested upon my eyelid.

On rainy days
it does not rain
enough.

Where water
is wasted
it waters
weeds.

The quince tree
has blossomed
in an abandoned house.

White chrysanthemums
watch
the full moon.

An injured horse
without an owner.

White foal,
red to its knees,
skipping
in the poppy field.

Little by little
the old elm
disappears
into darkness of night.

White morning.
Black night.
Grey sadness
between.

Sunrise
on the white foal's carcass
in the golden eye of the old eagle.

Half-asleep and drowsy,
thinking of the meeting
next Monday morning.

A river, flowing.
A tree, fenced in.

How high,
how magnificent
soars the hawk
searching for a small carcass.

How easy was the path
once I crossed over into madness.

Aimlessly,
quietly,
an angry ox
crossed
a roaring river.

Sun
removed the carpet of dew
a moment after sunrise.

Indigo mountain
and white poplar
prevent sleep
at early dawn.

Where
is the piece of cloud
that can weaken
the cruelty of sunshine?

No one recognises
the glowworm
in the light of day.

How hard it is
in the middle of summer
to believe in snow.

A wolf
on watch.

One hundred dry springs.
One hundred thirsty sheep.
An old shepherd.

Only three drops of blood,
the work of three hundred mosquitoes
busying themselves one hot summer night.

How hard it is
to contemplate the full moon
all alone.

The owl hooted ceaselessly
from the middle of night
until daybreak.
The rooster never crowed.

A harmless mosquito
spends the night with me
until morning
inside the mosquito net of my room.

Of one thousand worms
only one shines light
into the heart of night.

Thousands of bats muttering
on the longest night of the year.

Flight
is the reward for a caterpillar
who weaves around itself
a wall of silk.

Who decided that
the green leaf of the mulberry
should be food for the silkworm?

The wounds of thousands of needles
on a silk cloth.

A lock covered in rust
guards
a rotten door
of a roofless building.

I envy
no one
when contemplating
wind
through the poplars.

Three knife wounds
on trunks of three poplars.
Souvenirs of three foreign soldiers.

Image of a cypress broken by wind
on blue waves.

The tornado
rolled
the shepherd's whistling kettle
across the hilltop.

Wild rue on the fire.
Air filled with smoke.
Mysterious anxiety
in a clay hut.

Spring rain
extinguished the fire
that the old shepherd had lit
with difficulty.

Smell of walnut.
Fragrance of jasmine.
Smell of rain on dust.

A girl awake,
head on hard pillow.
An imitation bracelet
amid hay bales.

A young girl
passes through the lettuce field.
Smell of fresh walnuts
in the air.

The ant
scales the tree trunk
with difficulty.
Where is it going?

A piece of wood
on the waves.
From which boat?
From which river?
Where is it going?

Desert.
Hundreds of big and small fish
dive into
the hot mirage.

Spring storms
swiftly extinguish
every candle
in the shrine.

Green
turns to yellow,
air
to cold,
my thoughts
to death.

One person seen
in group prayer,
out of step
with everyone else.

How easy things are
when we win,
how difficult
when we lose.

The union
eventually decides
not to recognise
the spider's efforts.

The last marathon runner
glances behind.

A fly
guilty of eating too many sweets
was killed.

A small pebble
flew down the mountainside
and ended up
directly atop the anthill.

Monday morning.
Wind carries
the schoolgirl's scarf
from the clothesline.

A small fly
is nauseous
from the smell of pesticide.
Can anyone help?

On a foggy day
a drowsy child
goes to school
in the village of Pilevar.

I have been scared
of the wind's caress
ever since my ordeal
in the storm.

For three days
it rains
ceaselessly.
My belief in the sun
is gone.

Foggy day.
Difficult
to see the billboard
advertising sunscreen.

The compass
makes several complete rotations.
Only
a half-circle on the page.

Smell of smoke.
Smell of wild rue.
Crying baby.
Clay house.

How
do I sleep comfortably
when time stops
not even for a second?

Toiling night and day.
Enough food
for only half a day.

Yellow violets,
violet violets,
both white,
under spring snow.

Snowy morning.
I go outside
without a coat,
with the enthusiasm of a child.

The dandelion
carried a message
for the one hundred and twenty-four thousand prophets.
"Nothing."

Rain fails
during a bombardment.
Moonless night.

The young bride
bids
the fisherman
a tearful farewell.
Stormy night.

Sky splits
in broken mirror.

How good
that everyone walks his own path.

A stranger
asks directions
from a newcomer,
also a stranger.

I am sorry for myself.
I am sorry for you.
And for those I do not know.

The result of my deviation
is dirt roads
for those who follow.

Common feeling.
Mistress and servant.
Census day.

Cut.
Thrown away.
A malodourous
flower.

The weary villager
has fallen asleep
in the shadow of a scarecrow.

Bitter orange blossoms
in flowing river
after the rain.

At home in my refrigerator
is never anything to drink
except in winter
ice-cold water.

Sweat dripping
from the scarecrow's forehead
awakens the weary villager.

I left my umbrella somewhere.
A long trip ahead.
Many grey clouds.

Sunrise.
Five-fifteen and
thirty seconds.

New Year's Day.
Sunrise
exactly like
the last day of last year.

A boat
with no sail.
A sea
with no wind.
A sky
with no moon.

How accustomed we are
to not seeing that one pigeon
among the group
of flying crows.

In the eyes of birds
west
is where the sun sets
and east
is where the sun rises.
Nothing more.

At the foot of a majestic mountain
"God is Great"
is written
in small stones.

Believe it or not
even a mirage
would quench my thirst.

My fingertip,
covered in ink,
is pressed onto paper.
I feel less humiliated
after seeing all those patterns
on my fingertip.

It is written:
"Please do not touch."
My fingertip is tempted.

I look at Venus
and the Milky Way.
Glory
to the eye
that sees
all this.

I point my finger
at the mountain.
Glory to the finger
I am looking at.

With my hands
I make a cup.
I drink water
from a small waterfall.
Such glory
in my hands
.

With eyes open
I plunge my face
into spring water.
Ten small pebbles.

Sky
is mine.
Earth
is mine.
How rich am I.

I listen
to the whisper of wind,
the roar of thunder,
the music of waves.

When I returned to my birthplace
my father's house
and mother's voice
were gone.

A heavily pregnant woman
accompanies
five children of different ages
from Lower Koker
to Upper Koker
where they will be educated.

When I returned to my birthplace
the river had become a creek
and no children
were swimming in it.

When I return to my birthplace
my childhood playground
is covered
in scrap metal and quicklime.

A pity that
when I return to my birthplace
no one says hello to me.

In my birthplace
my childhood barber
didn't recognise me
and carelessly
shaved my head.

In my birthplace
everyone was now impatient.
The queue
twisted and turned
as it moved forward.

I greeted her in vain.
Her response made clear
she did not
recognise me.

When I returned to my birthplace,
the quince tree
bore no fruit
and white mulberries
were being bought and sold.

The young baker
of my birthplace
is old now and bakes unleavened bread
for customers he does not know.

The big sycamore in my birthplace
seemed small to me.
Officer Heidari
didn't seem particularly frightening.

The man who sold alcohol in my birthplace
had an old junk shop
full
of empty wine bottles.

When I returned to my birthplace,
schoolchildren
were working and trading.
Teachers
were impoverished customers.

Representatives
of the wood industry
meet in a wooded park.

When I return to my birthplace
mulberry trees
are being cut down
by acquaintances.

Noon on a summer's day.
The smell of fresh-baked bread
wafts over from fields of wheat.

A millipede
follows her companion
through olive trees.

The saddle
fell from the horse
and the rider from the saddle.

I measure
the depth of the lagoon
by the croaking of frogs.

I lie down
on hard ground.
Cotton clouds.

I have fallen
from the horse onto my back.
Leg pain.
Back pain.
The pain of thousands of recommendations.

Full moon
in water.
Water
in bowl.
Thirsty while sleeping.

In the silence of night
the lullaby of termites
keeps me awake.

From ash
I make an idol,
then in a fire
burn it again.

Heaven and Hell
beside each other.
How far one is from the other.

Finally,
a summer afternoon
listening to the scarecrow.

White smoke
from
clay hut
in blue sky.

I saw
nothing in this village.
No smoke
rising from a clay house,
no clothes
on the clothesline.

Twilight.
The lamb
observes
the wolf.

New moon.
Old wine.
Recent friend.

Several steps ahead:
cherry pit.
On my tongue:
taste of cherry.
Behind:
cherry tree.

Believe it or not
I have suffered
loss from profit
and have profited
from loss.

I no longer feel
for my master.
I disconnected
from followers.
I tread
lightly.

A drunkard,
silent.
A cleric,
whining.

I feel free
to choose
suffering.

Thorn in the eye.
Thorn in the heart.
Thorn in the foot.
Spring on the way.

Spring day.
Summer day.
Autumn day.
Winter day.
Be my guest.

End of spring.
The red flower blooms.
Realms of maturity.

Half of me,
yours.
Half of me,
mine.

I wrote
three poems.
I read
thirty pages.
I offended
a friend.
Third day of the month.

What should not be said
came from my tongue.
My feet took me
where I should not go.

Dozens of keys
from years ago.
I haven't the courage to throw them away.
Anyway, no lock.

Believe it or not
I got drunk
on a drop of wine.

Believe it or not
I quenched my thirst
with a dewdrop.

I determine
my destiny
in the pages of my notebook
in a half-darkened room.

I wonder
how all these scattered memories
have come together
in my mind.
Believe it or not
I photographed a tree
and it blushed.

It has been a long time
since the moon showed itself.
Endless dark clouds.

Longest night of the year.
Early morning exhaustion
of the glowworm.

Believe it or not
sometimes I miss
being given a good slap.

Behind the dark cloud.
Moon,
on which side of the sky are you?

The glowworm
is impatient
during the longest day of summer.

One side of the window
facing me.
The other
facing a passerby.

The moon shines
upon the made-up face
of an elderly prostitute.

Will the full moon
shine behind
a dark cloud tonight?

Nuns
among violets
reminisce
about childhood.

My suffering
is diminished
at daybreak.
My enthusiasm
is diminished
at sunset.

Who understands
the pain of a blossom
when blooming?

A friend,
in the form of an enemy,
appears in a dream.
My day darkens.

I blacken
one hundred white pages
while explaining homework.

The snake
moves past its shed skin
with indifference.

A thirsty man
sleeping beside the creek.
A beggar
sleeping on buried treasure.

A beggar
awake beside the creek.
A thirsty man
awake near buried treasure.

The bee
stung the wound on my foot.
The bee is all I got.
The wound is all the bee got.

A headless doll
floating in a river
flowing down from the mountain
heading slowly
out to sea.

During the toads' nighttime banquet
how well will
the snakes do?

At the bottom of the well
a lonely man.
A lonely man
at the top of the well.
Between them a bucket.

A man hanging
from gallows
in the freshness of morning.

The scarlet cloud
darkens,
mourning the sun's departure.

A nostalgic song.
A foreign land.
Men at work.

Reluctantly
I enter a house
in which
no light is burning.

What meaning
does the seashore have
for someone afraid of waves?

Among
hundreds of seashells
I search for my shell-like button.

What day
is today?
What month?
What season?
What year?

My memory overflowing
with useless things.
I choose to learn
nothing new.
I recall things
with difficulty.

The attic of my house
is filled with useless things
which I enjoy.

I don't know
if I should
thank or complain about
the person who failed to teach me
to be indifferent to things.

With a worn-out rope
I go down into the well
for stagnant water.
Complete waste of time.

I intend to circumvent
a large hole
using a slow and steady strategy.

I will write
an endless story
of my grief.

I think about explaining something
that is inexplicable.
How boring
to hear about things
you already know.

I sell something
that cannot be bought.
I buy something
that cannot be sold.

Bags are packed.
I don't feel like going,
but there is no carpet here
to stretch out upon.

How ridiculous is he
who knows yet asks.

The bitterness of day
features nowhere
in my nightly dreams.

The means of assuming greatness are here.
Leaning against the clay wall.

The game that runs
from Monday to Sunday,
on which day of the week will it end?

Counting down
to the day of my death
began
at the moment of my birth.

I have forgotten
my grudges and loves.
I have forgiven
my enemies.
I choose
to make no new friends.

I am scared of heights.
I have fallen from a great height.
I am scared of fire.
I have been burnt many times.
I am scared of separation.
I have suffered a great deal.
I am not scared of death.
I have never died,
not even once.

A wind
not from the north
or south
or west
or east.
From Heaven.

An excursion
among countless barren trees
is sufficient.

Who can
guess
the taste of a cherry,
half yellow,
half red?

On my ID card
is a photo
testifying
to the flight of time.

Among countless barren trees
I count
the years wasted.

One of my beliefs
today
is that life is beautiful.

One of my beliefs
today
is that God exists.

I was concealing
my longing
among those who conceal.

The apple fell from the tree.
I thought
about the apple's gravity.

I guess
the depth of the mirage
from the intensity of thirst.

I guess
the durability of love
from the intensity of excitement.

"When do you return?" I asked.
"Never," said she.
My watch stopped.

Today,
like every day,
was lost for me.
Half spent thinking about yesterday,
half about tomorrow.

One of my beliefs
today
is that it is impossible
to separate me from my shadow.

In science class
a small nameless flower
was divided
into five parts,
each with a name.

I have a meeting
with a new companion
on a path never taken.

The sable
lay anxiously
on sable fur.
The hedgehog
lay calmly
on spines.

Beyond good and evil
is a sky
of blue.

The wild flowers
do not yet know
that this road
has for years
been abandoned.

Flight of rock doves
at daybreak.

In my life
accidents
have been more influential than decisions,
punishments
than encouragements,
enemies
than friends.

Daybreak.
The thief
feels pity
for the sleeping policeman.

Aroma from
odourless flowers.
Joys of youth.

Searching for a word
my mind offered no help.
I went the wrong way
and became lost.

Eventually
what remained
was me and myself.
Myself offended me.
No one came to make peace.

On a dirt road
I saw a blind man
with no one to lead him
and without a walking stick.

Life
is an unjust smear
against the downtrodden.

My days
remain unfinished.
Weeks and months.
At autumn's end
I review the spring.

Grey men,
end to end,
restless,
at the memorial.

Grey men,
end to end,
restless,
at the wedding.

Reflection of daybreak
in a patch of water
at the bottom of the well.

I spend
too much time
angry with myself.
Time is gold.
Gold is bitter.

I dreamed
I was relaxing
all alone,
surrounded by grey flowers
under indigo sky.

Thousands of times
have I travelled safely from
sunniest day
into darkest night.

Wind
has carried
my family tree
from a rootless plant.

I am
free of limitations.
Completely free.
For how long
will this freedom limit me?

Exhaustion
comes not
from today and yesterday.
It is a legacy of my ancestors.

The word of my heart
flowed through my tongue.
It burnt her heart
and my tongue.

Awaiting a friend
to make peace,
through the window
I contemplate
a vast landscape.

I toil.
No happiness.
No sadness.

I close my ledger
as the four o'clock flowers
open.

Two trout
asleep together
on a bed of white porcelain.

The definition of love
in the dictionary of my life,
always changing.

Midnight.
A masterpiece
recorded in my diary.
Sunrise.
Complete rubbish.

To reach Heaven
one is obliged to pass through Hell.

Body
in the dust.
Foot
in mud.
Heart
on fire.
All is lost.

Every night
I die.
At daybreak
I am born again.

The death
of eternal love
in a stopped heart.

Sun
and moon shine
on a small pond
with two ducks.

I stretch out
under the cruelty of the sun
in the shadow of the moon.

How best to stretch out
in the heavy shadow of a barren cypress?

Bury
my heart separately.
How fragile
it is.

I worry
that odourless blossoms
will become fragrant
when the fragrance of the rose
is gone.

To the intense cold of loneliness
comes the Hell
of my imagination,
which warms me up.

A tortuous path.
Moving through night and day,
through righteousness and evil,
good and bad,
silence,
turmoil,
hatred,
anger,
love.
Love.

On a starless night
I go down a well
at the bottom of which
is a white flower
with five petals.

I worry
that Shirin's weeping goes
unheard
because of the sound of Farhad carving the mountain.

I despise
words.
Bitter.
Sharp.
Proscriptive.
Sarcastic.
Talk to me
in sign language.

I worry
that wild horses,
in fear of the wind,
will spend the night
in the sheepfold.

I worry
that children will sell
silver coins,
tarnished by time,
for half price.

To my ears
hungry sparrows in snow
sound the same
in spring.

In darkest night
at the end of a blind alley
on the clay wall
blooms a jasmine.

A piece of dark cloud
rains down
upon the lone cypress
on a scorched hillside.

Wind
swept through deserts
and narrow alleys.
Jasmine at the end of the blind alley
swept away.

In my imagination
is a tree
which at sunrise
is plundered
of all fruit.

Hungry wolf
in the snow.
Sheep
asleep in the sheepfold.
Guard dog
at the door.

I am trailed
by a shadow
that was my childhood comrade.
It grew up
with me.
It grew old
with me.
It trails me until death.

Loneliness.
The result
of unconditional agreements
with myself.

I am standing
atop.
Deep
in the valley
my shadow beckons.

With the Wind
Poems by Abbas Kiarostami

A white foal
emerges from fog
and disappears
into fog.

It snows.
It snows.
It snows.
The day ends.
It snows.
Night.

Traces of a passerby in snow.
Has he gone to do something?
Will he return
by the same route?

A cemetery,
completely
covered in snow.
Snow has melted
on only three graves,
of three youths.

Snows
are melting quickly.
Footprints,
big and small,
will soon disappear.

White of pigeon
lost amid white clouds.
A snowy day.

Sound of a drum.
Poppies, alarmed,
line the road.
Will they return?

One hundred obedient soldiers
entering the barracks.
Moonlit night.
Disobedient dreams.

A small patch of snow.
Souvenir of long winter.
Early spring.

Yellow violets,
violet violets,
together
and divided.

The white-haired woman
inspects cherry blossoms.
Has the springtime of my old age arrived?

Amid cherry trees,
an old nun
advises
young nuns.

Day-old chicks
experienced
the first rains of spring.

The butterfly
twirls aimlessly
in mild spring sunshine.

Notebook pages
turn in spring wind.
A child sleeping
on his small hands.

An old nun
eats breakfast alone.
Whistle of a kettle.

Wild cockscomb
biding its time
amid orderly lines of spring violets.

Jumps and sits.
The grasshopper
sits and jumps
in a direction that only it knows.

Six short nuns
walk
amid tall sycamores.
Cries of crows.

A drop of light
falls from a crack
in the grey sky
onto spring's first blossom.

The honeybee
hesitates
among thousands of cherry blossoms.

Trembling hands.
A stretched bow.
Moment of deliverance.
For a bird…?

A dream about the massacre of thousands of small birds
on a feather pillow.

A red apple
spins one thousand times
in the air
and falls into the hands
of a mischievous child.

Among hundreds of
big and small stones
moves
only a turtle.

The spider
has begun work
before sunrise.

Springs
in the heart of faraway mountains.
No one drinks the water,
not even a bird.

How fortunate
that the old turtle
doesn't notice the nimble flight of the small bird.

It sprouted.
It blossomed.
It faded.
It fell apart.
No one saw.

The spider
stops working
for a moment
to watch the sunrise.

Worker bees
work slower
in the middle of a spring day.

Such serenity.
How magnificent.
The moon rises
in the east.

How can
the old turtle live
for three hundred years
unaware of the sky?

The comet
falls through dark night
into the heart of a tranquil pond.
Song of burning metal
in water.

Growing.
Completed.
Shrinking.
Tonight,
a moonless night.

Dark sea.
Dark shore.
Am I to expect sun
or moon?

Moonlight melts
fragile ice
on the old river.

Beside a sleeping man,
a woman, awake.
No hope of a loving touch.

Thursday evening.
Five pregnant women
in the silence of the waiting room.

Rhubarb and mountain clover
converse with each other
and pay their respects to
mild autumn sunshine.

A sycamore leaf
falls lightly
and lands
on its own shadow
in the middle of an autumn day.

Sound of wind
echoes in alleys.
No passersby,
not even a dog.

A drop of rain
rolls off a box tree leaf
into muddy water.

One hundred big trees
broke
in the wind.
From a small sapling
just two leaves
were carried away.

The turn of which leaf
to fall
in the next wind?

This time
wild geese
land on cut reeds.

A pregnant woman
silently weeping
in the bed of a sleeping man.

Ten times
wind
opens
the old door
and closes it
noisily.

A tired man,
by himself,
only one league
from his destination.

The moon
shines on wet box trees
moments after rain.

Moonlight
shines on a pine tree
covered in snow.

A small, nameless flower
has grown, all alone,
in the cleft of a huge mountain.

Rumbling of thunder
above the village
interrupts
the dog's howling.

On a mountain trail
an old villager.
From afar a youngster's call.

The damaged bridge
scratches
the water's surface.
Wasted moonlight.

No one
can do anything
when the sky is so intent
upon rain.

Black dog
howling
for the newcomer.
Starless night.

New Year's Day.
Spring winds
blow the scarecrow's hat from his head.

Full moon
rises cautiously beyond the peak
of the volcano.

Hanging
fog.
Pale sun
eastward.

The key falls
without a sound
from the neck of a woman in paddy fields.
Kettle whistle
from kitchen stove.

Sixty-six long steps
to the end of the garden.
Steps of a short nun.

A pregnant cow.
Two empty milk pails
in the hands of a man on the road.

A loaf of bread
shared
among five hungry children
and a heavily pregnant woman.

Worker bees
stop working
for an enjoyable conversation
around the queen.

The bountiful cow
walks just like
the villager behind
who carries two milk pails.

A heavily pregnant woman
awake
among five daughters and a man asleep.

Two nuns
coldly
cross paths
among sycamores.

Moonlight
shines through windowpane
onto the pale face of
a young sleeping nun.

Autumn sunshine
on clay wall.
A lively lizard.

Scarecrow
sweats under his woollen hat
in the middle of a hot summer day.

Autumn sunshine
through windowpane
onto the carpet's flowers.
A bee bangs against glass.

Autumn storm.
One by one
pine cones
fall.

Sunset.
Flies buzz around the head
of the dead packhorse.

This time
the spider
connects
mulberry and cherry branches.

Rain
on dry trees.
Song of faraway crow.

Drought.
In the middle of the day
wind
divides a small cloud into two pieces.
One goes west, one east.

Among a cluster of ants
a tiny ant's celebration of thanksgiving
for having escaped the terrifying hoof of a horse
on cobblestone.

Children of the village aim,
without hesitation,
at the scarecrow's tin head.

Thick morning fog
in field of cotton.
Faraway thunder sounds.

Sunflowers with bowed heads
whisper
on the fifth cloudy day.

The spider looks
with satisfaction at its work
between mulberry and cherry branches.

Sun shines
its first golden rays
upon the magnificent spider web curtain.

Snow falls
from dark cloud
with whiteness of snow.

In the shrine
I thought one thousand thoughts.
When I left
snow lay everywhere.

The dandelion floret
made a long journey to the pond.
Nothing happened.

The spider
removed with great care
from the hat of
an old nun.

The nuns' conversation
goes nowhere.
Eventually
comes bedtime.

Snow
thrown from the roof
with a shovel.
How worthless.

Snow sits
on the clothesline.
In this cold weather
it won't dry
very quickly.

The black crow
in snow-covered meadow
looks at itself with bewilderment.

Night
          long.
Day
          long.
Life
          short.

The stray dog
showers
in spring rain.

The nun
caresses
silk cloth.
Could it be used for a habit?

The dog lies in wait
at the end of the alley
for the new beggar.

To look at the annoying mosquito
the sleeping dog opens one eye,
then closes it.

Hail upon the egg
of a small sparrow.
Flight of a tiny bird.

The dove
composes the first epic poem
while flying over the peak of a volcano.

Azure rain
on cherry blossoms.
Colourful blossoms.
Spring sunset.

Candle smoke
blackens
the butterfly's colourful wing.

Among all cherry trees,
only one
fails to bud.

Sunflowers huddled
one against another.
Rain showers.

A field being irrigated.
Scarecrow
being watered.

One of the nuns
said something.
Others laughed
loudly.

Two dragonflies, male and female,
pass each other
amid oaks.

Sunday afternoon.
Aggressive confrontation between two prostitutes
leaving the church.

A pile
of old, used tires.
A scrawny dog,
unpaid,
on watch.

The earthquake
even destroyed grain
stored by ants.

Of one hundred apples
ten are worm-ridden.
For each worm,
ten apples.

The small apple
spins
under a small cascade.

The stray dog
wags its tail
for the blind pedestrian.

Colourful fruits
amid the silence of mourners in black.

Among mourners in black
a child
stares at the persimmon.

The gravedigger
stops working
and eats
a little bread and cheese.

Two days of
the spider's work
is destroyed
by an old servant's broom.

The spider
starts
spinning,
this time
on a silk curtain.

Moonlight
through window.
Sound of crying baby.

Schoolchildren
put their ears
to an abandoned rail.

Scarecrow, lonely.
Barren field.
Early winter.

Birds   -
play
with the scarecrow's hand and face.
Job done.

Two hundred-page notebooks.
A sharp pencil.
A backpack filled with advice.
A child on the move.

The schoolchild
walks the old rail,
awkwardly imitating
the sounds of a train.

New Year's Day.
Wind
dances
the scarecrow's old coat.

Under the guard room's dim light
a child
draws.
The father
asleep.

The feverish child
looks through the window
at the snowman.

The old pencil sharpener
seems unhappy
beside the new pencil sharpener
at the bottom of the bag.

The child
is gentle with the doll.
The mother…
not so much.

A drop of rain rolls down the glass.
A small hand,
covered in ink,
wipes condensation
from the window.

Wind
will not return the kite
it took up into the sky.

Hundreds of fresh walnuts
surround a small child
with small blackened hands.

A shrine
one thousand three hundred years old.
The time
is seven minutes to seven.

The watch
on a blind man's wrist
has stopped.

The blind man
asks the schoolchild
for the time.

The villager
returns to his land
for the spring season
without so much as a glance at the scarecrow.

Not one coal worker
has ever seen
the first winter snow.

Collapse of the coal mine.
Flight of hundreds of white butterflies.

Whiteness of snow
stung coal miners
leaving the mine.

The more I think about it
the less I understand
why snow is so white.

The nuns
fail to agree
on the colour of the refectory.

The more I think about it
the less I understand
the discipline
and splendour of spiders.

The more I think about it
the less I understand
why mothers
so love their children.

The more I think about it
the less I understand
why dogs are so loyal.

The more I think about it
the less I understand
why the hands of the poor are rich with callouses.

The more I think about it
the less I understand
why truth is bitter.

The more I think about it
the less I understand
why the galaxy
is so big.

The more I think about it
the less I understand
why we are so afraid of
death.

Will my ears ever again hear
the roaring of the nearby river
as snows melt?

The last leaf upon the branch
longs
to see spring buds.

When I awoke with a start
it was the exact moment
spring had begun,
not a second off.

New Year's Day.
Blue sky.
The jet has drawn a line.

The honeybee drunk,
thanks to the aroma
from an unknown flower.

Spring rains
flood
the pigeon's nest.
The pigeon on its way to enjoy spring.

Will swallows
not return
to their starting point this year?

The snake
crosses the street
without looking left or right.

The train howls
and stops.
A sleeping butterfly on the rail.

Birdsong
accompanies the child's tears
until mother's return.

A piece of cotton cloud
guards
the crescent moon.

The ploughshare splits the earth.
The ox doesn't understand
why its limbs ache so.

Spring breeze.
Flight of dry autumn leaves.

Full moon rises
in the east.
My love moves
a little closer to great heights.

My shoes are soaked
when crossing
the clover field.

Ears of wheat
twine together
in strong spring wind.

The female jackal howls.
The dog replies
from far away
on a moonlit night.

The mirror breaks
in the hand of a plain woman.
One hundred springs flow
into the heart of a dark night.

My shadow
accompanies me
on a moonlit night.

Sunrise
in
the east.
My love
wanes.

The flame rages
on a stormy night.
No reaction
to the lover's persistence.

From within the wood casing of the cherry tree
the young bud
loudly announces its arrival.

The lily
filled
with spring rain.

Spring rains
pour down
onto unwashed plates.
A young girl
dries her hands
with a floral skirt.

Morning dew
concealed in folds of clovers.

No one knows
that the small stream
gushing from the heart of a tiny spring
intends to reach the sea.

Spring dawn.
A drowsy man's call.
The singing nightingale
takes flight.

Broken bottle,
full to the brim
with spring rain.

The horse hoof
crushes an unknown flower
among thousands of flowers and plants.

Rain on hay
carries the smell of spring
to the cow.

The packhorse
slowed down
while crossing
the clover field.

Summer afternoon.
The cow moos,
waking a tired man
with a start.

Wind howls
through deserted alleys.
No passersby.
Not even a dog.

Midsummer night.
Narrow crescent moon
shines its delicate light
on hundreds of weary sickles.

A dirt road ends
in the cloudy sky.
Rain
falls on dust.

A single year's harvest
gathered in one day
upon the back of the ailing animal
of an exhausted villager.

The dark cloud
goes to meet the moon
on a moonlit night.

Young ears huddled
one against the other.
Fear of wind
or sickle?

For years on end
the tired sickle
hangs
on a dark storage room wall.

Six bamboo chairs
recall
the last autumn storm
in the bamboo field.

Weeping willow.
Tall cypress.
Sad neighbour.
Autumn sunset.

The first autumn of loneliness.
A sky with no moon
and one hundred song verses
in the heart.

Thirsty crow,
its beak scratching in the dust.
A cloud on the way.

The starving crow
stares at crops around the moon.

Wind
carries the dandelion up
to the tip of the pine.
A pigeon's nest destroyed by wind.

Rain falling onto the sea.
A dry field.

Winter storms.
Crescent moon
moves faster
across the expanse of sky.

One thousand naked children
in the snow.
Nightmare of winter night.

Storms from the east.
The flight of crows
to the west
made faster.

Trout do not know
the river's destination
and accompany it
to salt water.

Dusk.
The small fish
slipped out of the fishermen's net
onto the seashore.

Wind
howling.
Wolf
howling.
Moon
hiding
behind dark cloud.

For the moon, the question is:
are the people down there
the same as those
one thousand years ago?

The glorious bridge
obscures moonlight
shining on the river of gold.
But for only a moment.

The ailing villager,
in step with an injured animal,
bearing a load of cotton.

Songs of rice farmers.
Happy and sad,
but always
the same beat.

At the shrine
I thought one thousand thoughts.
When I left,
none remained in mind.

"I cannot help you"
she said.
"I don't love you"
is what I wish she had said.

The baby
in the cradle
doesn't know the dimensions of his own bed
in a room of twelve metres square.

Autumn sunset.
I step
upon red and yellow waves.

I have never been so sure
of anything
as end of night
and end of day.

Where is she now?
What does she do?
She who I have forgotten.

I have arrived with the wind
on this first day of summer.
Wind will carry me away
on the last day of autumn.

I arrive alone.
I drink alone.
I laugh alone.
I weep alone.
I depart alone.

Powerful blows
drive the nail into wood.
All that remains
is a round board
on which is written:
"Here lies a nail."

The worm abandons
the worm-ridden apple
for a fresh one.

Full moon
shines generously
on the glowworm.

The glowworm
shines generously
on the moonless night.

It's the grandmother
who always loses
when playing games with the child.

The child
opens
one of grandfather's eyelids
to show him the marble.

Not east.
Not west.
Not north.
Not south.
Only the place I find myself now.

Atop a deep valley
I shout
and await the echo.

I weep
uncontrollably
when there is no place to weep.

I am forever supposed to meet
someone
who never shows up
and whose name I cannot remember.

Years
have I wandered
like straw
amid seasons.

I cross six paddy fields
on a moonlit night.
Mud
up to my ankle.

Chasing the mirage
I reached water
without being thirsty.

I return,
remove new clothes,
and again don
old clothes.

I leave behind me a life
lived in a flash.
I weep for myself.

Of one hundred passersby
only one stops
in front of my stall.

Always unfinished,
my conversation
with myself.

Forgive and forget
my sins.
But
not so that I forget them completely myself.

Wind and Leaf
Poems by Abbas Kiarostami

Tonight
I have a rendezvous
with the moon,
the full moon,
at seven minutes to seven.

The moon wants to show off
amid
scattered, brooding clouds.

There is a secret between
you,
me
and the moon.

Moonlight
upon
beautiful face.

They have harvested
wheat.
Moonlight
on straw.

Watched by the moon,
the snake
crawled into the nest.

When I left home
it was just
the moon and me.

Pale moon
against background of snowy sky.

The moon
is full.
My loneliness
is tonight
doubled.

I shared my secret
with the moon.
As the sun rose
the secret was revealed.

Frozen moon.
Winter sky.

Cold wind enters,
together with moonlight,
through a crack in the door.

The full moon
was wrestling
with the river,
which eventually
carried it out to sea.

Full moon
swimming in a pond,
hidden from sight.

Under moonlight
the wine glass was empty
and the heart barren.

Between the moon and me
is a conversation
that neither I
nor the moon hear.

How far you are.
How close you are.
You, the moon.

Meeting of moon and sun
at daybreak.

As the sun rose
the moon's face
turned pale.

A dark cloud
finally
embraced
the full moon.

Silence
from the moon
breaks my heart.

Insomnia
of moonlit night.
A useless conversation
with myself
until morning.

This morning
only one set of footprints
in the snow,
those of the snow sweeper.

At first snow
the crows,
completely in black,
rejoiced.

Never
was it that hard,
life
in the shantytown
under snow.

One messenger
with two letters
wandering in the snow.
Recipient unknown.

Never
was it so beautiful,
the shantytown
under snow.

In my life,
which hasn't been that long or short,
it has been snowing for ten years.

Snow stopped.
Rain started.
Rain stopped.
The bird sang.

It is not in my nature
to wait.
For spring rain,
however,
I have no choice.

First rain,
then snow.
Snow stopped at dusk.
Night arrived on time.

Under my car's windscreen wiper
a verse of the poem "Winter"
was frozen.

No trace
on frozen ground
of any passerby.

Early spring.
Weeds
among strawberry bushes.

A small sapling,
growing taller,
reaching for the sky,
unaware of the axe.

How do aged trees
look upon
small saplings?

A fire burns
in the woods,
witnessed by
poplars.

A tree
full of oranges
that are orange
in a sky
that is sky blue.

Daily diary
of a honeybee
in April.

Wild flowers.
No one saw them.
No one smelled them.
No one cut them.
No one sold them.
No one bought them.

Beside the lagoon
were white flowers
and a fetid odour.

On a pedestrian crossing
lies
someone's button.

Among
the riskier of skills:
making friends.

Awaiting daybreak.
When darkness came
he did not switch on a light.

Let's listen
to the conversation of two shellfish,
if there is one.

Sleepwalkers.
What did they say
at their nighttime meeting?

If there were a spring
in the depths of the ocean,
what would it be like?

The ground filled with mines.
Hundreds of trees,
full of blossoms.

Passing an explosion of cherry blossoms,
people in black
bid farewell to a corpse.

When the stone wall collapsed,
mighty trees
scattered.

Fledgling weeds
do not recognise
aged trees.

What is to be gained
in praising spring
and decrying autumn?
One departs,
the other arrives.

The bee
sat on the flower.
The butterfly took its leave.

One year has passed
since flowers blossomed.
Once again
flowers blossom.

The scarecrow
fell to the ground
because of small birds flying overhead.

In a slaughterhouse
one day
a bee
stung
a butcher's hand.

Among the fishermen's fare
were black bread and olives,
bottles
and tins of tuna.

Orange trees.
How do they feel
when the citrus market is bad?

Today
I sold my orchard.
Do the trees know?

One cypress.
One turtledove.
The cypress in the ground.
The turtledove on the cypress.

Relationships between shellfish
in their shells
should not be taken lightly.

For some
the mountaintop is a spot to be conquered.
For the mountain
it is a spot for snow.

Rails
buried under snow.
A train en route.

Out of negligence,
two parallel lines
brushed each other.

I was the only witness
to an apple
that fell from a branch.

I have lain down
on a smooth surface.
What difference if the earth is a sphere or not?

The apple fell from the tree
and I thought about
your gravity.

I still
don't believe
it's the earth
that rotates.

The first piece of poetry
raised from the heart
sat on the page.
Next lines…
difficult and useless.

Asked a child:
"Why do fish
love
swimming so much?"

This small child
in conversation
with the city's greatest man of letters
was using incorrect grammar.

One branch of a cherry tree,
without blossoms,
without cherries.

I give
my greatest respect
to the tree.
It lets fall a leaf,
perhaps in response.

Neither cypress
nor old pine moved.
Only the weeping willow
envelops itself.

After a mild breeze,
large trees
began undulating
on the pond.

Four trees
of four kinds
with one kind of shadow
for four tired travellers.

The truck
loaded with tree trunks
drives towards the sawmill.

Tree trunks
were delivered to the sawmill.
The timbers
will be ready on Tuesday.

A small raven
builds a nest
in a hollow tree.

Woodcutters
behind a pile of firewood,
with a small fire
and thick smoke.

None returned,
not the rivers
that flow to the sea,
not the soldiers
who went to war,
not the friends
who travelled to a foreign land.

The commander's uniform
in the closet
was consumed by moths.

How enthusiastically reserve soldiers
follow news
of war and peace.

Commander
and commanded.
Both injured.
Both hungry.
Both reluctant.

Youth
at the front.
Elderly
working hard on the farm.

The soldier who blew the trumpet
did it badly.
The sharp-tongued commander
hurled invectives
during morning parade.

The soldier who placed his fingers in his ears
while the artillery was firing
lost his fingers
and his ears
and his eyes
in the blink of an eye.

Two cones beside each other.
One on its base,
one on its tip.
Between them runs a line.

One bullet.
One brain.
One day.

An old woman,
hunched,
in the doorframe.
"Goodbye."
A tall young man
turned at the end of the alley.

Injured soldiers.
Wandering.
Groaning and bloody.

He began to struggle
once
water covered his head.

The drowning person,
at the last moment of life,
offering bubbles
to the world.

On that side of the river
are farmers working.
Women in paddy fields on this side.
Between them,
children growing up.

The word "glorious"
in the notebook
of a poor student
in a clay hut.

The bountiful cow
and cattleman
stare at each other.

An old donkey
with a heavier load
than normal.

The old villager
lashes the rump
of the ailing mule.

Persistent flies
on the old mule's wound
rode from one village
to the next.

In the office of vital statistics
they asked about everything
except vital statistics.

It's only the horse
made of bronze
that doesn't throw his rider
to the ground.

A stamp
with a laughing child on the envelope.
The letter
from an angry woman.

Cutting
and acidulous
and bitter is he.
Yet
he has a sweet
and luscious beloved.

Two workers, unknown to each other,
on either end of a handbarrow.
First encounter.

Orange peels
at the mouth of the sewer
swirl around themselves.

An evacuation
was ordered
from the house
with few furnishings.

An intersection.
On each corner
four blind men
with almost
the same income.

A beggar's bowl
in front of a magnificent church.

The travelling salesman
finally sold
a used suit
priced at
one thousand tomans.

Workmen disconnecting electricity
gave warnings to
twenty-nine deadbeat customers.

The bank cashier
received three hundred thousand tomans
for managing a deal
worth six hundred billion.

The scent of thousands of plants and flowers
in the apothecary.

The old-time steamship.
How admired it was
at the marine exhibition.

The stonemason's name
on a stone
from the fifteenth century.

The sun rose.
Dew dried
on the poppy.

A beauty can choose
from every hopeful
behind the wheel.

Under scattered stones
the beetles mate.
Maybe.

The wine jar
broke.
Wine
flowed like blood.

On the foggy window
forms a water drop
tenderly.

Forty shadows appeared upon the ground
when forty bulbs of the chandelier
were switched on.

The dandelion floret
that entered through the window
departed through the door.

The address of a holy shrine
on a scrap of paper
in the hand of an old woman.

Only one St. George
among
one hundred and twenty-four thousand prophets.

The young man with his feet upon the ground
dreams only of taking off.

Coal miners
finally called a halt
to the strike.

That man came.
That man came with a sickle.
You wheat all bound together,
it's time to disperse.

A man came,
tired,
from a foreign land
with a backpack filled with hope.

All compassion
lost
when he took power.

Socialism
follows
sausage
in the dictionary.

Student monitors
should behave themselves.

Impact of waves against rocks.
For how much longer?

He could not read
or write
but was saying something
that I had never read
and that no one had ever written.

The palm reader
stares at the palm.
The girl
stares at the palm reader.

In the dictionary
beside the word "nothing"
should obviously be written
nothing.

In the dictionary
"nothing" is defined as "empty"
and for "empty"
they have "hollow."

A simple teacher
from Kalah Gun am I.
I have
twenty-four students
with shaved heads,
shining eyes
and clean collars.

By the seventh day of class
the dull student
despised
school.

Puppeteers,
awakened at noon
by the commotion of children.

Asked the child:
"Can a hedgehog
feel itchy on its back?"

Shhh…
Daddy is sleeping.

Six artificial smiles
captured
in a flash
in a souvenir photo.

The glowworm
couldn't stand
the cold of the cave.

The meeting
of summer fruits
at the farmers market.

OK.
A flower from every garden.
In which pot?

The caravan departed,
the chief
asleep.

Relatives unknown to each other
prepare to travel together.

A tear was wiped away
by an old sleeve.
His grades from school, not so good,
in hand.

Magnificent day of birth.
Bitter day of death.
Some days between.

The bird that opened its wings
was given no opportunity to close them.
Free fall.

The story of night
came to a close.
The day came to a close.
Another day.
Another story.

The present,
in time,
became the past.

The present
becomes the past
before we can respond.

For two days
the final month of winter
pulled in
the first month of spring.

Four downcast pedestrians
passed each other
without a glance.

Only one match
in the box
of burnt matches.

A headless doll
in the hands of a sleeping child
in the lap of
a bemused woman.

The climax of this magnificent drama
was eventually
determined
by extras.

Through my window
I see two towers,
both the same.
Two dogs,
one white, one black.
One couple, both lonely.

Skeletons of small fish
beside the upturned boat upon the seashore.

The cook,
standing,
contemplating the vegetable's demise
while making soup.

The fork
wounded
a small trout
on the white plate.

What a revolution
in the pot
thanks to this combination
of uncollected material.

Different materials
in boiling water.
Unity eventually achieved.
"Soup is ready."

The trout
in the pan,
noticing that the cook was distracted,
jumped into the flames.

Disparate material
united
in boiling water.
Does bringing things together help them mature?

Pieces of spaghetti in a pot,
finally separated from each other.
Does dividing things
help them mature?

The cook
cut off its head
in front of my eyes.

All sacrificial rites
were done
in front of my eyes.
Knife and fork
at the ready.

Drinking wine
from a disposable cup.

Not so euphoric
in front of a glass
half full, half empty.

Wind
took the bird
in the direction it wanted,
in the direction
the bird did not want.

We have reached
the end of Ramadan.
A journey ahead.
Bare tablecloth.

Thirst.
A bloody
spring.

Dry land.
Waterless creek.
Powerless cloud.
Water in the water bearer's eyes.

Miles and miles of drought.
Miles and miles of rain
in the eyes of the hopeful.

Polluted water
moves towards a field
filled with red lilies.

With the wind,
from
west to east,
an autumn leaf.

From west to east blew
the wind.
From east to west went
the moon.
From sky to earth
the rain.
From earth to sky
the dust.

Green.
Hard.
Small.
Springtime persimmon.

One of the deaf-mutes
finally
broke the silence
and spoke.

A musical instrument
in a dark box
in the hands
of a blind man.

He was playing music
for the deaf
and dancing
for the blind.

Today
the product of yesterday,
tomorrow
the product of today.
The product of life is death.
And death
brings forth.

Ten stairs.
One landing.
Ten stairs.
One landing.
Ten stairs.
One landing.
No one opened the door.

I came.
You weren't there.
I left.

Two yellow lights
slicing and moving
through thick fog.

A short poem,
the product of insomnia during winter solstice night.

An unknown poet
in a forgotten corner
proclaimed this year
as the Year of Poetry.

That year
farmers
harvested poetry
instead of what they had planted.
In April
neighbours
spread poetry
on the clothesline.
Salesmen
were selling poems.

A line of poetry
was lost upon the seashore.
No one is searching for it.
Wind
stole
a fragment of a poem
from the neighbour's clothesline.
Destitute lovers,
in darkness of night,
far from watchers' eyes,
distributed tracts of poetry.

Mints
struck coins
of two and four verses.
Prostitutes
were accepting poems
from penniless clients.
Ladies
about to be married
were requesting poetry collections.
Banks
were considering
opening poetry branches.

Cashiers
were running out of poems
at their tills.
A barefoot youth
traded
a couplet
for a switchblade.
The council
that issued building permits
was accepting poetry
instead of blueprints.

Poetry merchants
in ships without sails
were smuggling poetry.
Seamen
were pouring
excess poems into the sea.
Pharmacies were giving poetry
as change
to customers.

A fisherman
familiar with poetry
pursued a fish
in the reflection of the moon.
Smalltime grocers wrote
"We do not accept poetry"
upon their doors.
Seasoned traders
folded their arms
for fear of stabilizing
the situation.

Politicians
consulted with colleagues
conversant in poetry
to find a solution.

Census takers
counted
one hundred and twenty-four thousand
youthful poets.

In ocean depths,
twenty thousand leagues below,
a fragment of poetry,
twisting
among weeds.

Someone on the other side of the wall.
Someone on this side too.
Neither one
nor the other knows.
Only the poet knows.

Eight or ten fish, big and small,
and a fragment of a poem on a page
in the fishermen's net.

When I have nothing in my pocket
I have poetry.
When I have nothing in my refrigerator
I have poetry.
When I have nothing in my heart
I have nothing.

In a cramped hotel room
I wrote a poem
about open plains.

At daybreak
my poetry faded.
At sunrise
my poetry passed away.

In my old childhood shoes
are always hidden
one or two unfinished poems.

The kite I threw to the wind
in childhood
today landed in my poem.

A word on a page.
The page on the
hook of a poetry-loving fisherman.

He was a politician poet
or a poet politician.
His poetry
was poisoned
by politics
and his politics
devoid of poetry.

He was an expert in poetry and a poet
and a connoisseur of wine
and a wine drinker.
He spent several months in prison
where he didn't compose a single line of poetry
or drink wine.
He recited poetry
for others
who knew nothing about wine
or poetry.

In both pairs of my white socks
was found
a line of pure poetry.

If I will it
the old shoes of my childhood
appear at my feet.

I make a mountain
from straw.
Ascending the peak of nothingness.

A knot in my work.
Angry.
Heading into the desert.

I am stubbornly
on the road
that leads to peril.

Hundreds of kilometres
from departure to destination.
Hundreds of people
I have nothing to do with.

There is no end
to the footpath.
Above my head
a small cloud,
a cloud like a pillow.
Shoes pinch my feet.

I asked someone for directions.
He misled me.

I have
no experience
of emergency exits.

The forbidden act of distancing oneself
from the wall of wisdom.
How troublesome.
How difficult.
How enjoyable.

I have on my foot a callus
that my companion knows nothing about.

I passed through cloudy woods,
from an indigo mountain to a blue sea,
yet still
I am sad.

Intending to fly,
I experienced
free fall.

How pleasant,
the turmoil of the ugly city
and strange ugly faces
when I return
from open plains.

Morning fog.
The tree in my house.
Visible and invisible.

My house
is rainy.
In the kitchen, living room
and my bedroom
falls rain.
And I, on the porch,
stare out the window.

Overnight
hundreds of bitter orange trees
have grown in my house.
The kitchen covered in leaves.
The living room filled
with the smell of bitter orange.

I take refuge from
the heat of the alley.
A watermelon bush
grows in my refrigerator.

Today,
in my back yard,
a cat
ate a pigeon.

Wet matches
in a house
abandoned.

Rooms facing the sun,
for some time now
without sunshine.

Silence rules
my home
until the return of
a woman I know.

A minute of silence
from the house next door.
The sound of children playing.

In my back yard
for years now
is a broken stool.

The neighbour's ivy
on the wall of our yard
grows and grows.

Always a commotion and
sometimes
a gift
from the house next door.

More respect
when far from home.

Neither in the front
nor back yard
is anything moving.

My house
is northeast.
My work
is southwest.
I pass west and east
and north and south
in a single day.

My house
has four bedrooms.
In one of the rooms,
to the side,
on a double bed,
I sleep
alone.

I am the breadwinner of a house
whose occupants have left.
They are opportunists.
Every man for himself.

Next door
is a celebration.
For what
I do not know.

Morning.
When I leave home, I am young.
Night.
I return aged
with a thousand-year sorrow.
The four walls of my house,
calm and patient,
shelter an old man who rises young
at daybreak.

A severed head
with glasses,
without blood,
in my desk drawer.

In my house
I was my own guest.
The ringing
of an uninvited guest.

I take my pulse.
Twenty-seven.
I multiply it by four.
One hundred and eight.

One today,
one tomorrow,
with a half glass of water,
on an empty stomach.
This before food,
this after.
Food, simple.
Rest, absolutely.

Today
the twenty-four-thousandth page
of my daily journal was turned.

I turned my eyes
from the mirror.
Infirmity
lingers in the mind.

In your eyes
the lines of my face
are twisted.

Communication,
voluntary.
Destiny, solitude.

I thought I had a fever.
I did not.
I thought I was in love.
I was not.
I thought I won.
I had lost.

I wanted to plant a flower.
The flower
and me.
No soil.

I wanted to plant a flower.
The soil
and me.
No flower.

In the near future
there are flowers
and there is soil.
I do not exist.

An excess of lovers
and beauties.
All too rare
are lover and beloved as one.

Thousands of responses upon my lips.
No one asks.

I said
I am ready to offer any response.
Someone asked the time.

The eagerness
of meeting.
Fragrant air.
A friend en route.

How restless I am.
when I have a date.
Accordingly
today I am restless.

Tonight the guest arrives.
I know
where she will sit.
I know
what she will drink.
I know
what she will say.

I said something.
A stranger heard.
He became a friend.

The fate of a story
I was excitedly telling
was sealed
by an untimely yawn.

I cannot handle love
and the drunkenness of wine.
I am so used to hangovers
that a hangover
is like being drunk.

Leaf speaks of wind
Wind speaks of leaf.

Fearful of wind?
I am rooted to the ground.

It was clear as day.
Dark night ahead.

Tongue-tied.
Heavy heart.
Mind wandering.

Even my thoughts
do not pass through
the four walls of my room.

The land of my imagination.
Limitless.
Barren.

Reality drained us.
Truth,
hidden from sight.

The only certainty
is
that I am me.

I am neither bad
nor good.
Badness is foreign to me.
Goodness also.
I am me.

Let's not talk about good and evil.
You are my good,
you are my evil.
Let's not talk about friends and foes.
You are my friend,
you are my foe.

Let's not talk
about benefit and loss.
You are my benefit,
you are my loss.

Say nothing.
You are you.
I am me.

In the end
the conversation grew into an argument,
the argument into silence,
silence into bitterness.

It started with understanding
and ended with misunderstanding.

Both of us,
you
and me,
were burnt in the fire
while others watched.

Like me,
back in the day
you were married.
Today neither of us is.
Yet
we pass each other by.

When she laughed,
I laughed.
When she wept
I wept.
When she spoke
I listened.
When I spoke
she ran.

When she arrived
it was spring.
Afterwards summer and autumn.
We passed the winter.
Anyway...
The day she left
spring arrived.

Left side
or right,
in front
or behind,
be with me.
Do not deprive me of your presence.

All day
it rained.
All day
I slept.
All day
she wept.

Summer for you.
Winter for me.
Spring for you.
Autumn for you.

When you arrive
you have arrived.
When you are here
you are here.
When you leave
you have left.

Friend,
don't argue with me.
Talk with me.
Listen with me.
Stay with me.

One thousand times
I would have left
if you had asked me just once.
I asked you one thousand times.
You did not leave.

I wanted to go.
She said stay.
I stayed.
She said leave.
I left.
She came.
I came back.
She left.

When she came
she came.
When she was there
she was there.
When she left
she was still there.

She accepted with difficulty.
She responded with bitterness.
She left with tenderness.

Nothing taught
nor learned.
Good riddance.

Friends
always offend me.
Of enemies
I recall nothing.

Last year
the deaths of three friends
and births of three foes
were registered
in my daily journal.

I looked back and saw
a dagger
and a smile.

We were lifelong
friends.
We have been enemies
for a couple of years.

With the arrival of an unexpected guest
the palace of my loneliness
collapsed.

There will surely be
an end to this grief.
Otherwise to me.

Of my nightly silence
termites
are jealous.

Night,
all night,
I leave half my bed
empty.

It was me, at night,
with a mouse.
I slept
on one side of a carpet
as the mouse
skipped about on the other.

If I want,
a cloud will come between
the sun and me.

I like to play
but do not take part in group games.
And I find one-person games boring.
Advise me, please.

With long legs
and a short rug
how do I stretch my legs
so they fit?

Between good and evil
I chose good.
It was a path
full of evil.

I thought of sweetness,
then tasted it.

I placed my leg
beyond the rug.
Nothing happened.

I reject
death.
At a seventieth birthday party
death reveals its patience.

My friends
do not understand me.
Understanding others
is not easy.

I went to the farm.
There was no farming
and no farmer,
just a headless scarecrow.

I drove two hundred kilometres.
Then,
while still behind the wheel,
asleep for twenty minutes,
drove twenty more.

No sadness.
No happiness.
I just
walk.

If I continue along the river
I will arrive at the southern sea.
But I do not want to go to the sea.
I go right.
I follow the sun.
I will set with it.

My shadow
grows longer and longer
on the sands
of the seashore.
Fainter and fainter
is the sound of waves.

This shore
is the same shore.
This sea
is the same sea.
I am not
the same me.

I am at the start
of a main road
which ends in a footpath
which connects to a main road
which ends in a footpath.

In darkness of night,
as in *The Odyssey*,
I took the Silk Road.
At daybreak
I lay
beside the dimple.

I rush
in darkness
to the White River
only one hundred leagues away.

The wind,
blowing at six hundred miles an hour,
from west to east,
eventually settled
in barren hills.

The water took my passport
in the direction
I did not intend on travelling.

If I drive twenty kilometres
the ground will turn white
and sadness
will depart the heart.

Searching for the source of the spring,
I reached the spring,
a muddy spring.

When I arrived in the garden
it was spring.
At the end of the garden
was winter.
Between them,
summer and autumn.

Days
longer and longer.
Nights
shorter and shorter.
Ahead,
a long, hot summer.

Night arrived on time.
Daybreak appeared on time.
The rooster crowed on time.
Falling asleep,
my timing was infelicitous.

At the start of spring
I left home.
Midsummer.
I slept under the tree.
Autumn.
All is lost.

Sincere friends,
each unique,
scattered somewhere.

Half my friends
are dead.
Childhood friends.
A half-empty bottle.
Sadness and happiness
prevail.

I get up
and lie down.
I get up
and lie down.
Until daybreak.

Upon my eyelids
one night
towers a mountain of sadness.
Behind my pupils
one night
wells a sea of tears.
In deepest thoughts the sea dried up
one night.

I thought all night.
The result?
I slept all day.

I dreamed
I decapitated my spouse.
Such a bizarre nightmare.

I dreamed
I was testing
my friends of thirty years.
Such a bizarre nightmare.

I dreamed
I live with strangers.
Such a bizarre nightmare.

I dreamed
I sold my house.
What a nightmare!

I dreamed
a millipede
swallowed
one of my shoes.

I dreamed
my arms
were rotting away.

I dreamed
a spring of blood
gushed from my pillow.

I dreamed
my eyes
were swallowed
by an old turtle.

I dreamed
small roaches
nested
in my larynx.

I dream
I am a soldier,
headless.

I dream
you cherish me
like
a small baby.

I dream
a caravan of camels
has taken refuge in my solitude.

I dream
I am a butterfly
without wings.

I dream
when I divide
one hundred by two
the result is nothing.

I dream
I am a silkworm
weaving thorns
around myself.

I dream
my friends and acquaintances
are together,
knitting me a scarf.

I dream
two hedgehogs
have laid eggs in my eyes.

I was asleep
when the grass turned green.

If I allow it,
sleep
will take hold.

Too soon
to awake.
Sleep
is impossible.

There are many
sleepless like me,
each
in his own loneliness.

Between Tuesday and Wednesday
was a particularly long night.

When I sleep
I have slept.
When I stand
I have stood.
When I go
I am going.

I take refuge
from the house in the street
and from the street
in the house.

The sound of grass growing
woke me suddenly.

One thousand arrows in my palm.
One thousand insults on my lips.
I neither shot an arrow
nor uttered an insult.

I have plenty of reasons
to be bad.
Alas!
No one understands.

I am the hero of a tale
that has neither a hero
nor a story.

Today I stay home
and open the door
for no one.
But the house in my mind
has no door.
They come
and go,
those annoying friends
and unpleasant acquaintances.

I ascend
the peak
of a cone
and descend
from there.
I lie down beside the base.

Someone laughed
in a crowd of mourners wearing black.
I watched.

A kite
just above my head.
Faraway,
the end of the line
in a child's hand.

Wolves howl.
Dogs bark.
I feel cold.

Everyone is floored
by drunkenness.
Me, by clarity.

A rebel without a cause
was executed
with cause.

I was reading a history book.
When the earth shook
the pages turned.

Nighttime trial.
Poetry saved me.

I look at the empty half
of the glass
and the full half.
Anyway...
Things aren't so good.

Neither you nor I
can do anything
to improve the situation.
Drink some wine
at least.

I smile
without reason,
I love
without proportion,
I live
without caring.
For some time now.

Such suffering.
I died.

The doorbell is broken.
Please knock instead.

Let's move beyond
happiness and sadness.
Let's move beyond
division and reconciliation.
Let's move beyond
pointless and unpleasant words
and empty love stories.
Let's move on.

Wine
Poetry by Hafez

Selected and adapted
by Abbas Kiarostami

Love and Youth

I am famous in the city for being in love.

My heart follows no path other than the love of beauties.

God's place for us was among the lips of beauties.

I will never forget the love of black-eyed beauties.

Everyone, mindful or drunk, seeks the beloved.

Upon the tablet of my heart is carved nothing but
    that letter which denotes the statuesque beloved.

We are drained, in need of wine and a minstrel.

Love, privation, youth and the arrival of spring.

I have a gem and seek someone who knows its worth.

I, rogue and lecher, am in love and conceal it from no one.

Speak to me of no one else.
I worship the beloved.

With all these beauties do I flirt in my imagination.

Contemplation.
My heart took flight like a bird.

I, beggar, long for a beloved as tall as a cypress.

Love, youth and mischief are all there is.

I am in love with the gorgeous face and beautiful hair.

A city full of flirtation, with beauties in all six directions.

A city full of delicacies, one from every direction.

Making love.
Being young.
Red wine.

For some time now have I worshipped only beauties.

Wherever be the beloved is the wellspring of joy.

Her sweet lips.
Her sweet lips.
Sweet lips.

O God!
At the time of flowering, forgive the sins of peasants.

Do you know what good fortune is?
Catching a glimpse of the beloved's face.

A face as beautiful as a flower is sufficient for us,
    in the garden of the world.

Who will be loyal to me purely out of generosity?

In Praise of the Beloved

May your beauty be ever increasing.

My love for you became a source of wonder.

Many has your beauty enslaved.

In your unsettled hair does beauty settle.

From your light will one hundred beams touch the sun.

Life orbits your beauty mark.

All beauty, inner and outer, nourished by your vigour.

Your lips are at the centre of everything gorgeous.
Everything gorgeous orbits your beauty mark.

See the flirtatious daffodil which blossomed
      in front of you.

Best that you hide your face from the eager.

Not even the moon has the light of your face.

Flirting suits only you.

All goodness, in every world, flows from your goodness.

From you, at every moment, comes a new love.

With you as bandit could one hundred caravans
      be robbed.

You, queen of beauties, and yet praised by beggars.

I wish your face would be always tulip red.

May your body be free
      from the touch of indifferent physicians.

You have mixed water and fire on your red lips.

May the evil eye be far from you.
You are both soul and beloved.

You could be no more enchanting.

Both worlds are one light, one of many lights,
    radiating from her face.

Your pure gem does not need our praise.

Her labyrinthine hair is the plaything of morning breeze.

Union with her is better than eternal life.

Let my lips be among those stealing a kiss
    from her face and shoulders.

Let her body be healthy, her heart joyful, her mind happy.

Behold those gorgeous lips, shining like a gem!
And her smile!
The begetter of chaos in my heart.

Either our forehead touching the ground she walks on
    or our lips against her mouth.

Disheveled hair, sweaty face, a drunken smile on her lips.

Drunk, she walked past and threw me, the dervish,
    a glance.

The time of Majnun has passed.
Now it is our turn.

Desire for Union

I, beggar, desire union with her.
Pity me.

Hafez!
Not every beggar's hand will touch that waist.

We await your face, hope in hand.

Last night I said her shining lips will cure me.

Leave it to lips to remedy the weakness in our heart.

I seek until I am fulfilled.

Hands eventually reach the tall cypress.

My heart and faith.
My heart and faith.
Both stolen by her.

If providence instructs, I will grab her skirt.

This, too, shall come to pass, as it did in the past.

Mosque or tavern, the aim is to reach you.

What if I pick fruit from your garden?

The Breeze of Paradise

O cupbearer, come!
The beloved removed the veil from her face.

She emerged from behind the curtain into festivities.
Go, mop her brow.

In the hidden house of joy I have a beautiful beloved.

Two-year-old wine.
Fourteen-year-old beloved.

She comes out at night, aggressive and bitter,
    the colour of flowers.
Drunk.

Union.
Kissing and hugging.

I have a beloved.
Her face like a flower, in shadow because of the hyacinth.

Your words revealed the secret of lips,
    your waist that of the body.

With every twist does the breeze of your labyrinthine hair
    keep me drunk.

Our beloved beholds no one.

At our festivities the moon of the beloved's face is full.

Worshippers of the sun are unaware of our beloved.

From now on, my hand and the skirt of that tall cypress.

The beloved offers me the best seat in the tavern.

Cherish the night of union.
Go wild with joy.

Hey candle!
Cherish union with the butterfly.

Only the nightingale knows the value of all these flowers.

Divine night, of which hermits speak, is tonight.

Glorious dawn.
A happy night it was.

From the garden blows the breeze of paradise.

Departing the Body

The beloved departed, unbeknownst to lovers.

She left.
My joy turned to woe.

Unfortunate providence took her from me.

I was watching as the soul departed my body.

The black-eyed gazelle escaped our trap.

She stole my heart and hid her face from me.

My moon departed this week.
It already feels like a year.

Hey caravan chief!
My baggage has fallen.
God help me.

My dear Joseph has departed.
O brothers!
Have mercy on me.

Flirting, she revealed her eyebrows, then drew the veil.

Heart broken, eyes bloody, body weary.
The soul broke away.

As you walk by, your eyelashes cause
     the blood of onlookers to flow.

Without rhyme or reason she became upset,
     stabbed me, then left.

They brought me rest and left me restless.

Like the wind, she leaves destruction in her wake.

Because of you I took to mountain and desert.
Until today.

My unfulfilled desire for your lips.

Her strong winds buffet my heart and faith.

The beloved.
Behind both my suffering and relief.

Night of Separation

We were counting on friends for help.

Separation from the beloved,
     whereof I simply cannot speak.

We collapsed with the grief of separation.

Do not be surprised if this story makes a stone weep.

Unkindness from the beloved turned my tears
    the colour of evening twilight.

Unable to see the beloved, my heart began to bleed.

My head lost and eyes burnt, all because of waiting.

With fire in the heart and grief for the beloved,
    my chest is burnt.

The world-weary soul wants to meet you.

Either loyalty or news of union with you
    or death of the rival.

In whose arms does she sleep?
In whose room is she?

Sleep escaped my eyes because of this painful thought.

Alas!
How I suffered during separation.

Sleep does not suit my blood-filled eyes.

Every night I am preoccupied with every star.

What is rest?
What is patience?
Where is sleep?

Last night a flood of tears flushed away my sleep.

I fear that tears will unveil the secret of sadness.

How befitting that the morning candle and I
    shall together shed tears.

Separation from the beloved set my body ablaze.

Who can erase our suffering with just a glance?

Day and night we deal with tears.

With the bow of truth I ward off
    one thousand arrows of calamity.

O God!
I wish no ill will on any wise man.

For how long will you suffer
    because you worry so about life?

The bitterness of grief has poisoned my tongue.
Every piece of my heart is a story of sorrow.

O wind, carry my bloodstained poem to the beloved!

Poor, wandering and pointless.
Morning breeze and me.

To covet the lips of the beloved means to risk death.

For a kiss from her lips I would give my soul.

My desire is to tell you the story of my heart.

The endless hazards of your black hair.

How could joy ever enter my sorrowful heart?

Our severed heads,
    like balls rolling around on your estate.

Such painful love have I suffered.
Do not ask me.

O God!
That ecstatic cupbearer with such sweet lips.

Love doesn't exist without the beloved.
Where is the beloved?

The beloved, drunk, gives no thought to lovers.

Much time has passed since the beloved sent a signal.

How wonderful!
The weary one has news from the beloved.

The only way I can love her is secretly.

It gleamed brightly but momentarily.

Life passes by with neither wine nor the beloved.
Such a waste.

O morning breeze!
The heartbroken wait upon the path.

Early morning.
I was telling the wind about the dream.

Why does my flirtatious cypress
    not want to be near the garden?

Desire for the beloved is the essence of our life.

In the face of cruelty from the rival,
    what is there to do but be patient?

The beloved and wine would be a life well spent.

We are extravagant in our neediness, yet ask for nothing.

Separation destroyed me.
There is no path beyond the curtain.

On dark nights I long to dissolve myself.

Bitter Wine

I want bitter wine, the power of which can ruin a man.

That sweet dream of mine.
A cup in my hand.

Fate carries me to the tavern.

Could it be that the doors to the tavern are flung open?

A morning breeze welcomes the old man selling wine.

Come to the tavern and make rosy your face.

Weeping, seeking justice, I will go to the tavern.

On days of distress, grief should be shared with wine.

Life's foundations rest upon wind.
Bring wine.

Our solution was reliant upon two-year-old wine.

O cupbearer, bring me wine!
The eternal order cannot be changed.

Beware the days.
Seize hold of the cup of joy.

Like lilies we lie beside the stream, cups in hand.

From now on just me, drunkenness, isolation from all.

In times of plight, go for joy and drunkenness.

In drunkenness is breached the pearl of secrets.

Drink a cup and walk gracefully in contemplation.

Such a moment!
The self-sufficiency of drunkenness.

In this illusory world, seize hold of nothing but the cup.

Should the sage of the Magi tell you to,
    make the prayer rug colourful with wine.

I did whatever the king of eternity told me.

Drink wine.
Being in love has nothing to do with entitlement
    and free will.

For how long will you suffer this worthless world?
Drink wine.

Ask drunken rogues about the secret behind the curtain.

I long to sacrifice the mortal and immortal world
    for the beloved and the cupbearer.

Do not suffer this world.
Do not forget my advice.

Eliminate old grief with old wine.

The glazed cup of wine is an obstacle to sorrow.

Never step disrespectfully into a tavern.

The tavern is where Hafez rests.

Last night I saw angels knocking upon the tavern door.

O sage of the tavern!
Rescue me!

Come!
Come for a while and be ruined by wine.

Rinse the notebook of our knowledge with wine.

O cupbearer!
We wait at the edge of the ocean of annihilation.

For God's sake, cleanse my robes with wine.

Come, drop our ship into the river of wine.

Felled by the pain of love and hazards of the hangover.

Begging at the tavern door is a glorious elixir.

Let wine decide the direction of the soul.

The robes of Hafez, forever collateral for wine.

From the cup's smiling lips comes the smell of the soul.

Use wine to turn our dust into clay.

Hafez!
Kiss nothing but the lips of the beloved
    and the lips of this cup of wine.

O cupbearer, serve the light of wine until sunshine!

O cupbearer, such appreciation for your service!
May your cup be full of wine.

Drunk, I knock upon the door of prudence.

Open your heart, like a cup of wine.

Wine's sun rose from the east of the cup.

Ramadan.
But bring a cup anyway.

Although we are far away,
    we grasp the cup in remembrance of you.

You made me drunk, so unveil yourself.

Safe place.
Pure wine.
Close companion.

You should also take wine and the path into the desert.

Hafez!
Quit the tavern when you are old.

Garden joyful.
Weather pleasant.
Wine pure.

Without wine comes no springtime joy.

Last night I walked drunk through garden festivities.

O wind!
From that wine, to me a breeze.

I heartily applaud the efforts
    of earnest consumers of dregs.

Drinkers are we.
Bewildered, roguish, lecherous.

God's grace is greater than our sins.

The Flaws and Art of Wine

The price of red wine?
Essence of reason.

I consulted with reason.
"Hafez, drink wine," I was told.

Do not speak to me about how reason prohibits drinking.
Bring wine.

Hey busybody!
Go cure yourself.

Conversations with kings are darkness
    on the longest night.

Do not decry me were I to walk from mosque to tavern.

Whether I am good or bad, go be yourself.

It was not my decision to move from mosque to tavern.

Do not ask obedience, dependability and righteousness
    of me.
I am drunk.

I never refuse wine in the spring.

As you speak of wine's flaws, speak also of its art.

Over there are good things in life.
And here am I, drunk.

Whoever tussled with the consumers of dregs
    lost the struggle.

Over here are we.
Over there an idle busybody.

O pretender!
Go, for I want nothing to do with you.

So tired am I of excessive piety.
Where is the pure wine?

Those who sell themselves cannot enter the realm
    of those who sell wine.

Me?
Refuse wine?
Inconceivable!

Do not ask a bat for a description of the sun.

O busybody!
Away!
Do not decry those who consume dregs.

O believer!
Away!
Heaven belongs to us.

A desire for wine will destroy the regretful believer.

Be not proud of sin and pretend not to piety.

Let her be ashamed before wine worshippers.

If he drinks enough, I salute the Sufi.

I will not forgo the beloved's red lips and the cup of wine.

Conversation in Absence

Tears brought water to the faces of the burnt.

Tears.
Talking to yourself.

Ruined, with a name sullied, although hopeful still.

O beloved!
How to deal with the sorrow of love between us?

You make no effort to cure me.
Do you not see my pain?

Better that you wound me than someone else heal me.

Return, and let past years of Hafez's life return.

To acknowledge the dervish
    is not inconsistent with greatness.

It is the custom of neither the dervish,
    nor those upon the path, to be cruel.

Do not abandon the dervish if he has no riches.

No one trades art these days.
But I have nothing else to offer.

You know that sighs will fog the mirror.

Aren't you afraid of my scorching sighs?

Do not make me, the wanderer, anxious.

Learning about loyalty and how to keep promises.
Both good lessons.

Enticement isn't only about destruction of the lover.

Destruction of this weary person by your sword
    was not fated.

There is no need to invent a story
    if you want to shed our blood.

A lion in thrall to your love will become a fox.

Do not expect patience, courage and consciousness
     of me today.

I shall never disentangle from the curve of your eyebrow.

Why cut me, a broken man, loose from yourself?

O cypress of the stream!
Be not proud of your waywardness.

I have fastened great hope to your labyrinthine hair.

Receive those destroyed by your flirtatious wink.

O sun, rise and deliver the morning of hope!

The smell of flowers wafted over.
Time to make peace.

Do not cut yourself loose from me.
You are the light of my eyes.

From the root of my every eyelash flows water.

Caress our injured heart with a breeze.

Every strand of my hair
     has thousands of attachments to you.

The message is that we do not want life without you.

Alas!
This is who I am, breathing without you.

I will not detach my heart from such a beloved as you.

Dissolving myself was the only way
    I could escape from you.

My desire for you unfulfilled, I stopped breathing.

Promise we might meet on the day of my death,
    if for only a moment.

Hafez, who did not listen to advice,
    was destroyed by your flirtatious wink.

Come to the mound of the one you have destroyed
    and lift him from the dust.

How unseemly it is to escape after leaving me in the dust.

Lift your skirt out of the dust and blood as you walk by.

She sent a message that she will sit with rogues.

Years and months, and still I did not age.
The beloved is disloyal.

Sorrow of Love

"What benefits does love offer but grief?"
    asked the busybody.

Upon the path of love, from the direction of annihilation,
    come one hundred dangers.

Beware!
The source of the spring is far from this desert.

O heart!
The path of love is filled with chaos and calamity.

Every dewdrop on this path is one hundred fiery oceans.

You are tired.
The frontier of love is nowhere to be seen.

The caravan departed.
You are asleep.
Desert ahead.

Night.
Dark in the desert.
Where will we end up?

For how long will you be lost in the desert
    of selfish desire?

Dark night.
Fear of waves.
Fearsome whirlpool.

How unwise it is to leave the mind in fragments.

Lovers have no powers of decision-making.

There is no sign of promise and loyalty
    in the smile of a flower.

The notebook of the physician of reason
    contains no chapter on love.

Ups and downs in the desert of love.
They are traps, every one of them.

Such wintertime cruelty the nightingales experienced.

O how the nightingale wails, every which way!

Do not trade the heart's treasure
    for the lips and beauty marks of beggars.

For half a flirtation, they are asking one thousand souls.
That which has no beginning has no end.

No one upon the path of love knows the secret.

Do not give your labyrinthine hair to the wind.

Pity that the wise heart is anxious.

Beware of losing yourself in the darkness.

Heart burning.
Tears flowing.
Morning mourning.
Night sighing.

Not every tree can tolerate the cruelty of autumn.

Early spring.
Do your best to be joyful.

A pity that a bird like you is held captive in a cage.

I have lost my way this dark night.

For how long should I pamper the love
    of heartless beauties?

This is about our beggary and the riches of the beloved.

To whom should I aim my heart
    when there is no beloved?

Joyous will be the day when I pack my bag
    and leave for the next stage.

O God!
Send rain from the cloud of guidance.

The puzzle of love goes beyond our knowledge.

The story of my beloved and me is endless.

Hafez's pained heart desires the lesson of love.

O heart!
Don't be such a loafer and gadabout.

Hafez, out of selflessness, seeks the beloved.

Secrets of Love and Drunkenness

Whoever became trusted of heart
    remained within the sanctuary of the beloved.

Do not trespass on love's estate without reason.

The pampered will never reach the beloved.

O heart!
Do not give up on hope.
Graciousness from the beloved may yet abound.

Love is an enterprise that requires guidance.

O friend!
Many are the wonders upon the path of love.

Make no effort and this path will take you nowhere.

Yes, yes.
Words of love take an unmistakable form.

To love is the fashion of suffering rogues.
To be chained is the fashion of being roguish.

Consider the mysterious perfection of kindness,
    not the defects of sin.

Those with hearts awakened by love will never die.

Crude and simple-minded is not the usual disposition
    of warriors of love.

The door to the sanctuary of love
    stands higher than that of reason.

O heart!
Be steadfast.
Making love takes time.

To behold purity, first purify yourself.

No one could have picked from her a flower
    without encountering the hazards of the thorn.

If you seek the face of the beloved, polish the mirror.

Burn bright and dance wild like a candle
    in the face of cruel winds.

In love there is no escape from compliance and suffering.

The soul has no desire for this world
    without the beauty of the beloved.

The word of love is not the one that trips off the tongue.

There is a hidden heartening word from which arises love.

The game of love is no game at all.
O heart, lose your head!

Step beneath her sword of grief, and dance.

You are no less than a particle.
Do not be small-minded.
Practice love.

Be in love, otherwise there comes a day
    when the world ends.

An ocean, an ocean of love, with no shore.

No stage upon the path of love is closer or farther.

When it comes to love,
    there is no difference between monastery and tavern.

So many evil temptations upon the path of love.

The laughter and tears of lovers come from another place.

Knock upon the door of joy.
Do not walk the path of reproach.

Security and comfort are hazards
    upon the path of lovemaking.

Joy cannot be attained without suffering.

A wise bird, having fallen into a trap, must be patient.

Begging at the door of the beloved
    is more valuable than a kingdom.

Secrets of love do not sit comfortably in a monastery.

Do not share secrets of love and drunkenness
    with the pretender.

May the world never be emptied of lovers' cries.

We are told neither to tell nor listen to the secret of love.

Hear the story of love not from the preacher,
    but from Hafez.

When in love, accept the angelic beloved's blame.

O heart!
Do not complain of obstacles, as would a flower bud.

Professing love and complaining about the beloved.
Such falsity.

Be on fire.
O heart!
Your fire will do wonders.

Do not hesitate when it comes to righteous work.

Do not sleep if you seek joy.

The work of a bureaucrat requires reason and logic.

O heart!
Be steadfast when in love.

Every moment you give your heart to love is joyful.

On love's estate royal splendour has no value.
Worry not about dishonour
      when walking the path of love.

Better to stop complaining about the night of separation.

Although the thorn torments the soul,
      the flower compensates.

The nightingale suffered a bloody heart
      and arrived at a flower.

The rogue without possessions has no need for prudence.

The pampered will never reach the domain of the rogue.

Walking the path is faith.
Immaturity is a sign of blasphemy.

The palace of paradise is given as a reward for work.

Do not worship in hope of reward, as do beggars.

Attain wholeness by thinking not of disunity.

Be loyal and she will too.

Yes, in this garden no one picked a flower
    without a thorn.

Ascending to heights of distinction is difficult indeed.

Hafez!
Do not bother her heart with your wailing.
Stop!

No lover ever spoke harshly to the beloved.

Hafez!
Be afraid of the beloved's delicate mind.

Forget separation and union.
Seek only satisfaction of the beloved.

Come to the garden.
Let the nightingale teach you to sing a love poem.

I speak to you in signs.
Be like a flower.
Emerge from the bud.

Hafez, you are your own veil.
Remove yourself from the midst.

Message to the Beloved

Today I understood the value of advice
    from those close to me.

Never will I complain about your cruelty.

Although you washed away my honour,
    I shall not turn my face from your door.

Judge us not, although we are bad.

Hope of union with you keeps me alive.

My heart resides at your door.
Be gentle.

Today I am in your hands.
Take me in.

If the price of union with you is my life, I shall pay it.

Whether in peace or war,
    I will die in the face of your glory.

Whoever has good news knows the language of secrets.

The bird of the heart is again in love
    with a beloved of curved eyebrow.

A captive of love, upon the path to freedom.

The captive of your love is free of both worlds.

I will destroy the universe if it turns against my wishes.

I stand like a candle.
Do not make me afraid of fire.

I heard nothing more joyful than words of love.

I saw the sky's verdant farm and the sickle of a new moon.

Like the wind, I intend on travelling
    to the estate of the beloved.

Because of my love for you I long for exile.

My longing for your estate will never diminish.

If like Farhad my soul tragically departs,
    fearless will I be.

I shall not stop her if with a sword she seeks to slay me.

We did not travel to this door
    in search of splendour and dignity.

An eye that can see the soul is needed to see your face.

In old age I desire youthful love.

No!
I am not the kind of person made tearful by your cruelty.

Love is the pearl.
I am the diver.
The tavern is the ocean.

Although I am old,
    please embrace me tightly this one night.

Ask us about nothing but stories of kindness and loyalty.

I will let down my shield when an enemy raises his sword.

I would do anything to pursue my longing for you.

All hazards will disappear.
The thousand-year-old dream will be fulfilled.

O God, protect her, wherever she is!

I swear to God that wherever she is, I am with her.

When will good news of union with you arrive?
My soul shall rise to the occasion.

The day of separation will soon end.

Worry not.
Lost Joseph will return to Canaan.

Happy days when the beloved returns.

Make a distraught Hafez whole again.
A good deed.

Cherish us, for life is unpredictable.

Whatever you consider.
Whatever you decide.

Good News of Union

Good news was received!
The time of sorrow will soon be over.

They gave us good news:
Soon you will pass by.

A message was received:
Spring arrived, grass grew.

At daybreak good fortune arrived at my bed.

O heart, good news!
Someone with the breath of the Almighty will arrive.

Last night the sounds of love between us
    echoed within me.

Thank God peace was made between her and me.

Day and night of separation from the beloved was ended.

Hafez!
The night of separation departed.
The pleasant aroma of union arrived.

Her wanton heart felt sorry for delirious me.

I sense an improvement in the condition of the world.

Divine Night

The book of separation is closed.
Tonight is divine night.

We reached the sun.
Dust settled.

A harp.
Joyous music.
The stage at the festivities.
A place to dance.

Morning breeze.
The tulip sensed the aroma of delectable wine.

Tonight is divine night,
    about which people of truth speak.

Water's edge, beside the willow tree.
A gift for poetry and a beautiful beloved.

What better than springtime carousal and companionship
    in the garden?

The ocean of her festivities.
Cherish the swim and find the pearl.

The flower is dear.
Cherish her companionship.

Cherish moments of joy and find the pearl.

Watch how the beggar of the city became
    king of festivities.

After one hundred bloody hearts,
    finally was the beloved's skirt reached.

"Hey, old lover of mine!" she asked.
"Are you sleeping?"

An intimate celebration.
Close companion.
Endless drinking.

You, like morning.
Me, the candle of dawn's solitude.

The unwitting ponder our lecherous nature.

One morning I happened to pass through the garden.

At every turn
     is her kindness towards my burnt heart renewed.

The beloved is here with us.
What more could you ask for?

Nightwatchman of the heart's sanctuary am I.
Night after night.

Separation

Desire for sweet union is beyond our means.

O heart!
Did you see what love's sorrow has once again wrought?

An explanation of desire is beyond words.

The soul was burnt, helping the heart fulfill its desire.
Failure.

I was bound by chains, beset with pestilence.

O God!
Save my heart and faith.

Midnight call.
Early morning prayer.

The smell of my charred heart wafted across the skies.

Should I not be of bloody heart, like the tulip?

Morning.
Dew drips from wintry cloud.

I should weep, like the wintry cloud, for this garden.

I walk.
Companions ride.

Blood must surge through a reddening heart.

Alas!
My contracted chest cannot bear the great weight
    of sorrow for her.

While in exile, separated and of sorrowful heart, I aged.

Better to hide my pain from pretender physicians.

I tell the story of the beloved to no one but the beloved.

Without you, in my barren hut.

How joyful to dance to fresh poetry and the cry of a flute.

Does fresh poetry flow when the mind is sorrowful?

Distress of long nights and sorrow of heart.

Many tears to prevent her from leaving, to no avail.

I thought perhaps that through tears
    I could turn her heart to kindness.

My tears could wash away none of her heart's enmity.

I no longer complain about strangers.

We played many roles, to no avail.

Hafez!
A long-lasting union is impossible.

There is no wisdom in these people.
O God, show me the way!

The shining heart of the beloved is a crystal ball.

May my dear life be sacrificed for dust
    under the door of the beloved.

Shame prevents me from looking the beloved in the eye.

Separation from the beloved.
Patience embittered the soul.

Regret

Being roguish and in love seemed easy at first.

One hundred thousand flowers blossoming.
No birdcall.

By day's end, my reputation in shreds
    because of selfishness.

They prevented us from entering
    the realm of respectability.

I encounter no one less respected than me.

The eagle of oppression extends its wings across the city.

The angel's hidden face.
The demon has taken the stage.

Suffering, my soul perished.
Desire unfulfilled.

This is the commandment of the Almighty.
There is nothing you can do.

In the circle of fate, we are the compass point.

O heart!
Youth departed.
You picked no flower of joy.

A pity that a nightingale like me is now caged.

Someone like me, with such a beautiful voice,
    does not deserve this cage.

Remembrance of the time my home was on your estate.

Remembrance of when I was
    a drunken resident of the tavern.

How can I speak of myself
    when I am so unaware of myself?

Fly!
Simorgh's realm is no place for you.

Hard times.
Wondrous work.
A world in turmoil.

Suffering, such suffering.
Toil, such toil.

Serenity for us was considered inappropriate
    by the beloved.

Mine has been an entire life spent in prayer.

My faith wavers like a willow tree.

No hope for fidelity from this unstable world.

Honour departs.
Rain.
O sin-concealing cloud!

My place was always at the heart of the tavern.

Thank God.
At least your cruelty is consistent.

I throw the burning light of eyes into the wind.

Awakened

O unwitting one!
Try to awaken yourself.

Where is the mystic who understands
    the language of the lily?

There is, at this moment,
    great commotion behind the curtain.

That you are a man of knowledge is sin enough.

Fate fulfills the wishes of the ignorant.

Fate breaks apart the ships of artists.

Trust in God.
Be happy.

Drink wine.
Forget the story of Aad and Thamud.

There is nothing troubling upon the path.
Bring wine.

Spill a drop into the dust
     and enquire of glorious kings beneath.

The curved harp invites you to joy.

Go do it all.
Regret nothing.

Worries of the world rob you of life.

Things change.
Don't be upset.

Life is not worth a moment of grief.

Key to the treasure of desire
     is nightly weeping and morning prayer.

Prayers of the recluse prevent catastrophe.

What can human beings do?
God will provide.

Cherish the incidental.

Trust not the wind, even if it blows in the right direction.

Sit beside the stream and watch the passing of life.

This world, so crude.
Its generosity cannot be relied upon.

What do you expect from the world as it moves?

Look at something after the fact
    and perhaps see some benefit to it.

People of sight lose both worlds at a glance.

Life gives nothing that it does not also take back.

O bride of art!
Complain not about fate.

Endless joy and comfortable living
    are not the fashion of love.

Nothing remains, neither those united nor union itself.

Happy is the heart that does not always follow the eye.

Calamities rain down from this decorated ceiling.
Move on.

Strangers do not hear the angel's message.

Do not bother your mind with existence
    and non-existence.
Be joyful.

True fortune must be embraced without a bloody heart.

Seek beyond your fate and you will be of bloody heart.

You cannot rely on the affairs of the world.

Who knows where Kavus and Kay Qobád went?

Neither the age of Khidr
    nor Alexander's kingdom remain.

Who knows how the kingdom of Jamshid
    was swept away?

A summing up:
Life is unstable.
Do not trust in it.

Every building in view could be destroyed.

Open your heart and think not of destiny.

Silence!
How can destiny know the secret behind the curtain?

Ask not why the world is beneficial to rascals.

Hafez!
Silence!
No one knows the secrets of the Almighty.

What is this high, simple and ornate ceiling?

Not a soul was at rest under this blue sky.

No one knows the outcome.

Hafez!
Your only duty is prayer.

No one is aware of the hidden secret.
Do not invent stories.

It is out of our hands which of us plays each role.
Recluse or drunkard.

Be content like Hafez.
Do not involve yourself with the inconsequential.

Although no gold treasure exists,
     there is a corner of contentment.

Because of his high spirits,
     Hafez removes himself from the heart of things.

Next to a spring.
Beside a stream.

From this world Jamshid took nothing
     but the story of the crystal ball.

You cannot trust in the world's generosity and manner.

Hafez!
Silence!
The art will reveal itself.

Contentment

Hafez!
You are the veil upon the path.
Remove yourself.

How can one fulfill the desire of others?
Forgo your own.

From now on, for me,
    submission and recognition of the rival.

Be happy and accept what you have.

I uprooted the image of the poplar tree
    from the garden of the heart.

For three months drink wine.
Be devotional for nine.

My garden needs neither cypress nor poplar trees.

From now on my heart shines light up into the sky.

No one could unveil wisdom like Hafez.

A serene heart is no place for a meeting of opposites.

The feast of joy.
Drink one or two cups, then depart.

I am supported by the foundations of the sun.

O God!
Make me a dervish, content.
Bestow wealth upon me.

A dervish in the corner.
Such a roguish existence!
Not a care in the world.

The garden of Heaven is the sanctuary of dervishes.

I am a slave of the resolute rogue
    who disregards his health.

Our most frequented spot is a corner of the tavern.

The reclusive await the unveiling of beauty.

Whoever has chosen solitude has no need of exploration.

I severe myself from the crowd, free, like a cypress.

Since the beginning of time nothing has been asked of me,
    except to be a rogue.

I was moving calmly as a compass.

I listen to nothing but the music of the flute
    and songs of the harp.

I will also give my heart to the wind.
Let it be.

In our heart is hidden desire.

Who shall I tell what I see behind the curtain?

Where is the companion
    with whom I can depart this earth?

May followers of delusion walk the path
    for thousands of years.

We experienced much in this troubled world.

No astrologer could read my fate.

Disloyalty of the world keeps me wracked with disbelief.

The world and its affairs are nothing.
Nothing.

Life, futile and capricious.
All used up.

Only broken hearts, nothing else, are traded on our estate

We say nothing bad.
We do not seek to challenge goodness.

Never stop being a beggar and you will find treasure.

Thank God!
I am free of king and beggar.

My services, performed for no money,
    free of expectations.

Whether I am thorn or flower,
    there is a designer of this garden.

We drank whatever she poured into our cup.

From now on:
My hand, the base of the cypress, the bank of the stream.

Aside from pitchers and books,
    I am without friends and companions.

Free time.
A book, in the garden corner.

O heart, none go astray when on the straight path!

I am a slave of those words that summon fire.

The grand name of the Almighty does its job.
O heart, be joyful!

O God, bestow upon me the fortune of poverty!

Our sage spoke:
"Nothing wrong was ever written by the pen of creation."

Everything done by our sage must be believed in.

You will eventually become clay for potters.

Our home will eventually become the valley of the silent.

Time to say goodbye to prison.

On the day of death, make our coffin from the cypress.

Tears
Poetry by Saadi

Selected and adapted
by Abbas Kiarostami

The beginning of the book, in the name of the wise god.
God the creator, alive and powerful.

Night caravan, what news of morning?
Bird of Solomon!
What news from Sheba?

Honour prevents me from complaining about you
        to anyone.
I will not burden physicians with pain caused by lovers.

Whoever said that contemplation of a gorgeous face
        is wrong?
Not to behold a gorgeous face is criminal.

Whoever cannot withstand the pain of betrayal and
        commitment does not know the value of love.
He can never be an honest lover.

If they let me choose what I want
        on the day of reckoning, then the beloved for us
        and for you every gift of Heaven.

No one knows the value of a good companion as I do.
A fish understands the value of water
        when it falls onto dry ground.

People are drunk on wine but lack all desire.
So intoxicating is the beloved that I require no wine.

The imprudent elderly man experiences joy
        with a young love.
How foolish for someone so old to contend with
        the young.

The market for your youth
    lasts no more than a couple of days.
Cherish what you have, young man.
To delay would be disastrous.

You asked me not to contemplate the faces of beauties.
I will abide by your every wish,
    except when fate intervenes.

For some time now has apparent piety been
    blasphemy concealed.
I pulled back the curtain of hypocrisy.

Young man!
Your eyes let it be known that last night you drank wine.
Find a companion who can keep the secret.

The seeker of spring must be patient in winter.
There is no way for the seeker of desire to avoid failure.

The logical – those beggars – are unaware of Leila's secret.
No one, save broken Majnun, has such power.

Throw your lasso after someone else.
We are already enslaved.
There is no need to bind the feet of the tame.

Saadi!
Yesterday gone, tomorrow still unattainable.
Between this and that, cherish today.

Tell the one trapped on foreign soil
    that returning home is but a sweet dream.

Avoid the faces of beauties and stay out of trouble.
Look, and shake the hand of restlessness.

If you want to follow desire,
    give up on the idea of union.
If you want me, leave your liberty at the door.

We recognise our salvation in poverty.
Each should seek his own salvation.

From the confines of solitude I desire the desert.
From the garden the joyful morning breeze
    delivers the message.

A drink more bitter than the poison of separation
    is required.
Only that will make me forget the joy of union with you.

Reason was never of any assistance when battling
    the beautiful hands of the beloved.
To pummel on the anvil is the most foolish of acts.

Aimless suffering brings with it no treasure.
Here is fate inexorable.
A strong arm is irrelevant.

We will not be deterred by your cruelty.
One thousand thanks for each of your cruel acts.

Battle with someone as strong as yourself.
We are already broken.
What more have we to lose?

Our heart never empties of you.
Now that you have captured the city,
    do not proceed to destruction.

Should the light die, what worries has morning breeze?
Should the cotton fall, what worries has moonlight?

Sleep will never embrace us through the entire night.
You, who have been asleep your entire life, understand.

Last night, in my dream, we embraced.
Never in reality, only in dreams.

A pity to clothe that body.
An injustice to mask that face.

So busy am I praying to her
        that I have no time for myself.

The garden is no more.
You rose up, like a statuesque cypress,
        and filled the garden with clamour.

I heard that you take care of whoever is ill.
I have a fever.
My heart cries out for a visit.

You had no mettle for love, Saadi.
You lack the power to escape.
You have no tolerance for abuse.

Chivalrous am I, but lack the power to hide you
        from the eyes of others.

Images of you discourage sleep.
It isn't polite to close the door on acquaintances.

How worthy of admiration is he, loyal to just one.
Fixed in one direction, he evaded all others.

Miserable is he separated from you.
Rested is the body united with you.

I have no desire for a garden.
Wherever you are do I find my country matters.

Here, my body, wracked with illness.
There, my heart.
Here the sky.
There the itinerant star.

You are king, we are captives.
You are great, we are nothing.
You are rich, we are poor.
It befits the mighty to care for the hearts of friends.

Poison from you is a panacea.
Invectives from your lips are beautiful odes.

Saadi has no concerns about death.
The death of lovers is salvation.

Saadi, if you are resolute
    complain not about the beloved's cruelty.
So long as the world has existed,
    cruelty from the beloved has been heaped upon
    the lover.

We seek nothing from you but you.
Give the sweet to someone who has never tasted love.

You consort with everyone but run from us.
It is not your fault.
Untamed fate is to blame.

Better that the wall collapses all at once.
Then the beauty of the garden
    will be immediately apparent.

Of words spoken, those of the beloved are most joyful.
Messages from the beloved nourish the soul.

If the beloved is not there,
    tell the candle to extinguish itself.
When she is there, even if there is no lantern,
    a light still shines.

Faults of friends are strengths.
Words of enemies cannot be trusted.

We are a collection of the scattered.
Our beloved is absent, yet stands before us.

Not everyone has a vision.
Making love is one thing.
Worshipping the ego is another.

If I complain about the beloved, I am being dishonest.
Whoever is full of himself is unaware of the beloved.

If it comes from the hands of the beloved,
    no matter whether a sweet or bitter drink.
Hand it over, my beloved.
The water seeker is thirsty.

Strike me with a sword and I shall not stop loving.
I am no friend of whoever is the shield
    between your sword and me.

I will never leave this prison.
The chain with which you bind my ankle
    is a crown upon my head.

I shed tears because of separation from the beloved.
The beloved brought forth my sorrowful tears.

Saadi!
Why complain about the beloved
    when happiness and sorrow are so fleeting?

Saadi will no longer go to the corner.
Solitude is joyful.
Being with friends even more so.

A patient heart can be made only of stone.
One thousand leagues from love to patience.

The roots of the cypress are in the dust of the garden.
Ours are in the heart.

They claim the lover is ignorant.
Whoever is without a beloved is ignorant.

First stop on the path of love:
Abandonment of wealth, fame and dishonour.

O friend!
Heaven is a good friend.
Such a disagreeable companion is Hell.

Living in the world is fantastic, being rich is delightful,
    and good health is important.
But friends always come first.

Come to me, despite your enmity.
Our friendship endures.

Powerful is the arm of your love.
Weak is the fist of patience.

To insult good friends is to divide body and soul.

Loyal were we, but still banished.
Go, Saadi!
This is your reward.

Don't you know that old age is no time to battle youth?

Within our solitude fits nothing but a pearl.
Go!
Whoever is not my beloved is a burden.

The true lover does not perish from a wound
    made by the beloved.
Bring me burning poison.
To me it is clean water.

Past midnight.
All eyes, save mine and those of Parvin, at rest.

If your eyes are upon the beloved, listen not to the enemy.
Saadi!
To be in love and considered honourable
    is like a heavy stone beside a glass jug.

For me there is no difference between
    your cruelty and your loyalty.
Whatever the beloved wants.

The beloved arrived, ecstatic, with smiling lips,
    like the blossom in its sepal.

Whoever consorts with drunkards has nothing to hide.
Reputation is of no use in a tavern.

Saadi!
If you are a seeker then walk the path and suffer.
Patience in the desert will deliver you to the Kaaba,
      where the beloved can be found.

The heart comes alive through
      hope of loyalty from the beloved.
The soul dances to the sound of the beloved's words.

Only the scent of the beloved can heal the lovesick.
And if the lovesick truly means to depart this world,
      he dies only in the name of the beloved.

I wish no ill will upon my enemy.
To see the beloved and lover together
      is punishment enough.

Sit with me and my heart settles.
Leave me and your imprint remains on the heart.

Have you ever heard the beloved
      describe someone as patient?
Patience and love cannot exist together in a single heart.

Patience is the only way of enduring cruelty
      from the rival.
Everyone knows that to be with a flower means also
      to be with a thorn.

Saadi!
To whom will you complain about the beloved?
Be patient with the beloved, although the beloved
      knows no patience.

Distressed, often I turn to the wall.
For afflictions of the heart there is no better confidant.

Saadi!
A treacherous creature is whoever says he has a heart
      but no beloved.

I fear my loneliness shall bring dishonour upon myself.
It is not dishonour I fear but loneliness.

Do you shed tears for the thorn in my foot?
Do you care about the pain absent from your soul?

Bliss is time for yourself.
To sit upon the throne without the beloved
      is hardly invigorating.

Unbeliever and blasphemy.
Muslim and prayer.
Me and love.
Everyone around you believes in something.

The door to the garden of Heaven was opened.
It seems that the wind had the key.

Saadi!
Let go of life.
Impossible to have two beloveds in one heart.

Saadi!
Accept divine judgment when afflicted.
The ocean is the pearl and the coral is fear and panic.

Love remained in the heart.
The beloved was lost to us.
Friends, give me a hand.
All is lost.

The heart of whoever sets eyes upon the beloved
    will have no rest.
Those caught in this trap can expect no freedom.

Thinking of you.
We were lovers in love.
You unveiled yourself.
Our work was done.

What you have goes beyond the statuesque.
So extraordinary!
This is not a smile.
It is a miracle.

Time spent without you does not count.
In my remaining years I will be making amends.

Laying eyes on you, the traveller's resolve evaporates.

Statuesque is the cypress.
Beautiful is the face of the moon.
You are both, yet neither.

Come!
Time for peace and benevolence,
    so long as we tell no stories of the past.

No face can contain as much meaning
    and no verse as much significance.

Everyone sheds tears for others.
Saadi sheds tears for himself.

Remove the hat of vanity.
Stop flirting and stay awhile.
Never have I seen such a cypress in clothes as yours.

As the passion of love arrives,
    so departs the collected mind.
Can two kings rule one country?

The story of love is too long for a scroll.
A description of the beloved is too long for words.

You cannot be in love and stay secretive.
The tavern is no place for abstinence.

Everyone who drank with you howled.
Everyone who saw your face fell in love.

Enemies are hot for combat.
Our fire is never cold.

Would anyone ever forgo his beloved's love?
Perhaps him, with a heart harder than stone.

Our death will come in the desert of love.
Who is courageous enough to travel with us?

Why should our distress concern you?
Why should the morning breeze worry if the light dies?

Those who have freedom, a beloved and a cup of wine
    have fortune, joy and a life filled with meaning.

Love is the scar which only death can remove.
Everyone's face bears this scar.

Wind arrived, carrying a pleasant aroma.
The almond tree blossomed.

Whoever dies with the beloved comes alive.
Dead is the heart of whoever does not take a beloved.

If you seek love, find a heart soft as wax.
A black stone cannot become a precious gem.

My heart, forever desirous of the beloved,
    does not follow the path of reason.

If union is impossible, I will settle for separation.
If I cannot reach the date, I will settle for the thorn.

My life, so worthless if you do not choose me.
Do so and give value to my life.

Dawn uprising of nightingales.
The sleeper, unaware of morning.

The wise avoid affliction.
The religion of lovers dictates otherwise.

Do my prayers to God count if you are on my mind?
You, the beloved, prevent me from praying.

If you do not desire us, send your dream
    so at night I can share with it my hidden secrets.

Whoever cares about his own skin
    can never desire the beloved.
If the beloved is reached, it is through sacrifice.

Those who seek God do not follow their own desire.
A voyage made by the needy can never be false.

No harvest burns without fire.
The idiocy of the pretender has no such effect.

This passion in our head will depart
    only once our head is gone.

It is not the way of friendship and friends
      for you to be unaware that I am dying of love.

Whoever is oblivious to words of love is like a mural.

Best to just look without speaking
      so that the rival has no need to put his ear to the wall.

Whoever sits in a corner and wanders not like a compass
      shall attain great treasure.

I want wine, the beloved, and a place and time
      where there is just me and her and no one else.

Whoever finds treasure in his home
      will have no need for the bazaar.

The perfumer spends all day with rosewater.
No surprise that the springtime flower garden
      holds no interest for him.

A fight started by the beloved can never upset the heart.
The impatient lover is no true lover.

With no suffering comes no treasure.
Morning arrives only once night has departed.

I will not tell the story of the beloved to the enemy.
No pretender is ever worth sharing secrets with.

Your face like a fairy.
Your body like the moon.
Your scent like jasmine.
Your body beautiful and shiny.
Strange that your beauty has caused no turmoil
      across the earth.

Merchants upon the ocean profit only when taking risks.
Whoever longs to reach you will endeavour
        until breathless.

The lives of those with no beloved are spent in vain.
He is still raw, whoever is not cooked in the fire.

The beloved returned.
The enemy mourned.
Spring breeze arrived in the midst of autumn.

O soul!
Reward me.
Hard times are behind me.
O body!
Be not sorrowful, for the soul has come alive.

The insane never heed advice.
Lock him up and he will tear apart every chain.

Today you know not whether I am on fire or in water.
When I turn to dust, wind will carry the news.

Desire for you guides my heart.
God understands that I follow no other path.

Halal wine for those in Heaven,
        especially from the hands of a heavenly beloved.

Your beauty will not last forever.
Your drunken lover will not be hungover forever.

Saadi!
You ecstatic!
Why so restless?
Because you seek something that knows no rest.

Love is not for men of letters.
Divine judgment rears its head.
There is nothing left to decide.

I have never met anyone who heard love's secrets
    and heeded the advice.

The tree blossomed.
Drunken nightingales.
The world became young.
Joy spread among friends.

Compared to the single tree in our solitude,
    every cypress in the garden is short.

You cannot blame the sweet-lipped
    for the spilling of blood.
It is the clear-sighted who let their hearts be ambushed.

Should anyone ask, tell them I am at the tavern.
Those who forgo can be found elsewhere.

Win the favour of the beloved.
No one else matters, however crafty they are.

Our path is that of admitting weakness
    and altogether surrendering to you.
You tolerate no one with whom you clash.

Sunrise from behind the mountain.
A beloved knocks at the door.

Do not abandon me because I am a stranger.
Loyal friends are better than kin.

Whatever the beloved desires must the lover accept.

Be patient with friends.
The stems of flowers may bear thorns.

A different beloved each night will cloud your day.

Behold the desire that moves the cypress so!
Look!
That cypress intends to walk into the desert.

The beloved, unfaithful to us.
Innocent am I, yet she has abandoned me.

O Muslims!
Come to my rescue.
That one is unfaithful.

The snow of age whitens my hair
My temperament keeps me young.

Slaves neither reject nor escape your command.
What can they do?
Slay or respect them and still they are at your service.

What can the seeker of the beloved do
     but tolerate his enemies?
Treasure and snake.
Flower and thorn.
Happiness and sorrow.
Together all.

Be with the beloved if all under the sky are enemies.
If anyone stings, she is the remedy.

Cruel beauties can be loyal.
They inflict pain, but can also cure.

I cannot understand this aversion to Hell
    and longing for Heaven.
Wherever you settle the people of love will come.

Morning breeze carries the scent of my beloved.
I want to follow her scent like the wind.

God!
Allow only the hands of the beloved to slay me.
I want to behold the beloved at the moment of death.

He is wise who fears affliction
    and worries about being slain.
But the path of Majnun moves in a different direction.

Our final goal is to be dissolved within you.
Our death is unimportant because you will live forever.

It is no fault of yours that we suffer so.
Where would Majnun go if he departed Leila's home?

Be patient, you resident of love's estate.
The cruelty of beauties is directed
    only towards close friends.

Only he who has suffered separation
    knows the value of union.
Whoever has been left behind cannot sleep well at home.

Whoever is without the beloved will not venture out.
The beloved gone, the lover stays home.

The precious gem, found in the mouth of the whale.
Whoever cares about his life never voyages
    upon the ocean.

Saadi!
Bear the load.
Forget not the beloved.
The love of Vameq does not end because of Azra's cruelty.

Saadi!
Tell the story of the sorrow she brought forth
    and night will end before your story does.

We gave up on the world, on exploration and wealth.
Love is like an engraving that will last forever.

A beloved as tall as a cypress walks into the desert.
Look how she moves, how beautifully she moves.

Reason is not powerful enough to defeat love.
Compromise is for the weak.

You, darling beloved!
Return and you will be welcome.
My tears are heard from earth to sky.

Different stories are told about
    the soul departing the body.
With my own eyes I saw my soul departing.

The beloved is not the one who enters my home.
Love is not a story my heart can ever forget.

Fate dictates that you agree with us,
    that everyone envious, shot through with arrows,
    will know about it.

Whoever is in love with the garden, and so considers
    flower and thorn as one, will undoubtedly be able
    to explore in early spring.

Saadi, enslaved by madness.
Freedom for those who follow reason.

If I fear thorns, I will never reach the flower.
One should seek desire in the mouth of the whale.

O beloved!
Do not leave.
We cannot settle without you.
Do not abandon us.
We will not abandon you.

When I am with you I care nothing for myself.
Whoever lays his eyes on you cares nothing for himself.

The story of the beloved's love cannot be told.
Tell it only to whoever has suffered a similar fate.

Ask those not asleep how long is the night.
It seems short to those sleeping.

Did I tell you that our fasting will one day be over?
Austerity will pass.
Hardship will end.

After hardship inevitably comes comfort.
But one must be patient.

To withstand the pain of separation,
    one must have a heart harder than stone.
My heart remains unsatisfied by passion.

I am hopeful that my predicaments will come undone.
Because our union ended, so will our separation.

The opposing force of life took away my flower.
Perhaps the accompanying thorns will no longer sting.

If I live longer, this sorrow and regret will end.
If the nightingale doesn't die,
        the blossoming tree shall bear fruit.

The colour of lilies reminds me of the beloved's face.
Curves of grass remind me of the beloved's shape.

Expect no union without separation.
A hangover always follows drunkenness.

Separation from the beloved stripped me of all patience.
I do not know
        when the springtime of union will blossom.

After hard times I long for union.
Morning comes from night, antidote from the snake.

Friends ask me why I have such longing and weep so.
Desire is born of love, tears of sorrow.

I shall never sour, even after one hundred bitter responses.
Whatever comes from your mouth is sweet and joyful.

We were a servant to no one.
But still we desire.
From such a benevolent character we expect generosity.

Saadi!
Should your heart bleed at the hands of friends,
        know that there is nothing gracious about
        heaving your heart into your mouth.

Who walked by radiating such a pleasant scent?
What desirable creature is walking by?

What moves from heart to mouth is never love.
Whoever is made impatient by the beloved is no lover.

Whoever sheds tears after being blamed by others
    should step away, into the refuge of the corner.

The lover dances towards the sword of affliction.
Unaware of himself, he is in thrall to the passion of song.

The mandates of love require that no one complains
    about the beloved.
Yet passion pushes the tongue to touch the lips.

Your head never nods in agreement with us.
Our heart never beats patiently for you.

If I utter no hopeful words while talking about you,
    meaningless is this story of love.

With one look she stole from us one thousand hearts.
Look at her, bringing such value to the bazaar.

O friend!
Either hide or be ready to give your life.
Love is a gunfight.
Forgo or accept.

"Life is nearing its end," I told a friend.
"Can those moments without the beloved
    be called life?" he asked.

"Saadi!" they said, "be patient or give away your wealth
    or make your escape."
Love requires either wealth or patience or exploration.

Unable to leave.
No honour in remaining.
The beloved upset.
We, the afflicted.

We will never sell our Joseph.
Keep your black silver.

When a lover cannot embrace the beloved,
    no matter if he sleeps on silk or thorns.

You are free of us.
We seek you.
You do not need us.
We need you.

We let down our shield.
We surrendered.
If you slay us, you are victorious.
If you forgive us, you are triumphant.

Awake!
Cherish the spring wind, the musical song of the bird,
    the joyful aroma from the tulip garden.

Today is spring.
Arise and explore with us.
Do not presume that life will bring you another spring.

The lover, patient in the face of cruelty from the beloved,
    forgoes all happiness to make her happy.

To take a beloved for the sake of one's ego is not the path.
We erase our ego for the sake of the beloved.

It seems our companions have taken to the desert,
        tormented by accusations and cruelty
        from the beloved.

I walk no path but the one to the home of the beloved.
I shall kneel only at the feet of the beloved.

We tell no one about the pain of love we have for you.
Stories of the beloved are told only to her.

Everyone wants something.
Everyone desires someone.
We ask for nothing but you.

Vameq, in love with Azra.
Today me and you, another Vameq and Azra.

The impatient butterfly will not keep its distance.
Up close the flame will scorch.

Saadi!
If you want honey, live with the bee.

You, so magnificent, free of us and in need of no one.
We, poorest of the poor, seek you.

We are impoverished foreigners in this city.
We are hunted by you.
All of us, caught in your trap.

I claim not to be distressed
        but the colour of my face reveals inner secrets.

Saadi!
Cling to the hair of the beloved at every moment.
Leave your enemies alone and they will bring forth
        the day of reckoning.

She gives fruit to no one.
Her garden is for touching only.
The apple hanging from the statuesque tree
        is for contemplation only.

Saadi!
Do not wait to hear about the health of he
        who departed in search of heart's desire.

Should the honest lover take offense at admonitions
        from the beloved, do not look upon it
        as her wrongdoing.

Our vow to you never changes.
It is a garden that autumn winds can never besiege.

I cannot embrace you, so let me kiss your foot.

A pity to die without being in love.
Endeavour so long as you have life and breath.

A head that fails to bow at the feet of the beloved
        is a heavy burden to bear.

Everyone has whims and duties to attend to.
Trapped as I am by whims of the heart, I have no duties.

I never thought you would be with me,
        you, the beloved, beyond my power
        yet finally attained.

I ask about the pain of love.
From everyone comes the same response:
"Do not ask me.
My home is in a state of disrepair."

I thought reason could control love.
No longer shall I rely on my thoughts.

Let everyone say what they want about us.
We will never remove our hands
    from the skirt of the beloved.

If my beautiful and cruel beloved returns,
    the thorn will turn to flower,
    the thorn will be removed
    from my foot, and my foot will be removed
    from the mud.

From reason come thoughts that corrode.
O you, so full of reason!
If you seek safety, go be in love.

Our punishment for being so ungrateful
    for the day of union was sleeplessness.
A night of separation.
Consumed by thought.

It is not unusual for a gazelle to be held captive by a man.
Unusual is a man captivated by a gazelle.

You don't know it, but you are on the riverbank.
Those upon the path to the desert know
    the value of water.

They are wasting their time,
    those advising me to leave the beloved.

There is no need to tell the story of love.
It has been written in bloody tears.

Everything has meaning.
Your beauty means God is powerful.

Do not expect a lover to heed advice.
Are you giving me advice?
I am not listening.

The connection between
        me the lover and she the beloved?
Victim and slayer.

Better that from my lips you hear our story.
A waste to deliver it through a messenger.

Everyone, including me, longs for a benevolent beloved.

You offer wine then invite me to reveal myself.
Love and secrecy.
Such things never mix.

Whether you invite us or turn us away,
        we are at your service.
I care not whether you draw us in or drive us out.

O cupbearer!
Bring entire oceans, east and west.
It takes time for whoever drinks steadily
        to become drunk.

I am not the one who cannot tell the difference
        between halal and haram.
With you, wine is halal.
Without you, water is haram.

When listening to such a sweet-lipped beloved,
     who cares whether this is prayer or blasphemy?

The time is upon us.
Today, a man of reason, fifty years of age,
     can become crazed in only five days.

When standing with you, I am fearful of no one.
A close friend is unconcerned
     about being blamed by others.

No one has seen such a beautiful and eloquent moon.
O blessed moon, rise up!
O beautiful cypress, stand up!

Fulfill my desire, I beg you, for even a moment.
Many inhalations of breath, but desire still unfulfilled.

I have neither the opportunity for union
     nor a chance for separation.
I have neither the power to depart nor a place to stay.

I could never imagine myself able to turn
     from the beloved.
O friend, leave me alone!
I can bear it no longer.
Yet I remain steadfast.

My body crushed.
My reason gone.
My love remains.
If I am unwilling to sacrifice my life, I am no true lover,
     instead a liar.

Winter.
Trees barren.
O my spring wind, come!
Here is desert and darkness.
O my moon, come!

Religious law forbids a drunkard to pray.
Who will accept my prayer, drunk as I am day and night?

The world's chains made sorrowful my heart.
Bound by your chains, I was liberated from all.

Thank God my heart was hunted by sorrow.
Me, liberated from suffering and scattered sorrows.

Your arrival was enough for me.
I had already told my story.
Whenever you stand proud,
    the polite thing for me to do is humble myself.

I have been free since the day I was bound by your chains.
I am your prisoner.
I am king.

Saadi!
To love one's homeland is expected, but living there
    has for me been a burden more difficult than death.

We promised to sacrifice our life for you.
Were I ever to break this promise, I would be a scoundrel.

I made one thousand promises not to be around love.
At every moment the dream of your face
    appears before me.

I arrived in a garden.
I could not resist.
I picked no flowers but was stung by
     one thousand thorns.

You came through the door.
I departed from myself, as if I left this world for another.

I put my ear to the road
     to hear who brings news from the beloved.
The awakened arrived.
I was lost to myself.

I told myself that if perhaps I saw her,
     the pain of love would be allayed.
I saw her, and my desire soared.

I was asked what made my red face turn yellow.
The elixir of love turned copper to gold.

Bring me the wine of your union.
I have drunk from the cup of separation.
Plant the tree of love.
I have ripped out the roots of my patience.

"Time spent with the beloved."
This is how I will respond when asked,
     on the day of reckoning, what I have achieved.

Two weeks since I have seen my two-week-old moon.
Not being with her brings me ever closer to death.

On the day of reckoning, when brought to trial,
     amid all that angst, I contemplate you.

O sky!
Keep closed the morning window for one moment more
    and block out the sun.
My moon and I are having a joyful night together.

I know not whether this is divine night or morning star.
Do you stand before me, or it is my imagination?

What sin led to your silence?
What have I done to deserve this separation?

Although you have broken your promises,
    I am grateful still.
Although you have been unkind, I seek you still.

I tell the story of the beloved to no one but the beloved.
There is only one who knows my secrets.

I am not that person who would ever turn his heart away
    from the beloved, even when the enemy's spite
    costs me my life.

I cannot bring myself to leave the home of the beloved.
Unlikely would I ever get permission to stay.
Nor do I dare go.

My heart, bound up in love.
Where can I go?
Friends, travel when you can.
Me, I am captivated.

Passion for union with you burnt my heart.
What base desires have I!
All these big dreams of mine.

I am hungover once again.
There was wine last night.
Beside me a flower
    from the garden of union with the beloved.

O cupbearer, bring wine!
I repent the sin of piety.
O minstrel, play!
How shameful is repentance.

How much longer will you maneuver me, like a compass,
    around yourself?
I wander, yet stand still.

I have no access to the beloved.
Nor do I have the patience.

Fate is the reason for your cruelty towards me.

If being a voyeur is sinful, excessively sinful am I.
What is to be done?
I cannot stop watching.

I have neither the time to settle nor patience for packing.
I have neither a place to stay nor a means of escape.

God!
Such a night is tonight.
A star rose.
I no longer love sun or moon.

I cherish all cruelties heaped upon me by the beloved.
Difficult to abide by, but – rising and falling –
    I accept it all.

Patience, a balm for love pains.
Crazed am I!
No relief for my pain.
And no balm either.

O caravan chief!
Move slowly.
Stick close to the weak.
You bear the beloved's burden.
I bear the burden of separation.

If I die because of your love,
    I will find you on the day of reckoning.

It is possible to escape this world and the next.
But there is no avoidance of the beloved.

Blame me, taunt me, one thousand times,
    and still will I never seek revenge.

On the morning of the day of reckoning,
    when I rise from the grave, I will speak with you.
I will search for you.

With patience can the cruelty of enemies be tolerated.
Might it also help me endure the cruelty of the beloved?

One thousand times I tried to hide the secret of love.
Each and every time I was defeated by fire.

The only way to suppress rebellion
    is for you to hide your face.
I am unable to shield my eyes from you.

You sold me for nothing.
But I would not sell a strand of your hair
    for all the riches of the world.

Better to walk the desert path than sit idle.
I shall endeavour, even if I am to fail.

Even with all my knowledge,
    the remedy for the pain of passion evades me.
Even with all my wisdom,
    ignorant am I of how to solve the problem of love.

Before all this I felt fine in body and soul.
Your love inflamed my harvest, burning it absolutely.

I never argued about union.
I never complained about separation.
All commands are yours.
I follow the commands.

O you, more beautiful than Leila!
I worry that your love will transform me into a wanderer.
Like Majnun, I shall cross mountains and deserts.

I hear your advice, dear friend.
But never ask that I be patient for the beloved.

You question my passion.
I question those with none.

My friends travelled, each to a distant land.
I have taken the desert path instead.

Separation is hard for me, but I must be patient.
If I escape hardship I will be an unfaithful lover.

A moment alone with the beloved
     is better than one hundred years of joy.
I seek no freedom from this prison.
I am held captive alongside Joseph.

O wise one!
I am not to blame.
Me, unable to turn my back on love.

Everyone you see is alive in body and soul.
I live in hope of joining with the beloved.

Should you summon me, I shall come to your door.
Should you ask me to leave, I will follow your command.

Either you accept or not.
My remedy is prayer.
I pray.

I cannot tolerate these distant lands.
You have no desire for union.
My heart is patient.
There is no other way.

Your every command shall be followed with ease.
Banish me not.

You have no desire for union.
Such is my fate.

Should you, statuesque and beautiful, seek to banish me,
     your wish shall be my command.

Wherever stands a statuesque cypress
     will I long to be hunted by the lasso of her hair.

Whatever I have read is gone from memory,
    save stories of the beloved, those forever in mind.

Someone asked about separation, about pain and sorrow.
"In such a state am I," I explained,
    "that I know not what state I am in."

Sugar doesn't need to say how sweet it is.
Saadi, show us your art!
Don't talk so much.

Many times have I kissed the ground.
Much service have I given.
I kiss the lips of the beloved and behold her face.

I will not listen to advice.
The ears of my heart are open only to the music of dance.

We have no need of a garden.
We have the faces of our beauties.
Whether spring arrives or autumn winds blow,
    we are at rest.

Great suffering.
No rest.
We ended our search for rest.
Now we are at rest.

We closed the door of solitude to all.
We disconnected from everyone.
We sat with you.

We severed ourselves from everything unconnected
    to the beloved.
We broke all promises, save those made to the beloved.

We are respected by all,
      yet standing before you we are nothing.
We are looked up to by all, yet you look down on us.

For how long will you insist that everything is about you?
Stop!
You aren't the only beauty here.
I'm not too bad myself.

We searched the world.
The beloved was at home.
For years we searched with our soul for treasure.

In separation is passion.
In contemplation of the beloved is cruelty.
Let there be cruelty, for passion is unbearable.

People complain to friends about enemies.
When friends are enemies, to whom shall we complain?

With God's grace we become more alive
      each time the beloved slays us.

A slave never names himself.
We are whatever they call us.

When desiring the beloved, some scatter gold.
We give our heads.

Like a nightingale, we are in love with every flower
      born into this world.

The narrow-minded contemplate fruit.
We contemplate the garden.

We regret all we have said, save our stories of the beloved.

To forgo our valued life is possible.
To forgo our valued beloved is beyond us.

We promise not to voyage into the desert
    without the beloved.
Without her beautiful face
    there is no enjoyment to be had in exploration.

Others embrace everyone.
We sit with just one beloved.
Our hearts can never be stolen by another.

Enough just to open my mouth.
Endless stories of sorrow.

One thousand years are needed
    to tell just one of one thousand stories.

Such stories are not told of my own free will.
My eyes tell tales of my life.

If I speak of my suffering, of separation from the beloved,
    the hearts of many will burn.

Where are my friends?
Every morning we used to drink wine together.
I should tell them about this miserable hangover.

O gardener!
Plant this cypress.
If you were wise you would pull that other tree
    from the ground.

Moon and sun make bright the world.
Our world, bright because of you.

If you want our head, here it is.
Life and head.
If you desire us, here we are.
Wealth and body.

Someone, his heart weary, is shouting.
Do not blame him.
He is selfless.

Those made ill through separation are strengthened
    only by seeing her face.

No treasure without a snake.
No garden without a thorn.

The butterfly killed itself.
Is the candle guilty?

Arise!
Winter departs.
Open the garden door.

Early spring morning.
Scent of flowers.
Joyful song of nightingale.

A sufficient punishment for our enemies
    is to see lover and beloved face to face.

Let us shed tears like spring clouds.
Even stones weep when lovers separate.

Whoever has tasted the wine of separation
    knows how hard it is when
        the hopeful turn despondent.

Saadi!
During your years of life a love has settled in your heart.
Only years spent will remove it.

I am to be swept up into Heaven with righteous people
    but without the beloved.
Better to cast me, with sinners, into Hell.

Deep are you in the well of Canaan
    with narrow-minded people.
Come to Egypt and the buyers of Joseph
    will show themselves.

For him who separated us from our beloved
    I wish only for separation from his own companions.

My heart, worn down in the prison of loneliness,
    like a caged nightingale in spring.

You make people drunk and in love, as I am now.
Time to show your face to the righteous
    and make the pious drunk.

Take my robe, bring me wine.
Bring wine and take my sorrow.
The logical, oblivious to the joys of drunkards.

That tribe blames dancing and love.
Whisper a joyful song and those ailing folk will depart.

Those sleeping beside the beloved have no idea
    how long this night seems to those on watch.

I gave my free will to love,
    like the bridle of a camel in
    the hands of a caravan chief.

Attack us by sword and arrow, by all means.
Our only defense is to let down our shields.

We let down our shields when standing before you.
In battle against the beloved we will always be wounded,
      never able to draw our sword.

To depart and return destroys passion.
To make and break a promise contradicts love.

The beggar's love for the king is but a joke.
It is not possible to be without her.
It is not possible to tell her.

So strong is my love for you that I cannot be with you.
Love is perfected when desire for the beloved
      is unfulfilled.

Khosrow's desire was to embrace Shirin.
Farhad's work, carving Mount Behistun, was true love.

Easy to give up on life.
Impossible to give up on the beloved.

A pity to use a messenger
      when uttering secret words to the beloved.

This description does no justice to your beauty.
The words of someone in distress cannot be trusted.

If a statuesque beloved sits with you,
      forgive her those thousand acts of cruelty.

Whoever cannot appreciate moments of union
      should spend a few days alone.

Whoever seeks but is powerless must be patient.

There is no honour in complaining
        about the beautiful beloved.
Tell her to be cruel at every hour of the day.

When faced with arrows of divine judgment,
        use no shield but contentment.
If you turn your eyes to the beloved,
        do not turn your ears to the enemy.

Although your arms are strong, battle not with iron.
Saadi!
Do not battle with her beautiful hands.

With you everything is possible.
Without you I have nothing.

After you, one thousand regrets.
My meaningless life.

With every breath the beaming light of your face
        connects with an eye.
But never is it my turn to connect with you.

Enough thorns!
Plant a tulip in the garden of my hope.
Enough injuries!
Heal my wounded soul.

Candle and butterfly are lover and beloved.
If you do not long for death, circle not the flame.

Majnun, in love with Leila, was burnt.
Strange how untouched was Leila's heart.

Is that a quince or your chin or a beautiful apple?
Are those lips or sugar or your sweet soul?

Whether you show me kindness or cruelty,
    I shall not abandon my love.

I wondered about God's creations.
Morning rose in the east.
Spring winds blew.

O my dear!
Is it one night or one thousand years?
Ask the eyes of the afflicted how long is the night.

Facing the wall of patience,
    with all our wisdom we let down the shield.
Our fate, decided by her, lay before us.

Those slain by the beloved feel no pain.
Their souls keep them alive.
We live because of her.

She complains that we move too quickly.
Strange how close we are to death because of her tarrying.

I defend against my enemy's tongue
    by preventing him from knowing my secret.
I direct my gaze towards someone else,
    but still my heart is aimed at the beloved.

They tell me to avoid her,
    that I should take the path of escape.
"Where should I go?" I ask.
"I do not know the way."

A pity!
Such a bitter response from your sweet lips
    and the blackened heart of your crystal chest.

The miserable were burnt in the fire of your love.
Alas!
Your stone heart!
How unkind you are!
Alas!

Best not play with a raucous drunkard.
Best not battle with her beautiful hands.

You gave her your heart and received her love.
If she disagrees with you, better that you agree with her.
There is no other way.

My life ended, although I never quite perfected it.
Whatever achieves complete perfection will perish.

A drunk beloved, simple and delicate,
    in her hands a cup of wine.

A wolf with bloody lips.
Joseph standing tall.
On your estate I am famous.
I am deprived of your face.

Impossible to battle your beautiful hands.
We departed.
We prayed.
We heard cursing.

Do not be cruel.
The wailing of those with burnt hearts
    will circle the world and infect you.

There is no way forward, save to let down the shield.
The enemy has a stone in hand.
All that we grasp is fragile.

Life is too short to fulfill all promises.

As you veil and unveil your face,
    so my day becomes night and night becomes day.

Jewels adorn beauties.
But your beauty, my beloved, adorns jewels.

Whatever comes from your lips, however bitter, is sweet.
If you will not pray for me,
    at least acknowledge me with curses.

Such a beauty are you, so lovely and gorgeous,
    yet so unfaithful and uncaring.

There is no one else to be in love with.
After you comes nothing but loneliness.

What can a person who prays for riches do
    if his prayers go unanswered?
We are eager to serve, but you never call.

Like someone dying of thirst who imagines
    a pool of water, news from you
    worsened the wounds of separation.

What gifts have you for friends?
Nothing better than to offer yourself.

You departed with my heart and cast me into sorrow.
Night and day you are in mind.
I know not where you are.

My innermost feeling was that
I must remain loyal to the beloved.
Avoiding dishonour makes you no lover.

Better to beg from friends than be honoured by strangers.

Tell the pious that Saadi turned his back on piety.

I am less fearful of wine, merriment and music
    than of deceitful piety.

I did not know you had been unfaithful
    and unkind from the start.
Better not to promise at all than break a promise.

I told you that when you arrived
    I would share the sorrow of my heart.
But what is there to say?
When you arrive sorrow does depart the heart.

I am not the only one trapped inside
    the hair of the beloved.
Everyone connives with a beloved.

Lasso in hand, wisdom hunts love.
The weak cannot defeat the powerful.

Crowds wandering, exploring, in the garden.
You are our purpose.
We have no need for elsewhere.

If someday I were given the opportunity to plunder,
    I would still touch nothing but your hair.

"Ask something of the beloved," they tell Saadi.
I ask of the beloved nothing but the beloved.

How would you know anything about it?
Night of separation.
Day of loneliness.

Desire can never be fulfilled through work alone.
If she does not want you, all work is in vain.

Impossible to have two beloveds in one heart.
If you truly seek her, sacrifice yourself.

Ask the eyes of the afflicted how long is the night.
You, on the riverbank, do not know the value of water.

No heart can bear two beloveds.
It cannot contain two loves.
If you desire her, sacrifice yourself.

Tonight seems endless.
The sun takes no interest in rising.
Many things fly through my mind.
No sleep.

I am not so sinful
        that I should be turned over to the enemy.
If you want to punish me, do it yourself.

You made no promise you didn't break.
You set me on fire, then departed.

You broke my heart.
You turned against love.
You departed.
Be careful.
You have cracked something fragile.

This hangover will linger for a lifetime.
I did not exist when you settled in my heart.

You are unlike the sun.
Sometimes present, sometimes absent.
Others come and go.
You are here always.

O wise cleric!
Leave us to God.
You and piety and wisdom.
Me and love and drunkenness.

Remember, you opted for war.
Your decision.
War or peace.

A wrongdoing.
The beloved withdraws her love from the lover.
You made a mistake and removed your heart.
But there was no wrongdoing.

The commands of love and reason
        cannot be followed at the same time.
Two kings in one land.
Such chaos.

O morning wind!
How joyfully you blow.
My soul healed by you.
From you to me, a message from the beloved.

Enter into the garden one morning.
See how it scatters morning flowers.

Given the chance, I want to die beside you.
If not, let me die on your estate while longing for you.

Before this, in my solitude, calm and collected was I.
Suddenly you arrived, and I fragmented.

Saadi!
The time for a good reputation is past.
Now is the time to be in love.
Have a heart of iron for a time, I told myself,
    and avoid falling in love.

I found the water of life.
Let the envious perish.

By sword she wounded.
She glanced behind her.
She told me I had not turned away from love.
She told me I had received the fate I deserved.

Come back!
Patience and separation burnt us.
You, absent from all eyes, are present in spirit.

We are from love's estate,
    not merely observers on this path.

I said I would give my heart to no one.
I want to avoid love.
I long to be oblivious.

I have not the luck of the mirror you stare into.
I am worth less than the dust of the bazaar
    beneath your feet.

Sleeping, your eyes stay closed.
From our chest is early morning wailing released
    into the sky.

You care not about pain unless you experience it yourself.
Those asleep are unaware of the pain of the awakened.

A beloved wants to inflict cruelty upon me.
The powerful seek to battle with me.

With the beloved, poverty is Heaven.
Without the beloved, wealth and riches are nothing.

We searched as best we could.
What could be enough if fate is against us?

I am not free to turn my eyes from you to me.
Whether you look at us or not, you are free.

The advice of the wise no longer matters.
What can be more powerful than a roguish whisper?

For how long will you hide?
You veil yourself but reveal our secrets.

Stay away from me.
People will be jealous upon seeing a precious gem
    in the hands of a beggar.

Your ears and neck require no jewelry,
    colouring or perfume.

Saadi's wailing moves the mountain
    but makes no impact upon your stone heart.

You behave like a cypress.
You stand like a poplar.
You look like the moon.
You appear as an angel.

Without you, problems everywhere.
Without you, mourning in every home.

Saadi!
Bitter medicine from the hands of the beloved
    is better than sweetness from any other.

After separation another life is needed.
This life, spent in hope.

Every pain has a remedy.
For Saadi's, it is peace with the beloved.

Whoever has no beloved knows no joy.
The heart not hunted by a beloved is no heart at all.

How joyful to see lover and beloved in the garden,
    face to face, far from the jealous.

How joyful to walk, with the beloved, into the garden.
How soothing to speak to the compassionate
    of heart's sorrows.

Those with no desire waste their life.
You, with the power of decision, cherish desire.
Only this is true freedom.

You, delicate as a flower, consort with another.
You, valuable as gold, held in the hands of others.

My heart, captivated by the love of a beloved.
How gorgeous, with a face as beautiful as a flower.
Yet so cruel.

Cruel.
Riotous.
A troublemaker.
Disquieting.
An artist.
A wonder.
Wonderful.
A source of suffering.

Hair like violets.
Body like jonquil.
Scent like jasmine.
So beautiful is she that no one wants to look at the moon.

I cannot sit with her.
I stand aside.
I am content just to look.

All but the beloved can be avoided.
What is to be done when ensnared by passion?

Keep me safe from the rival
    and poison from you will feel like honey.

Ask the eyes of the afflicted how long is the night.
You think that whatever comes easy to you
    is easy for everyone.

Majnun's story is like my own.
We found nothing.
We died searching.

I am not the only one hunted by the lasso of desire.
Everyone wants you.
Who do you want?

King.
Moon.
Darling.
Love.
Beauty.
Springtime.
I wonder what your name is.

Only upon my death will I avert my gaze from you.
You settled in my heart.
You seek to own it.

Free of all sin am I, save my love and kindness.
What crime do you seek to avenge?

Act like a peacock and not only will my tower
    become your nest, but the entire world too.

This one facing the desert, that one facing the garden.
I turn only in your direction.

You told of stealing one thousand hearts.
Better to take care of just one.

In the presence of enemies you dishonour friends.
This is not friendly behaviour.
It is the act of an enemy.

If the person who burnt my harvest comes to you,
    you will learn that you cannot be in love
        and remain hidden.

Different stories were told about love, poverty, separation.

Fate cannot be challenged.
There is nothing you can do.

Banish him angrily and he will return with kindness.
Melt gold again and again but still it remains gold.

Union with you takes time.
Me, held captive by desire.
Proud, beautiful, poised are you.

I pray for you, although many promises have you broken.
Banish me with fury
     and you will embrace me with kindness.

Until today there has been no talk of suffering.
I was not hunted by the lasso of desire.

No words nobler than yours.
No face more delicate than yours.
No one more innocent than you.
How to truly describe you?

None to whom I tell my story have any advice for me.
No expert knows how to heal the pain of love.

The bow is stretched.
We let down our shield.
If you are happy with this, no matter about our heart.

You, sword in hand, is the best thing possible.
Others jealous when you slay me.

The enemy does not know the reason for our tears.
Silence is the only remedy for those wounded by love.

Our two natures match.
You, settled in my heart.
I imagine your embrace.

How fortunate are those who speak with you.
I have neither the courage to speak
    nor the patience to be silent.

How is it that this unsuitable rival sits with you?
He is poison, yet you drink him completely.
O statuesque moon!
Every now and then
    ask how those down below are doing.
Be thankful to God.

Even after one thousand good deeds I am still sinful.
You shed the blood of one thousand people
    yet still are faultless.

Nothing disappears from your gaze.
Whatever disappears is still always in mind.
It disappeared.
You won't let it go.
It returned.
You won't let it in.

You, stranger, are no friend, unless you accept and receive.
If truly you seek union, let everything fall away.

Saadi!
Obey the command.
Submission is the lover's only option.

I have nothing to gain
    by sharing with you the sorrow of life.
You have never experienced a night that lasts a year.

Your heart of stone.
Your promises breakable.
Everything else about you is perfect.

The irresponsible do not accept blame.
Leave me alone with my life.

I am not jealous of status or wealth.
I envy only him, who stands with a beloved.

One year with her was like one single day.
Waiting for her now, a day is like a year.

I wish you no sorrow, harm or pain.
You are the heart's companion.
You calm my soul.
You defend against sorrow.

Much travel is required for someone raw
    to be properly cooked.
A Sufi cannot become pure without a cup of wine.

O nightingale!
If you want to shed tears I will weep with you.
You love a flower.
She who I love is like a flower.

I cannot tolerate the stones of blame
    thrown by the ignorant.
You, a light behind the fragile cup in Saadi's chest.

You cannot expect me to be patient when separated.
Separation is a stone, the pained heart a fragile cup.

I sit here until morning, when the message of the beloved
    reaches my heart.

In beauty are you incomparable, in kindness infinite,
    in love inconsistent,
    in making promises untrustworthy.

My mind, at rest.
You, always in mind, whether you send me a crown
    or by sword wound me.

If you want to give your heart to no one, close your eyes.
The arrow of fate needs a shield of iron.

Tell the pretender we are broken.
No need to battle with us.

Saadi!
If you cannot be king, be humble around the powerful.

Fighters of the world break the hearts of enemies.
Why break the hearts of friends?

Joy without you is joyless.
What is a body without a soul?

Only two possibilities:
Either your heart is made of stone
    or your ears hear nothing.

One statuesque beloved in a crowd is better than
    seventy cypress trees in a garden.

O heart!
If this separation and the fire of my passion for her
    leaves you cold, you are no heart at all.
You are iron.

My heart and soul are busy with you.
I look right and left.
Rivals will never know that you are my goal.

To die with you would be more joyful
    than living beyond you.

Impossible to remove sorrow from the heart,
    save by longing for happiness.

Call out to me with kindness and I remain your slave.
Banish me angrily and still are you king.

Do you know what love told piety?
"Do not battle with me.
You can never win."

Those bound to selfishness know nothing of real love.

The story of love is endless.
Patience visible, pain hidden.

If you are the beloved of the dervish,
    put aside your pride.
A good-natured demon is better than a ferocious angel.

If you banish me and I do not depart, forgive me.
I seek not to disobey you.
Me, so weak.

I neither avoid nor escape you.
The solution is patience.
You, both pain and remedy.

Do not ask me how I am.
I am whatever you want.
Do not ask me my name.
I am whatever you call me.

I burnt in your fire.
Smoke of passion.
You departed before extinguishing the fire.

It is no sin for me to contemplate the young.
The elderly know the value of youth.

Morning breeze.
I do not know the way to the estate of the beloved.
Have a safe trip.
Give her my best.

Saadi does not want to free his head from your lasso.
He is your captive.
Slay him the way only you know.

I look you in the eye and confess:
I am your slave.
Kindness or cruelty.
Either works for me.

Contradict not what men of standing tell.
Do what is fair to us, not what is possible.

The hearts of mystics, stolen by their beautiful faces.
The tranquility of the pious was shaken.
You used your face and spirit.

O friend!
Offer me no advice.
I turn my face towards her.
You know nothing of the secrets we share.

Saadi's pained heart, bloodied by his love for you.
You neither let him in nor free him in death.

I contemplated you.
You are unique.
All others just names.
You are flesh.
All others flesh.
You are soul.

You will never understand
     why someone would gaze at you
     until you find someone like you to gaze at.

The slave who serves you is free.
The land you travel to is joyful.

I will show you no less love and loyalty
     the more cruelty and enmity you show me.

Better that the cypress stands upright when you pass by.
Better that the parrot keeps quiet when you speak.

No one willingly falls into your love.
You, hunter, set the trap.

You said that watching is a misdeed.
But what virtue is there in stealing hearts?
A sinner you are, yet accuse others of immorality.

You show your face, then withdraw, taunting us,
    feeding the fire of our passion.

In the time of separation no one will ask me how I am.
Is someone with a burnt harvest ever asked how he feels?

No one can fault who you choose.
No one can reject who you like.

Night.
The beloved.
A candle.
Wine.
A taste of honey.
A night like this is an opportunity to see friends.

What is to be done?
I have no patience for you.
I was angry when I left, miserable on my return.

O beggar!
The gardener forbids you to pick apple and flower.
Be content with the colour and scent of spring.

O Muslims!
I cannot forbid myself the sight of beauty.
Your religion for you, mine for me.

O heart!
If you are in love, there is nothing you can do about it.
O body!
If you desire, seek and strive.

On this path either give your life or depart.
On this door either nail your soul
    or go seek someone else.

I saw patience versus passion, fire versus cotton,
    stone versus fragile pitcher.

Treasure and entourage of kings.
Dancing and chanting of mystics.

"Wash your hands of the beloved," you told me.
I won't do it.
You wash your hands of me.

Be cruel because kings are cruel to their slaves.
A fox can defeat a trapped lion.

My life is ending.
My love continues.
I am not so drunk from wine as I am
    from my love for the cupbearer's face.

No book can ever contain every story of the injured heart.

This book is finished.
But the story goes on.
The diary of someone in love fills endless volumes.

Water
Poetry by Nima

Selected and adapted by Abbas Kiarostami

I do not know to whom I should tell
    the story of my suffering.

While living and breathing I remain a servant to solitude.

What can the afflicted do but accept?

My heart is the message from beyond,
    where dreams and souls go to die.
Outwardly, it is the laughter of life.
All tears hidden within.

I am in love, in love, in love.
Being in love is pain and sorrow.

Movement of the sea, roaring waters.
Moonbeam.
Moonlight appears.
Rain falling, silence in the valleys.
The flight and wandering of moths.
The wailing of owls.
Darkness on the mount.
The weeping of a magnificent waterfall.
Birds calling, the sound of wings.
All this when I think of such things.

A small wooden hut near a place of ruin.
Do you remember?
An old woman of the village, spinning cotton, in tears.
Silence and darkness of night…
Outside rumbled cold winds.
Fire burning at the heart of the hut.
A girl – talking, wailing – bursts through the door.
"O my heart, my heart, my heart!"

Such flames that burnt through those dark nights!
Sheep and mountains nearby.
From time to time disturbance and commotion
        induced in the flock.
The call of shepherds.
The sound of murmuring.
The call of sheep bells.
The call of the flute.
City life abrades me.
City conversation torments me.

Separated from my origins, I have never been at peace.
I have become a seeker of suffering and adventure,
        quarrelling with my own evolution.
When it comes to life, I remain doubtful.
Now you, restless waves, take me, in sorrowful solitude,
        towards farthest hidden points.
It is here where those who have failed
        can retreat no more from salvation.

I wish the soul had wisdom and intelligence.

Simple thought.
Basic understanding.
Insignificant sorrow.

Homeless am I in the sky.
This is hidden from the serene heart.
Lagging behind time and space.
Whatever I am, I am for lovers.
I am what you say.
I am what you want.

O lover, arise!
Springtime!
A small spring welled up from the mountain.
Flowers on the plain resembling flames,
    dark river like sun storm.
Flowers have made colourful the plain.

Who can love me and not selfishly profit by doing so?
Everyone races about for their own benefit.
No one picks a flower with no scent.
Love without enjoyment and benefit is a dream.

Everyone cast you away, not knowing you are eternal.
Who are you, cast away from every place?
Have you come here with me as would a friend?
Are you a teardrop?
Are you sorrow?

Annihilator love.
I am love!

I am the flower of love, born of tears!

The time of love and passion will pass.
Blaze of mind.
Blaze of soul.
Pain of separation.

The mass of snow split.
The mountaintop formed into two colours.
The shepherd emerged from the catacomb,
    laughing contentedly.
Time for grazing.

Such a night!
Smiling moon.
Smooth grass.

I am a lover, asleep and unaware.

O my heart, my heart, my heart!
My poor, needy, worthy heart!
All your goodness, value and pride.
Yet what came of my time with you,
    save a tear upon the face of sorrow?

We could all be as obedient slaves,
    but love seeks flight at every moment.
It always notices the puzzles.
This conflict has embroiled us all.

I am a lion, king of all animals, leader of the warrior army.
Since my mother bore me she has roared
    and taught me not to groan, but to roar.

Me, fearless, when approaching the enemy.
My strong head and shoulders never bowed.
A benevolent mother raised me.
Out of wisdom, hoping for a courageous child,
    she kept me at a distance.

I prey upon things everywhere.
I sleep where I want.
My place of rest is any woodland.
I do not concern myself with poor and feeble tricksters.
Why should I worry?

Can you name the enemy that can challenge me?
What victory could ever slip through my fingers?
When the creator was bestowing traits
	he put victory into my paw and
	endowed me with dignity.

I am in love with whatever moves.

My foot, tired.
In the desert.

O beloved!
I have no idea how to respond to your letter.
You wrote poetry, I write poetry.
I think of you endlessly, either too little or too much.

When was it that human beings
	perceived their immediate surroundings?
Whoever saw what was in the distance raced towards it.
Those who do not fully appreciate you
	are among your relatives and close acquaintances.

O myth!
I do not want to be chosen and loved.
I was born up in the mountains, brought here by clouds.
Better to let me be in nature, in embrace of spring.

My name will never be known throughout the world.
I will never be respected in any company.
Best that I avoid artless rascals.
I am better than them all.

If you want to get on in the world, don't be so loathsome.

Disengage from yourself for one single moment.

The more people desire something,
    the more they are made ill and are slain.

Is it fair that when a hungry lion is asleep
    the fox gets whatever it wants?

Lucky are those who do not know,
    who do not understand, who do not read.
They are people oblivious to all problems,
    unless those problems are their own.

Even when dust gets everywhere,
    when it falls upon the path
    before me, even upon me, my way is never lost.

My straightness gives me strength.

What should the poet do with his fear?

With every broken rule comes an opportunity
    to find a path to life.

Many words were said, but many more are hidden.

When things are not working out, try as we might,
    should we not be more carefree?
If you are unable to win the fight,
    remove yourself from it.
If you cannot kill the snake on the road with your fist,
    do not kill yourself trying.

Failure all over.
Everyone lacking dignity.
One person a success, yet still stripped of all dignity.

Me, so heartbroken.
How sad that this heartbreak will fell me.

Destruction of this garden kills twilight.

Three hundred and nine will pass before our mind's eye,
    just as did three hundred and eight.

Happy for what we have found,
    although still hidden from everyone.

Shame on us for not helping ourselves.

None but the dead have completely surrendered.

A horse arrives, separated from rider.

Cold wind blew in from the mountain.

A branch from the roof, stripped, without leaves.

Everyone told him not to go, but he chose not to listen.

My journey is not to my heart's content.
I need to journey to my heart's content.

Although many searched and did not find,
    no one stopped searching.

I am my only companion.

Unless old yourself, you cannot understand.
Elders' words are not those of youth.

There is no hesitation in the world.
This mirror will one day strike a stone.

When destruction overwhelms your home,
    take it to the mountain.

Hope should be found in every dream.
All hopes began as dreams.

When willing to serve,
    one must free oneself from comfort.

In indigence is a man's brightness lost.

Finding is the payoff of wanting.

Jobs are unobtainable and employers rare.

For results, go to the root of the lily.

Again and again the world opens and closes one curtain,
    then shows its face from behind another.

Alive is the soul that arrives satisfied, then departs.
Dead is the soul that arrives covetous, then departs.

Why are you sitting in this cramped place?
Why not escape into the wide open?
For how long will you sit inside this cage,
    suffering and singing in remembrance of springtime?
For how long will you be like Harut,
    down in the bottom of the well?
If you are a miraculous moon, come shine upon us.
No cloud ever settled in one place.
No bird ever nested in a single spot.
Why close the door to contemplation?
It is like sitting at home in a grave.

O it is said that when one day passes,
    all things will pass with that day!
It is said that life is but a dream,
    that one should not bother one's mind about it.
But this is all nonsense.
Nothing passes in front of my eyes without burning.
I draw its image.
I remember everything.

How can you be so ambitious on this narrow path,
    where so many tears are shed?
You there!
Free yourself from ambitious dreams.
Lighten the load.
Calm yourself.

I take no benefit from her kindness.
Why am I so pained by the wound she caused?

A man never breaks his promise.

Every pattern, thanks to the delicate touch of the pen.

Since learning the language of night,
    my heart has understood the reasons for many things.
Heart darkened, hair whitened.
From dark clouds above, water rained upon the farm.
A pen the colour of night writes brightly.
A pattern appears from the darkness.
Contemplating this all night,
    by morning the key had dropped into my lap.

If you arrive at a mirage instead of water,
    be thirsty and cherish the moment.
Embrace life as I do.
If life offers you a drink of bitterness, taste it.
What could be more inspiring
    than drinking from the cup of life?
Why all these complaints when life is going so well?
Why all these tears?

Let no one in.
Separate yourself from good and bad
    if you are not party to this corruption.

Be like a river, moving through life.
Sometimes raging, sometimes at a standstill.

The ultimate desire of fruit is to ripen.

Old wheat is better than fresh barley.

Life itself is an indication of will.

Years of suffering have seasoned me.

Although you guard treasure, you have no treasure,
    while I, with my ailments, at least have pain.

I wish I had not spoken to her.
By doing so I broke her heart.

I emerge from my corner, finding reason to push on.
I stand, once again facing the desert,
    as powerful as when I began.

Hey caged bird!
Where do you imagine yourself?
On which box tree branch?
The city of happiness, with all its sparkle, is cracked.

Remove yourself from the dark house of imagination
     towards your true path.

Although many words were spoken, better not to speak.
The best words are of the path.

In this house I play a guest.

Although you are unable to touch her,
     why not at least take a first step?

Innocents are not born of dust and water.
A true sinner will eventually self-destruct.

O better to stop speaking,
     for speaking is the curse of the soul!
The truth is that language is a curse.

So long as there is hope, no heart is free.

Too much treasure and too many treasure maps.

The beloved was nourished by me.
Then she departed.

So many pointless treasure seekers.
Treasure fills their pockets, but still they search.

Amid the bewilderment of a mind maze
     we search for a shadow.
There is nothing more.

The storyteller left.
His story remained.

Of conflicts around the world, one strikes your eye
    and one hundred strike the soul.

She led me from the path and I followed.
Had I not been misled, I would be free.

"No one will see my house," someone once said,
    "although my door is open to people unknown.
Better to drive visitors away than host unwanted guests."

Even if I wear just one article of clothing
    from the thousand you have given,
    there can be no doubt of your generosity.
If I am miscast in this story, search only for meaning.
The story is merely words on a page.

My heart and the hope that nourishes.

This is a human being en route.

How foolish to give up on treasure
    because of the troubles involved in finding it.

Is it for our pleasure that the bird on the cypress branch
    sings so beautifully?

Keep your body in prison.
Release your mind from prison.

The curtain is a barrier.
You can be one person in front, another behind.

A bird sits on the roof of our house,
    singing a faint and strange story.
Uncaged and free, still it sings a story for us.

Of the dervish nothing remained.
Neither wife nor child, nothing more, nothing less.
Yet how good to remember him.
He reached the end of the path
    and brought the story to an end.

Alas!
Where in this dark night can I hang my tattered gown
    and so remove the arrows from my injured heart?
Alas!

Be straight as a flower and carry a weapon.
On this path wear thorns upon your head.
Even if a flower has one hundred thorns,
    its value is undiminished.

I wish he could come through this window.
I would call him from afar.
"Come!"
"Woman," I would tell Aliyeh, my wife,
    "my father has come, so open the door."

In the city of the blind my vision troubles me.
How futile it would be
    to blow a horn and announce my arrival.
Such childish behaviour that would be.

Should life be unsullied, free of mendacity?

Do not abandon me, helpless, weeping, in this rain.

Life is the darkness of night and morning light.
A different manifestation in every direction.
What, then, at the end?
What rider can tame this wild horse?

Victory belongs not to winners but to the free,
    even those behind walls.

Night hides our imperfections, as it does our strengths.

I escape what once I chased.
I have reached the point where I battle against myself.

I have been friendly with poets since childhood.

Did not those who broke their promise
    come together once again?

I am an honourable neighbour
    from the slopes of nearby beautiful mountains.
Do our cows not graze together?
In spring we milk them side by side.

All day beneath the green willow tree he sat, head bowed,
    like the branches of the willow.
His grief caused by heart-rending love.
Everyone heard his tears.
O cheerless lover!
Sing beneath the green willow!

Whoever battles against evil is entwined with evil.
This is an ancient ritual, part and parcel of life.
Such deceitful people!
O meaningless life!
O futile life!

If we enter hurriedly through one door, we depart,
    unhappy, through another.
When the heart is consumed with profit and loss,
    life drains out.

Truly beautiful is life in mountains and villages.
Yet a day will come when humans are powerless,
    when the beauty of nature appears as but a scourge.
There can be no remedy for his pain.

My farm dried up.
All solutions proved useless.
The enemy, so cunning, has discovered my weakness.
Alas!
He prepares to shoot arrows tipped with hatred
    into my heart.

In our mountains is a bird that sings
    atop silent lonely rocks.
It knows no language but its own.

Poetry is important.
The poetic life is one of the richest to be had.
Whoever walks this path never searches in vain.

There is madness in my nature.
If people are not at rest, I cannot be at rest.
If one day I weep because I have no bread,
    it is because I cannot give life to others.

For a moment
    my acquaintances are near enough to talk to.
Because I cannot place fire in their hearts
    and none of them understand my words,
    they walk away.

Is it really true that life is free of corruption?
The end of this night is nothing but the light of bright day.

I light my candle in darkness so that if I again collapse
    I can burn in my tears.

The fabric of my life, woven from regrets.
Alas!
I fear that humans, tiring of what they have in hand,
    constantly reach for things beyond.

There is a connection between the faces and nature
    of evil people.
In darkness of night they appear as the sum total
    of the world's ugliness.

Friendship and enmity are actually the same thing.

Whatever is designed to grow
    will grow because of clouds.

Searching, growing, gushing.
The heart.

Deserving of a father like me is a son like you.

Tuberose under dew.

After coldness of winter days come days of spring.

If bitterly I sit on silent lips,
    if regrettably I add to or relieve suffering,
    I am the smile of bitter and painful days.
Me, the lone lover.

O meaningless life!
In the springtime of her laughter
      the newly blossomed flower passes away.
Pleasant morning lives for only a moment.
Human beings, alone with their pain.

Two years have passed since his sad loss.
Autumn leaves, twice upon his grave.
Three weeping broken shadows
      hanging from the branches of another shadow.

O you, sitting upon the seashore, happy and laughing!
Someone is dying in that water.
There is always someone that you know
      struggling in this angry, dark, solemn sea.

This time, his wing deep in blood.
The owl, silent, sitting on the stone.

With so much hidden pain, it became clear to me:
Much suffering must be endured
      when courting the beloved.
Many untrodden paths must be walked.

If you have day, you will have night.

So long as I live will my ignorance bring me suffering.

Here I sit, having fled dark weather –
      with its polluted heart, its cold breeze –
      and your poisonous breath.
Allowing my heart to be trapped in this quiet corner,
      my path leads away from your poisonous breath.
Wherever you are, hidden from people, there I am.

O you, welcome to the anguished hideaway
    of a wandering poet!
Bring that backpack filled with my poems
    so I might place it under my head.
I find myself beneath the sheltering sky,
    my feet far from familiar terrain.
No matter if my grief diminishes or not.
My deep sleep ravaged, as I intended.

At every turn I fear that nothing but a sigh
    will remain of me.

Time for the king of kings to meet a shepherd
    who hails from villagers.

I will never forget that sweet moment,
    on the slope of dark valleys.
A cloud was on its way to meet
    the early morning moment.
Movement in all that was silent.
Shepherds herding flocks with serene songs
    from tambourine and flute.

Dear friend!
Cherish the time you have with the beloved.
If in that lonely place
    you find a heart loyal and sympathetic,
    never peddle those moments to the unkempt.

Nothing happens in the heart of a simple and silent hut.
But there is news.
With each delay comes much good news.

Amid turmoil of endless suffering
    are qualities of men revealed.

The night is long, the desert dark.

I want no one to see me and want to see no one.
In the passion of my unquestioning contemplation,
    amid hordes of myriad agonies,
    the pain in my bones will do.

You seek war so as to benefit from antagonisms
    stirred up among everyone.

Life is nothing but a hustle, so stop worrying.
Whenever things are tough, be more carefree.

Every step is afraid of the next.
A naked man, hand in hand with orphan child,
    en route to the village.
Shhh!
Dark night endures.

Ding-dong!
It is within the meditation of life.
It is the path to the day of deliverance.
The key to morning appears with it.
Dark night ends with it.

Ding-dong!
What's that noise?
A bell!
Who died?
Who still breathes?
Many times, like dancing shadows on water,
    have one thousand experiences been unleashed.
Yet the sleeper never once awoke.

Ding-dong!
Every breath offers a path to life, from dawn of existence
        to dawn of nothingness.

Passion for the race.
Escaping the bad.
Engaging with good.

The secret is revealed!
Things change.

Hand in hand with the one you know.
Shroud yourself in happiness and joy.
Listen to a love poem.
Praise her beauty mark.
Spend a night not thinking about
        what does and does not exist.

Unless the rust of an empty mind
        is eliminated from the heart,
        we are undeserving of desire.
Ha!
No door is opened before our eyes without purpose.

Keep your window open before my eyes.
My heart longs to be with you for a moment.
I have it in my heart to sing for you.

Why close our eyes to this lively world?
Whoever has known no beauty in his life
        himself boasts no beauty.

I stretched out my hands, near and far,
      towards the joyful musicians of the wind.
They brought a message
      from the newly blossomed spring.
To break the bitter silence of the valleys I asked for help
      from those whose heart-warming music
      brings rapture and adds intensity to joy.

Shame on me, miserable me!
In the heart of this dark night, who watches over me?
What can remedy this?
O God!
What brought me to this tearaway sea
      with hands empty of daily bread?
The beams of what longing have brought me here?
From weary seashore afar comes no burning light.

I should walk my path.
No one will care for me.
Although they would deny it, in this bustle of life,
      everyone is actually lonely.
My work protects me.

I am innocent.
Fishing is my work, hoping for daily bread.
My life has gone to waste.
No one in this world, this world in which we live
      with bloody hearts, can be more impoverished
      than me.

Hands move upon the crest of waves.
Naked bodies – dancing and flowing – entwined.

Tide upon tide.
High to low, low to high.
The sea at work.

I was received into the circle of love.
A pity that my weary heart isn't also rested.
The flood of tears carries me along.
The homesick heart envelops.
What if my path leads not to the home of the beloved?

Where should I go?
Who should I be thinking about?
You, my eyeliner, are at this moment my cure-all.
I shall not stop loving you.

Why such pretense?
Even if life isn't about the search, it must still be lived

Hey Rana! Rana!
Your body like a gazelle, Rana!
Magic-eyed Rana!
Hey Rana! Rana!

A neighbour is a companion of a neighbour.

Empty house.
Ecstatic guard.

Moon emerging, concealed by cloud.

Late stepped the man from the path.
He arrived by morning.

You may know how painful is the moment.
A human being understands
    but is unable to express things,
    as do poets, in words.
My heart, filled with grief.
I am in the same boat.
I appreciate the sorrow of the poems of the poets.

No one sees the end of these days.
No one knows how far these wings will fly, to what land.
They are all blind.
Suddenly, something startling!
The wrong man, energetic, rises.
The wise man, dispirited, sits.

The dark path, an enemy of my feet.
At every moment dirty water
        and stones make for hardship.
But I walk the path using eyes as feet.

The wind, wandering.
Door open, light off.
Every house in the village is empty.
The one with a load on his shoulder, walking the path,
        over the bridge, is afraid.

I come from dust.
I love the sea.
In every direction my eyes see nothing but sea.
It steals my heart.
Where will my path reveal itself to me?

My arrow falls to the ground.

Your arrow finds the heart.

It is reward enough for you
        that not everyone knows your pain.

So long as the world moves, everyone is on his own path.

Morning light burns in the distance.
I think about it.
Come, companion, sing with me!

From now on keep the door closed.
No one wants to meet anyone.

The old hazelnut tree stands, casting shadows
    across the ground, where the creek stops flowing.
A branch withered, a leaf turned yellow.
The wind came and swept it all away.

Why is the door split and window broken?
Why is every room dark?
Why is it that a friend never asks about friends,
    about how they are?

The heart should be the eye,
    able to find meaning in every colour.

The heart of the blossoming forest awakens.
The jasmine sleeps, soft in its embrace.

Turn towards the valleys, asleep in mountain embrace,
    the shining dream of morning, towards everything
    barren or fertile, every open plain.
Call him!

It is up to us if something stays or goes.
Those who proclaim they want nothing
    are in truth avaricious.
The immobile long to fly.

Moonlight creeps through.
The glowworm shines.
Nothing can shatter anyone's sleep.
But thinking of them causes me to awaken
	with tearful eyes.
The names of certain people
	have become my soul's daily bread.
At moments of melancholy
	I stretch out my hands towards them.
They give me courage.
They empower me.

All life's worries disappear in the middle of the night.

I have arrived from the desert with ravaged feet.

The creek weeps.
The moon laughs.
She laughs at my heart's desire.

Damn it all, including this and that letter of the alphabet,
	if I make mention of her.

Ruins contain treasure.

Shining moon.
River calm.

I stretch out my hands to open a door.
I am wasting my time.
Broken walls and doors collapse upon me.

Be patient with me when fatigue overwhelms.
Open the door to dialogue.
But please, no blame or bitterness.

A quiet forest path.
All that remains is a string of stones forming an oven,
    full of cold ashes, from nights long ago.

Wind knocks and swipes at the frightened road.
A woman remains silent.

Who remains?
Who is weary?

Above the plain it rains a wonderful rain.

Beside the river rambles the old turtle.
Sunny day.

When will the iron melt in my hands?
When will I forge it?
Such stubborn iron.

I have no pain.
A stubborn fever has laid me low.
I know why the threads of my body feel stiff,
    as if at every moment each were lashing me
    from top to bottom.

I retain all suffering in my heart
    and all arrows of blame in my guts.
I long for that day when, picturing your face,
    I smile and ask of those travelling to the city,
    "What news of her?"

A mercenary's work is best done for free.

It should be clear to you when I say that
    many hands make light work.

We have committed no crime,
    except to tread upon the path.

My boat has run aground.
I am upset.
I am in pain.
From my pain spills blood.

He hands over the keys of the locked locks
    of the dirty rusty chain to be repaired.

She who weeps when night is all around
    has a secret conversation with me.
She laughs with me.
She arrives laughing and laughing.

Such an honour to be free with life for a moment,
    to desire fearlessly, to talk about desiring fearlessly.
Such happiness!

Silent is the man who each day
    peered through the window,
    awaiting a rainy night, like tonight.

Everyone's spouse but mine has returned home.
My spouse is far away, working.

For some time now a bad feeling
    has been growing deep within.
My friends, my intimate friends!

I am focused on my work, he is focused on me.
I seek a homeward path, he seeks a path to nowhere.

My home is cloudy.
Clouds always hang heavy.

For a long time my neighbour's home has sat empty.

The host sits alone at home.

The sky rains down continuously upon the port.

I experienced the learning curve of youth.
My youthful days immersed in love as sweet as promises,
    but also bitter love.
Anyway, now my youth is behind me.

I am melancholic.
The guesthouse kills those who inhabit it.
I wish misfortune upon it.
Let its days be dark.
It has thrown together a crowd of people,
    some drowsy, some disagreeable,
    some absent-minded.

Turbulent sea envelops impatient boatman.
Night, filled with danger, is frightening.

I have closed the door.
The night is upon me, my night, dark as the grave.
Although I am not that far from it, it is far from me.

Night.
Valleys, still and sleeping, like dead snakes.
The hands of morning glory
    grasp the feet of the mountain cypress.
Whether or not you remember me,
    my memory of you remains strong.
My eyes upon the path, watching for you.

A drought upon my farm, beside my neighbour's farm.
"They weep upon the nearby seashore," we are told.
    "Mourner upon mourner."
Tell me, messenger of cloudy days, you tree frog,
    when do the rains arrive?

Spread across the floor are all my unwanted things.
In my darkened hut there can be no joy.
The walls of bamboo, dry as dust, about to explode,
    like hearts of lovers separated.
Tell me, messenger of cloudy days, you tree frog,
    when do the rains arrive?

At every moment is the white flower,
    like a beautiful face, smiling.
It tells a myth to the night.
The bird of happiness, anguished, shaken with suffering,
    talks nonstop.
It spreads a wing, the colour of blood,
    then sits, unhappy, on an overturned stone.

But the road is empty of everyone.
Debris upon debris.

The unawakened have many worries,
    but for no good reason.

Poetry is a sign of our desert dream.

Unlike all others, my ears are my eyes.

I do not listen to words of hypocrisy.

We are hanged by a hair.

O God!
Contemplation of those blue eyes.

My heart wanders because of your love.

With poverty comes one thousand wrongdoings.

Nothing has gone as I had hoped.
Meaninglessly, I continue chasing my dreams.

I am the poet of another people.
Among all others, I am the other.

Friends who travelled together have all left the festivities.
Grieving for them is the best thing to do.

A free man accepts no chains.

Shoes over here, feet over there.

Destroy timeworn foundations.
Today I sing alone.

I would rather be mute than a famous speaker.

Better than any words are those of the heart.

Fire
Poetry by Rumi

Selected and adapted by
Abbas Kiarostami

Although guiltless, I am a slave to she who punishes.

Consider it a blessing if misfortune befalls you
    on love's estate.

Because of love I ended up in a place
    unknown even to love.

Blessed is the righteous one whose beloved is at home.

Fight with me.
How sweet is this fight.
Make excuses, for excuses are the fashion of beauties.

I expect no loyalty.
Cruelty is the nature, habit and religion of beauties.

Night.
Not the time to let anyone in.
The lovers' *qibla* became the moon.
O moon worshipers, how the moon smiles!
O night walkers, arise!
Time to walk the path.

I am here, advice over there.
Cupbearer, share the wine.
Pour that cup, the cup which nourishes the soul,
    upon my soul.
Cupbearer, you who take care of lovers,
    place that cup into my hands,
    hidden from lips of strangers.

Things of wonder for the eyes.
Happiness and joy for the soul.
Drunkenness caused by beauty, and suffering
    thanks to the beloved, for the head.
Love should be forever soaring into the air.
Reason chases knowledge and good manners.

Such a day of bliss will be that day
    when we host the beloved.
Gazing at her face, our eyes become a gallery
    of beautiful paintings.
If there is pain because of injury caused by separation,
    we treat it with sunlight from her face.
She will torture our hearts however she wants.
We will do whatever she says.
We follow the commands of her heart.

I have come to take you by the scruff of the neck,
    to make you fall in love, to be selfless,
    to seat you in heart and soul.
You, blossoming tree, I have come to you
    as blissful spring, to embrace you with joy,
    to shake you up.
I have come to beautify you in this house, to raise you up
    into the sky, like prayers of lovers.
You are my ball, driven by the command of my mallet.
Although I guide you, I am running after you.

When you are with yourself,
	the beloved appears to you as a thorn.
When you are selfless, do you even need the beloved?
When you are with yourself, you are the prey of a fly.
When you are selfless, the elephant is your prey.
When you are with yourself,
	you are bound to clouds of grief.
When you are selfless, the moon embraces you.
When you seek rest, only restlessness will follow.
Seek restlessness and find rest.

Those troubled by love's passion are carefree,
	liberated from honour and dishonour.
Even after one hundred thousand stones,
	the crystal of love is intact.
Sky, earth and many others are frustrated
	when faced with love's hurried pace.

You need more than just patience when in love.
Reason offers no assistance.
Selflessness is a land of bliss,
	under the command of no one.
The caravan of life passes by.
No bell call is heard.

The heart spoke.
The beauty of her face, magical hair like narcissus,
	eyebrows like hyacinth, sweet-tasting lips.
O love!
People have given you many names and titles.
Last night I gave you another:
Incurable pain.

You shed tears out of weakness.
You fail to count your blessings.
Either stop asking God for a blessing or complain less.
O heart!
Look not at every branch, or remain embittered.
Contemplate beginning and end while extremes unite.

I am a sword, both soft and sharp, that sheds blood.
I am like the mortal world.
My appearance appealing, my conscience dangerous.

Do not stir muddy water.
Your soul will be made clear.
Your dregs will settle.
Your pain will be remedied.

Dignity and dishonour washed away by the wine of love.

Follow the rules of love properly
    and you will act improperly.

Burn the essence of our existence
    with your flirtatious ways.

Bewilderment!
Inescapable when confronted with such beauty.

Why ask loyalty from someone
    who has lost his heart to love?
When the heart departs, so do loyalty and cruelty.

Where is the cupbearer of the soul to disrupt us,
    to sweep away from the heart
        all worries of yesterday and tomorrow?

Have you ever seen a lover replete with love?
Have you ever seen a fish bored by this ocean?
Have you ever seen a painting escape its painter?
Have you ever seen Vamegh refuse Azra?

Just as there is existence in non-existence
     and non-existence in existence, a fire struck his soul
     and burnt his very existence.
O heart!
Although you hunt that lion, be afraid of this gazelle.
In her eyes, lions are fragile.
Her eyes are the eyes of a gazelle.

I have neither work nor business.
In this world I am in the employ of no one.
I need no employer but you, my love.
Night or early morning?
I don't know.
What news?
You count the days, my love.
Seeing you is my day.
Separation from you is my night.
You make my night day.
My love, you are springtime.

"What is it that rests in your heart?" asked the nightingale
     of the blossoming tree.
"Share it with me now.
There is no one here but you and I."
The reply:
"As long as you are with yourself,
     do not hope to understand such things.
Try to eliminate the self from this house.
The needle's eye of desire is narrow.
It lets in just one thread."

Of your soul-nourishing face are we admirers.
Bless us, for we desire you.
Your face is like sun and moon.
We are all particles in your air.
Do not slay us with no good reason,
     as you would an enemy.
We are your acquaintances.
Our death would satisfy you.
Your satisfaction is our only objective.

You, in love with me.
I make you unhappy.
Build less, for I will destroy whatever you build.
If you build two hundred houses, like the bee's
honeycomb,
     I will make you homeless, like a fly.
You long to hold people in captivity.
I long to make you drunk and restless.
For how long do you wish to be a prisoner
     of this and that?
If you emerge from this, I will transform you into that.

Much daily bread is hidden
     behind the daily bread that people seek.
O soul!
There is much baked bread beyond the work of a baker.
You have closed your eyes and ask:
"Where is daylight?"
The sun strikes your eyes saying, "Here am I, open the
door."
O soul!
The seed of a tree drinks.
Branches and leaves appear.
They are the soul of that tree.

The beloved of the tavern came to take us home,
    displaying for us refreshing spring.
She reveals herself, dons armour, then draws her bow,
    all to rob us.
She tells us things, throws out traps and tricks,
    and is deceptive, all to devour us.

Like a statuesque cypress is she.
Go, be her shadow.
Although she will eliminate us young trees,
    run before and after her.
O lover!
If her heart is of stone, flee not.
Whether at the start or at the end, we will be slain by her.

We walk, without feet, around the Kaaba.
Headless, we pray prostrate,
    our head and feet bewildered because of her.
We walk around the beloved's Kaaba without feet.
She arrived drunk into this world,
    emerging from non-existence,
    and broke down our door.

Either union with the beloved or wine.
If you cannot reach the ocean,
    place your feet into the creek.

Be silent and search ruins for love's treasure
    as it blossoms in spring.

The flower says more than the nightingale.

A dove calling for prayer.
Trees standing in prayer.

A statuesque beauty is the shortest route to the beloved.

O traveller!
Let your heart not be bound to any single place.

O rooster!
Cease your announcing of morning's arrival.
Morning declares itself with light.

While searching for the beloved's happiness,
    it is blasphemous to search for your own.

Love is ascension towards the estate of the beloved.
Read the story of ascension upon the face of the lover.
In life we see bodies hanging, many people like Hallaj,
    as ripe fruit does from the tree.

Born are we from divine judgment.
Divine judgment is the mother of all.
Like children, we scramble after divine judgment,
    flowing like water amid flowers.
This thirsty dust will give rise to plants.

I am like a flower.
My entire body, not just my lips, in laughter.
Alone with the beloved I am selfless.
You have brought a lantern and dawn into my heart.
Take not my heart alone, but my soul and heart united.
Send a regal message.
O king, invite everyone!
For how long should this one be with you?
For how long should that one remain alone?

The garden and beautiful flowers smile because of you.
Milk and honey.
Let it always be so.
Wherever you turn your face,
    a flower grows in front of you.
Wherever you go, you return.
Let your red carpet be of gold.
O God!
Give her a big heart and long life.
Give her glory.
We then shall have glory too.

Entering non-existence, free of worry about life.
Becoming strangers to ourselves.
No fear of strangers.
Two feasts every year for you.
For us, two hundred feasts at every moment.
If celebration and joy is all around,
    then this world for you, for us the beloved.

We took an unexpected journey.
Selfless we became.
Our heart was made lively.
Selfless we became.
The moon that once hid from us
    placed her face upon our face.
Selfless were we.
Even without wine we are always drunk.
Happy are we.
Selfless are we.
We need no one to remember us.
Remembrance are we.
Selfless are we.

Do not pollute your lips with kisses from everyone.
Let only the beloved's lips sweeten and intoxicate.
Do not allow the scent of any other lips
        to emanate from your own.
Let love be ethereal, pure, unique.
Moses distanced himself from Pharaoh's wealth.
A miraculous hand, bestowed upon him
        by the ocean of generosity.

We set fire to desire and madness.
At every moment we encounter waves of blood.
We are companions of those drinkers from Hell,
        whoever breaks through the sheltering sky.
Self-awareness is Hell.
Desire less and lose yourself.

Break not the heart of a seeker.
Be not cruel.
O beautiful moon, have mercy!
Even the religious never sacrifice the fragile.

Give wine to the beloved, with cup always in hand.
She is both bitter and sweet.
Bygone and busybody is your logic.
Let it be rambling and carefree instead.

Do not speak into the mirror
        so that she becomes your companion.
If you speak as such, she will veil herself.

A blissful and strutting tree in the desert.
Whoever sleeps in its shadow will awaken drunk.

Whoever has a head is forever worried about losing it.

Every plant is a sign of water.

Although embraced by the beloved, restless am I.

From that liberated cypress whispered the wind
    good news into my ear.

Lovers exposed.
A beloved in hiding.
Has anyone ever seen such love?

When you see the dimple, remember that the apple tree
    is an inedible fragment.

The beloved is serenity and the source of all restlessness.
How can I be with beauties
    when burning in new and dynamic fires?

Remain oblivious.
The mindful are disgraced when lovers gather.
O friends, awake at night!
Candle, wine, the lonely beloved.
All await.

If a tree could move,
    never would it be wounded by the saw.
If sun and moon were fixed like a rock,
    never would they shine.
Rivers immobile as the sea are full of bitter water.

Our death is happiness and union.
If for you it is grief, leave me be.
This world is our prison,
    the destruction of which brings joy.
Do not seek loyalty in this prison.
Loyalty here is disloyal.

What can be learned when in union with you?
What can be learned when separated from you?
Either become lost in my pain or reveal the remedy.
You flee from me because of my ignorance.
Either become lost in me or teach me.
No one is the master of loyalty.
Loyalty teaches me to be loyal.

You are my world and my soul.
What is to be done with world and soul?
You are my treasure.
What is to be done with gain and loss?
One moment I am a lover of wine,
        another a lover of kebab.
Me, trapped in an endless circle.
What is to be done as time moves on?
I am startled by everyone.
I flee from everyone.
I am not hidden.
I am not visible.
What is to be done with this world?
Union with you gives me a hangover.
I have no feeling for other people.
You are my prey.
What is to be done with bow and arrow?

Every moment, every hour, despite mindful pleas,
    I drink one hundred measures of wine, without a cup.
With the help of an invisible world,
    with no politics or tricks,
    I reach for flying birds and divine eagles.
In my drunken state,
    from my palm appear wondrous birds.
From my lips flows wine.

Come! Come!
The garden has risen.
Come! Come!
The beloved is arrived.
Bring at once soul and world.
Give everything to the sun,
      with its shining sword-like beams.
Smile at the unseemly, those who hesitate,
      and shed tears for those separated from the beloved.

The earth responded in one hundred different languages
      to utterances made from the sky.
You, lover of sky, be friendly with those who tell
      the tale of ascension.

There is work to be done, but I have no beloved.
All work is pointless when there is no beloved.
To love in one's heart is endless work.
All work, except love, comes to an end.

When lips are silent
      the heart speaks with one hundred tongues.
Silence!
For how long do you want to try this?

Close your mouth.
Words are winds.
Dust from these winds conceal the path.

No escape, save madness when your hair enslaves.

So busy am I with the beloved, there is no time for myself.

Lips kissing.
How sweet!
A thirst for more.

Bliss attained.
Whatever my heart sought was found.

Become a lion and love becomes a lion hunter.
Become an elephant and love becomes a rhinoceros.

Sell your logic.
Purchase wonderment.
From such business will you benefit.

O musician, play music!
The beloved, loyal and blissful, arrived drunk.
Everyone chose someone to love.
Our beloved is love.
Even before our existence did our love arrive drunk.

My hope for union has feet of clay.
I grieve our separation.
A rule for the afflicted:
More pain, fewer tears.

Come, and become nothing.
Non-existence feeds all souls,
     save those which are nothing but sorrow.
Me without myself.
You without yourself.
We enter this creek.
In this land is nothing but cruelty.
This creek drowns but does not kill.
It is the water of life.
It is nothing but generosity and kindness.

I have much to say to you and about you,
    but silence is golden.
The donkey who stays silent because of you is a wise one.
Whoever turns his back on art because of you
    is a great artist.

Such a garden!
May its flowers live until the day of reckoning.
Such a beloved!
Sacrifice both worlds before her beauty.
From early morning
    are the most beautiful people hunting.
May our heart be hunted by the arrow of her flirtation.
We broke down the door of piety.
She, thirsty for our blood, cursed us.
"May you be restless the rest of your life."
Neither serenity nor the heart survived.
May God be with her.

I had no idea that such desire would make me delirious,
    turn my heart so hellish, my eyes into rivers.
Me, unaware that a flood would steal me suddenly,
    carry me, like a ship, into a sea of blood,
    splinter the ship with waves,
    each piece left twisting in water.
So many unknown things.
Unsure am I whether, when out on open sea,
    I consumed opium.

Until dreams of the beloved are with us,
    all life is contemplation.
Union of lovers turns the house into a garden.
When the heart's desire is fulfilled
    one single thorn is better than one thousand dates.

Love cannot be found in wisdom,
    knowledge, books, papers.
The path of lovers is not that of everyday conversation.
Branches of the tree of love begin before our world.
Its roots continue into eternity.
It rests not on sky or earth.
It has no trunk.
We turned our back on logic.
We punished desire.
Logic and desire deserve no honour.

After sorrow always comes happiness.
After happiness comes sorrow.
Be dust and give rise to plants.
Whoever became dust found treasure.

O heart!
Drown yourself in sorrow for her.
Patience is the key that opens the door.
She will reveal the remedy.
Patience is the key that opens the door.
Absorb all sorrow.
Her great throne suddenly stands before you.
Patience is the key that opens the door.

If you are not crazed, make yourself crazed.
Even if checkmated one hundred times,
    gamble another piece.

Blessed is the gambler who lost all he had
    save a desire for gambling.

Steal the art of self-sacrifice from the butterfly.

The naked, unafraid of the blind.

Pain.
Tears.
Justice to follow.

Eternal promise passed hand to hand.

Do not concern yourself if love is dishonoured.
It has other names and titles.

Many people are intoxicated by the beloved.
They never know what bread is.

The logical will never understand the drunkard's passion.
The mindful will never understand an unconscious heart.
A king awakened to the drunken revelry that occurs
    when lovers gather will turn his back on his kingdom.

I rest, but my soul does not.
I am at rest when I am restless.
Leave me be.
I will clothe myself in fire, as does the sun,
    and with that fire give light to the world,
    as does the sun.

We searched for a guide and found only your love.
We searched for a companion
    and found only a sign of you.
Tell us how to search.
We tried one way of searching but found nothing.
From now on we search for the beloved up above.
We searched for the beloved down here on earth.
No sign of anything.

Today there is a different tenderness in your beauty.
Today whatever the delirious lover does is correct.
I dance more than any tree in these gardens.
Me, the tree of fortune.
Morning breeze blows about my head.
Despite those who insist that the shadow is separate
    from the tree, we spin in the shadow of your sun.

We, from Heaven, are in ascent.
We, from the ocean, are descending into water.
We are not from here.
We are not from there.
We are from nowhere.
We go nowhere.
We are Noah's Ark in the storm of the soul.
We travel without hands.
We travel without feet.
Like a wave, we emerged from within.
We explore within.

Here am I.
Over there, the grief and happiness of this world.
Here am I.
Over there, worrying about rain and the gutter.
Why should I not return to my original world?
Here is my heart.
Over there the exploration of dust.
You, birds, have wings and fly skyward.
Here are you.
Over there roof and ascension.
Enter the tavern and close the door behind you.
Here are you.
Over there people good and bad.

Speak of new things and make these two worlds anew.
Free them from all limitations.
Let the darkness of dust settle upon
    those not reawakened by your breath,
    those not made colourful and musical.
Keep the secret inside.
Silence!
Silence is bitter, but bliss will eclipse the pain.

Why does Venus knock on my door each early morning?
She, the slayer of one hundred moons.
Why does Venus knock on my door each early morning?
Those who see her are both awakened and dormant.
Angel or human?
Why does Venus knock on my door each early morning?
This world, upside down.
Water above my head.
She has transformed a stone into a gem.
Why does Venus knock on my door each early morning?

All glass am I.
Blowing glass is my job.
O stone upon my heart of glass!
Gemlike are those reasoned and wise, yet of her unaware.
Such a tragedy.

Spring is here.
Spring is here.
Fragrant spring is here.
The beloved is here.
The beloved is here.
The patient beloved is here.
Spring is here.
Spring is here.
Fresh spring is here.
Flowers, plants and lovely lilies are here.

Love deployed its army.
Love conquered my soul.
Ask love how I am.
Do not ask poor old me.

O lover!
Here is logic.
Hide yourself.
Alas! Alas!
Logic and awareness weigh heavy.

Dishonourable are we.
Drunk are we.

I tried them all.
I liked you the most.

Desire for the beloved.
Union will result.
Good news.

When you make me suffer, you save me from suffering.

Those lost upon the path
    will use logic to find their way back.
Who will assist once logic is lost?

Blessed is he whose gold was stolen by a thief.
Blessed is he who divorces his wife.

The month of cold departed.
Winter is over.
Come, fresh spring is here.
Verdant, blissful earth.
Time for lilies.
Look at those trees, as bewildered as a drunkard
    shaking his head.
Morning breeze sang a magical word
    that made the garden dance.

My heart, impenetrable to sorrow.
My wine, unassailable by thirst.
My heart, permeated by love.
It befriends only lovers.

Smoke billows from my burning heart.
I shall scorch the curtains of all seven skies.
If autumn destroys the garden,
    my new spring will make the world smile.
"Come back!" says the world.
"O spring, the cruelty of autumn
    has made hundreds of holes in my heart!"

Sleep envelops consciousness.
There is no sleep for the crazed.
They know nothing of the night.
In the religion of madness there is neither day nor night.
Only the crazed know what they have.
Even with eyes closed they see everything
    and with the soul read the eternal tablet.

Separation.
Earth and sky wept.
This heart has sat amid blood.
Logic and soul have wept.
Alas!
Of this grief I can speak no more.
I can offer no explanation for these tears.
In place of tears, a gourd.
Every moment full of blood.
Every moment full of tears.
Alas! Alas!
Alas! Alas!
Even the eye of doubt has wept for that tearful eye.

Why did the beloved see me yet ask nothing?
Why was she so bitter when passing the lover's window?
Why?
What wrongdoing upset her so?
Since morning she has planned the lover's death.
Why?
Why did she raise her mighty sword?
We startled the heart of the beloved.
We startled the benevolence of God.
Why?

We plan but still know nothing of divine judgment.
It is written by God.
Do not fight it.
Seek the land of love.
This will make your land free of Azrael.
Be the king's prey.
Do not seek your own prey.
Death takes all.

Disunity is born of disharmony, victory of union.
Conceited, you and your beloved both.
Divorce is born of this.
This is the beloved, not a piece of wood.
Do not break her.
Do so and hear the sound of cracking.

Pity him without gold, unaware of the goldmine.
Those unaware of us speak of prayer having no effect.

The soul returned from a long journey,
    arriving in the dust of your door.
It had left without you, hoping to resolve things,
    and came back burnt, having achieved nothing.

I seem to be sleeping but am awake, aware.
Although unconscious, of you am I conscious.

Every sound of the world I heard rings hollow,
    except that of love.

Even if the pitcher is cracked, the water inside is intact.

That old table does not deserve your bread.

Stop upon the path and death will appear.

A heart filled with words, yet speech impossible.

No wine and cupbearer, yet drunk am I.
I am Kay Qobád, with neither thorns nor crown.

One thousand lives has the lover.
Expire without hesitation or fear.
The soul will never diminish.
Do not concern yourself with such things.
You are following the blissful soul.

My heart wants you.
My heart desires.
My sorrowful, withered face desires you.
I am in ascent.
I visit two hundred roofs
        and am caught in two hundred traps.
The gazelle of my soul longs for your garden.

Be blissful.
You know the secret:
Bliss brings bliss.
Be thankful and sweet like sugar.
At every moment are the thankful rewarded with sugar.
Consume her bitter drink, then smile,
        and there will be no bitterness left in your soul.

O cupbearer, arise!
The moon is here.
Hurry!
Her arrival is untimely.
Be quick!
The beloved has entered the pavilion.
We could never imagine such good fortune,
        so sudden was its arrival.

Our desert limitless, our heart and soul restless.
It was within this world that the world took form.
What form do you take?
When you see a decapitated head rolling towards you
    along the path, ask of it our secrets.
Then you will hear our hidden secret.

O soul, beware!
Sleep not tonight.
Tonight I am your guest.
You, heart and soul of the guest.
Beware!
Sleep not tonight.
Your face unveiled like a full moon.
Tonight is divine night.
You, queen of all beauties.
Beware!
Sleep not tonight.
You, the cypress of two hundred gardens.
You, the serenity of drunkards' hearts.
You stole the heart.
Steal also the soul.
Beware!
Sleep not tonight.
You, blissful smiling garden.
Without you are the two worlds a prison.
You are all this and more.
Beware!
Sleep not tonight.

May we dream big.
May our gourd be full of water.
May wind and water be for us.
May love command us.
The queen of beauties is our queen.
Ever-present love is ours.
The soul of fortune is our companion.
May fortune be with us.
Wild and blissful are we.
We pull people in, as would a magnet.
May our attractive soul attract secrets.

The beloved cast you out.
Beware!
Do not feel disappointed.
If today she casts you out,
    tomorrow she will invite you in.
If she closes the door on you, depart not.
Just wait, and she will reward your patience with a throne.
Even if she closes off all paths that surround you,
    she will show you hidden paths
    of which none are aware.

Beware!
May your head fill with bliss
    and your lips be forever smiling.
Beware!
May the heart of love be happy with you.
May the worshiper of grief who sees you
    and does not rejoice be ashamed, pathetic, cast adrift.

A smile tells the story of your kindness.
A tear tells the story of your fury.
These two opposing signs tell the story
    of the one beloved.

Love speaks:
"You are correct.
But never think that we are similar.
I am wind, you are fire.
I enflamed you."

The verdant tree knows the value of rain.
You, so dry, know nothing of the value of rain.

Smiling flower.
What would it do if not smile?

Be angry with the one who can set you free.

I need to see her face.
Parvin and the moon have nothing to offer.

Most likely you will discover treasure amid destruction.

The lover's burnt heart, longing for wine.
Will you send sorrow and tears?
Absolutely not.

Will this door be open?
Yes.
Will the beautiful beloved unveil her face?
Yes.

You, the antidote.
This world is poison.
You, the bait.
Life is a trap.
All desires but you fulfilled.
My life unfulfilled.

Stop! Stop!
Your actions shame you.
Without the beloved this garden seems a tomb.
Enter the Ark of the soul, upon the forever turbulent
        ocean of love, and invoke Noah.

Whoever believes that the thorn delivers up a flower
        will smile when a thorn of cruelty arrives.
An unexpected curse from the sweet beloved,
        but her cursing nurtures the soul.
The beloved destroyed our home
        as would the stone-hearted.
Any house destroyed by her will become a palace.

Love is the alchemy that creates gold.
It transforms dust into intangible treasures.
It can open doors to the sky and guide wisdom,
        as would a ladder.
Whoever blocks the path of lovers is ignorant
        and does dirty work.

Again I rose up.
I swear to you, I am in such a state.
I will dismantle whatever limitations you place upon me.
I swear to you, I am insane,
        the one who holds demons captive.
I know the language of birds.
I swear to you, I am Solomon.
I seek not mortal life.
You are my precious life.
I seek not the sorrowful soul.
I swear to you, you are my soul.
Ascending without you is like being a sorrowful dark
cloud.
In the garden without you is like being in prison.
I swear to you.

O sun, fill the house with light again!
Make friends happy and our enemies blind.
Rise from behind a mountain.
Transform stones into gems.
Ripen unripe grapes.
O sun, make the garden verdant again!
Fill desert and farm with beauties.
O physician of love!
O lantern in the sky!
Help lovers and find a remedy for the afflicted.

I swear to God that in the workshop of your love,
        whenever you are absent, my work on the loom
        yields nothing.
The world has four seasons, each opposed to the other.
Is peace possible when four enemies are in combat?
Come burn every season but spring.
You are the real spring, the essence of every season.

If my heart has sorrow it is because
        I long for your happiness.
If my hands are generous it is because of your wealth.
The sorrow I feel does no harm.
Even if it did, let it be.
The thirsty are content with whatever comes from water.
Does the beauty of the garden come from
        the morning breeze which breaks branches?

Saffron told tulip the tale of an apple, half red, half yellow.
Half delighted, half in pain was the lover
        when separated from the beloved.

My poem is like Egyptian bread,
        inedible after only one night.
Eat it while fresh, before dust settles.

The world is like a tree.
You are leaves and fruits.
With no leaves and fruits, what use is a tree?

The beloved, broken and drunk.
A blissful day.
What is to be done but drink and experience bliss?

Disconnect from everything.
Utter the name of the beloved.

Which gem are you?
No one is wealthy enough to buy you.

Everywhere we go do scales of justice
    offer up whatever is deserved.

Close your mouth.
Open the window of your heart.

You, caught in your own trap.
How is it that you are also a hunter?
You, a thief in your own home.
How is it that you steal yet also give?

Nighttime.
But for us it is like morning.
Alas!
Turmoil of early night.

You, you are the beautiful.
You, you are the sweet.
I can never be happy knowing that
    you are sometimes happy, sometimes sad.

O cupbearer, bring red wine!
Reveal the remedy for a homesick heart.
This is a day for festivities, not battle.
Dispose of the dagger of war.
Let the harp sing.

My peace of mind, ravaged by your love.
Your love liberates me from kin.
Bow your head, move away from all this.
The statuesque cypress is unattainable
        to those with short arms.
Burning love arrived, destroying all but the beloved.
Sit happy and smile a blissful smile as everything burns.

I live my life only to serve her.
Without her, what use is life?
The sky wept because of my cries and prayers.
Without fate on your side, what use is prayer?
O heart!
For how long will you boast about loyalty?
Enter the ocean of loyalty.
What use is your loyalty today?

You, with no love in your heart, deserve sleep.
Leave us.
We are deserving of her sorrow and love.
Go sleep!
We came apart under the shining sun of her sorrow.
Such burning desire never arose in your heart.
Go sleep!
Searching for union with her is like flowing water.
You do not care where she is.
Go sleep!
The path of love is found beyond
    the seventy-two nations.
Such great faith you have in deception and hypocrisy.
Go sleep!

As we enter into turmoil of night,
    we make waves in night's ocean.
Whoever has seen the moon escapes sleep.
Many hearts, filled with light.
Many pure souls, burning.
They are the slaves and commanders of night.
Day is for business and trade.
Desire for night is something else.

Your love applauds.
Many worlds created.
One hundred new centuries appear out of empty skies.
We are today your guest, intoxicated by your smile.
I swear to God that as I utter your name
    my heart is startled.
Which roof but your roof?
Which name but your name?
Which cup but your cup?
You, our sweet cupbearer!

O candle of the world!
Your light was unseen within our circle last night.
Tell me the truth about where you were burnt.
Wherever you were last night longs for you today,
      as does my heart, as does the magical mosque.
You are the shadow.
The entire world is your shadow.
Who has ever seen light separate from shadow?

Blissful spring arrived.
The beloved's messenger arrived.
So drunk are we, in love, hungover, restless.
O eye!
O light!
Walk towards the garden.
Do not keep beauties waiting.

Why are you such a brittle branch?
Contemplate the beloved's face.
Why are you such an autumnal leaf?
Contemplate this new spring.
You would benefit from entering into the circle of rogues.
Contemplate countless wines, beauties, cupbearers.

Be selfless.
You see one thousand blessings.
Be yourself.
You see one thousand troubles.

As we emerge she disappears.
As we disappear she emerges.

Here is wine.
A drunk beloved.
Me, in love.

Clashing swords do not make safe the path.

Turn your back on status, honour and pride.

Blissful are all things given and received from above.

A true lover follows only one will.

Those in love with beauties can never avoid sorrow.
Those incurable can never avoid pain.

O brother, let the fig seller sell his figs!
Business is of no interest to us.
O cupbearer of the soul!
Where is the cup of wine?

If in your heart and soul you are in love,
        accept cruelty from the beloved.
If you tease those burdened by a thorn bush,
        you are no true lover.
To attract the beloved, a gem should sparkle.
Dispel from the soul all impurities.
Hang them by the neck.

"You will lose."
So be it.
"You have no belief in God."
Correct.
"You are a fox, not a lion."
Or even a dead dog.
"You are unaware of the heart."
So tell me.

The moon emerged, welcoming a month of fasting.
O sweet beloved, time for nothing but kisses!
No hugs or anything else.
O sweet-lipped musician,
    let your music be heard by stars!
Our king arrived victorious from the hunt.
O king, you hunted everything!
Let your dog roam.
Let it hunt just one thing more.

O splendorous Joseph, you ascend our roof!
For us, such bliss!
You have broken our cup and crushed our trap.
You are our light, our happiness, our victorious fortune.
Excite our passion and turn grapes into wine.
You are our beloved.
So compassionate are you!
You, a trap for our drunken heart.
Do not leave us alone.
Take our turban as insurance.
The feet of my heart stand in mud.
I give my life.
There is no opportunity to give my heart.
Let the heart wail with burning desire.
Alas! Alas!

I will never leave this shining house
    nor travel from this blessed city.
Me, the beloved and being in love,
    all for the rest of my life.
Even when dead I will never leave her.
If the world became a turbulent ocean
    I would seek nothing but treasure.
Our beloved is the soul and ruler of divine judgment.
Only divine judgment can release me
    from this precious soul.

Love has nothing to do with talking and allusion.
The soul has nothing to do with names and forms.
Lovers are commanded by the beloved's mallet.
The ball has neither hands nor feet,
      going wherever the mallet sends it.
The ball feels nothing.

O my beloved!
Everyone with his soulmate.
Everyone with the beloved he deserves.
Those with sorrow for you in their heart are unwanted.
Those hunted by you are unhunted by all others.
A branch of one tree disconnects from all others.
If you seek union with her, forgo all others.

What could bring rest to my soul?
O beloved, union with you!
What could remedy my illness?
Union with you.
Through union is a brick turned into a palace.
Through union is a thread turned into cloth.

I am you.
You are me.
O friend, do not leave!
Do not envision me as someone else.
Do not banish me from your door.
Bound to you as a shadow am I.
Do not stab at your own shadow with a dagger.

No matter what, the shadow is blameless.

The crown of love upon your head.
O seeker of truth!
Walk blissfully with it.

The window decides how much moonlight
    creeps into the house.

In the Kaaba of night one prayer is counted
    one hundred times.

For a lover, the more silence the better.
For the ocean, the more turmoil the better.

The windmill never knows why its sails rotate.

Arise and dance!
We all applaud.
We men, free of women.

Among beauties I blossom like a flower.
Among those who believe only in the past
    I am as despondent as autumn.
Logic brings with it consciousness.
Me, turning my back on such things.
I despise logic.
It withers me.

O heart, such passion I feel for our union!
A stranger am I, drunk and in love.
My bags packed, I am ready to travel to our rendezvous.
If I desire anything but you, I deserve the gallows.
If I touch anything but your skirt,
    my hands deserve to be severed.

O musician, begin your lovemaking!
Play the stringed instrument.
You own the land of drunkenness and selflessness.
There is no need to desire what King Sanjar owns.
Ensure that love can intoxicate,
    for no grapes can ever come from dust.

It is cold today.
You desire us.
Your blissful heart seeks exploration.
Do not postpone bliss until tomorrow.
Peace is here and now.
Your face is like the sun.
Extend your shadow over us.

O soul and world!
Why do you flee?
O glory of kings!
Why do you flee?
You take off like an arrow, then return to us.
Why do you escape the bow?
You have one thousand treasures.
Why do you flee from those so soft-spoken?
Silence!
The tongue is nothing but harmful.
Why flee towards harm?

Dancing is for restless souls.
Quick, arise, no time to waste!
Do not sit here thinking so.
A real man would follow the beloved.
Don't tell me she isn't interested.
The thirsty man wouldn't care.
The butterfly fears no fire.
The soul of love disdains wisdom.

If he in love disappears, ask the beloved.
If he flees, search on the beloved's estate.
If the nightingale of my soul flies suddenly from my body,
    ask not the thorn.
Search instead in the garden.
I, on the estate of love, asked a sage where she was.
"Search the secrets" was his reply.

The worst of all endings is the one without love.
What gives life to the seashell is the pearl inside.
As the verdant branch withers,
        the leaves grow fearful of becoming brittle.
If a lover misses the caravan of love
        he will find Khidr as his guide upon the path.

A fresh branch am I.
How can I dance without wind?
I am the shadow of the cypress.
How can I move without it?
If she does not excite my passion, I shall fall silent.
She is the rider I run after.

The way I feel today, I am unable to distinguish
        a donkey from its burden.
The way I feel today, I am unable to distinguish
        a flower from its thorn.
Today the beloved shook me up.
I cannot distinguish myself from her.

In our heart we are in the sky
        although our bodies are buried in the ground.
Our soul is stirring although we appear as dead.

O you all, arise and applaud and be happy and drunk!
Bury sorrow and sorrowful thoughts.

How you long to rule over us!
The honour of being a slave will never be yours.

Flee from the one not in love.

If you are chasing after prey, it is you being hunted.

My face is all suffering.
All treasure inside.

Lips dry, eyes wet.
Pain of separation.
Today, union.
Nothing dry or wet.

We are lovers, poor and in love.
We are children, young and old.

To the souls of all drunkards:
I swear I am drunk.
O compassionate beloved, help me!
If I have desire for anyone but you,
    I do not deserve a head.
If I am without you, let me burn.

So drunk am I that I cannot distinguish Eve from Adam.
Because of my passion, the ocean is in turmoil.
Because of my bliss, the whole world is drunk.

The queen of beauties emerged furious.
Let my sweet life be sacrificed for that bitterness.
"Do not see things so askew," I told my crooked eye.
Who would believe a smiling flower could be so bitter?
Inside the palace the king smiles, but in the courtroom
    brings forth fury.

Go!
Head towards the queen of beauties.
Go!
Head towards the sun of all souls.
Go!
The plodding caravan is about to leave.
O you dawdlers, move faster!
Go!
Leave behind bed, home, kin.
Horse and mule.
Saddle and pack saddle.
Go!

Look at every face.
Yellow.
Exposed pain.
Look at that city.
So pained, like a garden in autumn.
Pain caused by separation and fear of divine judgment.
Hidden fires.
Tears.
We worry about the sky, about impending darkness.

You are like the seven oceans.
Bestow the pearl.
Make all this copper ripe for alchemy.
Every stone wept for us.
O beloved, remedy our pain!
Blessed am I, living amid riches.
Without you I am an orphan.
Cure me!
I closed my mouth and sat in sadness.
Open my hands.
Desire for union.

Whether asleep or awake, I thirst for the beloved.
I am a companion of her imagination.
Like a mirror I follow her face.
I revealed and hid her reality.
The moment she smiled, I smiled back.
The moment she became angry, I did too.

O beloved!
For you and me, meaningless is the word "beloved."
O beloved!
How ridiculous it feels when I speak of my "beloved."
Any sigh from me must return whence it came.
I close my mouth and do not sigh.
When the moon reveals itself
     there will be sighing and tears.
O beautiful full moon!
More blissful is contemplation of you.

We, a particle of the sun of love.
O love, rise up so we too can rise!
Search for us among valleys.
We, the tiniest of particles.

Do not deceive us with colours.
The dagger of love makes yellow our face.
One thousand cheers:
To pain!
The rest for us.
We, companions of pain.

A fish that knows the ocean will never survive the dust.
A true lover
     will not stay surrounded by colours and smells.

Love was a matchmaker.
I was pulled towards you.
I am first a slave to love.
After that, all yours.

What is the meaning of east and west in a void?

A life without love is no life at all.

How does a fish avoid the sea?

O beloved!
Stop talking such nonsense.
Do not delay until tomorrow.

We may be lost to the world, but are welcomed
    onto the estate of the beloved.

I closed the lid of the pitcher,
    but still wine seeped through.
Those who made the pitcher know its personality.

I have broken my cup with my own stone.
I have ripped my curtain with my own hands.
I have dug up my roots with my own fingers.
I have wept from the clouds of my eyes
    onto the farm of my soul.

Such impropriety.
We feel bad about so many things.
One hundred thousand sorrows.
Call the gang of drunkards to wash away all sorrows.
We will not face the cruelty of night.
No cloud can hide our moon.
There is no death for lovers.
We will not mourn their demise.

I have become selfless, yet long for ever more selflessness.
Me, longing to be as drunk as are your eyes.
I seek neither throne nor crown.
I long to submit and serve you.
My sweet beloved placed her hands around my throat.
"What do you want?" she asked.
"Only this," I told her.

I saw your face and spring arrived.
I saw that the flower was intimidated by your face.
As you rested in my heart I saw my heart restless for you.
I closed my mouth and heard so much more.

What route did I take to get here?
I want to go back.
Things here are not yet ready.
Lovers believe that not one single moment
        should be spent outside the estate of the beloved.
O homeless heart, stay away!
Sit over there, a much better spot.
The rest is just form and colour.
The rest is just war, dishonour, fame.

O soul!
Lust and desire strengthen your body of clay and water.
The challenge is to leave desire behind, at which point
        all problems will be solved.
Any delay will lead to one hundred different illnesses.
You, the cause of all illness, detach from yourself.
Make a promise and hold true to it.
If not, illness will linger.
There is no remedy.
Become accustomed to this way of life and you will find
        inside yourself one hundred thousand treasures
        that nourish the soul.

"Show me the ladder," I said,
    "so I might ascend to the sky."
"Your head is the ladder," she said.
"Place your feet upon it.
When you place your feet upon your head,
    you walk through stars.
When you crush all desire, you walk across the sky.
Come!
One hundred paths in the sky are revealed to you.
You will fly every morning, like morning prayers."

Who am I?
Who am I?
Filled with temptation.
Sometimes they pulled me this way, sometimes that.
I have become like a bow, pulled by my ear.
Even were I to close the door on fate,
    still it comes in through the roof.
One breath like burning fire, another a powerful flood.
Whence have I come?
From what season?
Could I be sold in a bazaar?

Accept accusations as did Joseph
    and experience prison as only criminals do.
Logic sits upon the courtroom throne,
    madness in the depths of prison.
Prison and accusations for the lover,
    throne and pulpit for the wise.

Garden scent fills the air.
The beloved's scent too.
Be loyal once and you shall benefit
    one hundred thousand times.
This deserves that.

O brother!
To be in love requires pain.
Where is pain?
To be honest and trustworthy requires a man.
Where is this man?

For how long will you ask me about frightful nights,
    those nights of separation?
Tell me.
There is no night during these, our happy days.

The cup broke.
No wine remains.
Me, in need of wine.

To give life for love is easy.

How wonderful it will be!
Us together, without you and me.

The moon is the measure of life.
Sometimes full, sometime half.

Unhappy am I with the light that creeps in
    through the window.
Tear the veil from the roof.
Tell the secret.

Kebab and wine on this side, smoke on the other.
A tree covered in thorns on this side,
    the beloved on the other.

The logical find joy in things effortless.
For lovers, effort is honour.
Love is fragrant.
It cannot remain hidden, its power cannot be masked.

O young man!
Hold your chest as a target.
Stand before the beloved, an arrow in her bow.
O young man!
Love is not for the pampered.
Love is for champions.

Take a look at my life, but tell no one about it being
      out of control.
I have no one but you.
Let me be with you.
Bring me a cup to quench my thirst.
You will never be short of wine.
I deserve no happiness.
Do not protect me from sorrow.
Your sorrow is my constant companion.

Last night the heart drank something wonderful.
What was it?
I have a hangover.
What caused such injury to the heart?
Such distress I am in.
At every moment the scent of my soul wafts from my lips.
Now so close to the beloved,
      the soul has no excuse for complaint.
Place your lips on mine and drunk will you become.
Go on, try!
As good as wine made from grapes am I.

Place yourself before my eyes.
You, who are more me than me.
I turn off the moon.
You are even brighter.
Enter the garden and embarrass the trees.
You are more beautiful than one hundred gardens.
The cypress is intimidated by your stature.
The lily must keep quiet.
You are the lily.
O candle of the soul!
In times of tenderness are you softer than wax.
In times of flirtation are you harder than iron.

So sweet is selflessness, whether poison or sugar.
Seek the hat and you will lose your head.
So sweet is selflessness.
When you are caught in her trap, when you have drunk
    from her cup of wine, the exit is nowhere to be found.
So sweet is selflessness.
You are cold as snow.
Become nothing, become extraordinary.
Worry less about the world.
So sweet is selflessness.
Although I am trapped, my cup is full of wine.
My life renews as I age.
So sweet is selflessness.

I was born of a mother of good fortune
    and a father of generosity.
I am a child of happiness, as were all my forebears.
Any wolf I encounter is transformed
    into handsome Joseph.
Any water well I encounter is transformed into a garden.
The most jealous person, with heart of iron and stone,
    is transformed into the most generous before me.

If you are drunk, join us.
We are drunkards, who reject praise and flirt with no one.
Over there the drunkard, over here thought and logic.
Either we sit upon the throne or guard the door.
Whoever is aware of the throne would be a doorman.
We, unaware of the soul, sit beside the beloved.

Only sugar from her lips can break your fast.
Blessings upon you.
You taste sugar from her lips.
On the last day of Ramadan it is written on her lips.
Blessings upon you.
Limitless wine.

You are the soul of the soul of the world.
Your name is love.
The one filled with you reaches highest.
Silence!
He whose mouth is sweetened by love
     should say nothing.

You need help from the beloved?
Make her happy.
You want to do business?
Make the customer happy.

Behind the curtain of secrets I am happy with myself.
Sometimes hunting.
Sometimes in prison.
Sometimes flirting.
Sometimes greedy.

O sleeper!
Awake in remembrance of the beloved.

O Sanai!
If you find no beloved, be a companion to yourself.

O brother!
To be drunk and selfless day and night
    is the most blissful of all possibilities.

You taste the red lips of the beloved.
Why such tears?

O sweet soul!
Give no thought to the one unable to distinguish
    autumn from spring.

A hard worker am I.
There are no hawks like me.
I express need and greed to no one.

Grab hold of any love that warms you.
None but she can help you.
Spend dark night until morning in remembrance of love,
    and no longer does night seem so dark.

O cupbearer of red wine!
O musician of blissful lyrics!
Ownership of eighteen thousand worlds
    amounts to nothing if there is no beloved.

I wear a habit out of fear and hope.
Bring me wine and free me from fear and hope.
Bring the cup that burns through logic.
Many thoughts of fear and hope fly through my mind.
Give me gold and bring forth bliss.
Fear and hope make my face a golden yellow.

Love, a physician looking for patients.
If this is not so, why am I ill?
Love, entwined in my head.
If this is not so, why I am in love and wearing no turban?
Last night the beloved kissed my lips.
If this is not so, why are my words so sweet?

Where is the one
    who can intoxicate my soul without wine?
Where is the one
    who can make my soul and heart crazed?
Where is the one to whom I am solely sworn?
Where is the one who made me break my promise?
Where is the one for whom souls shed tears
    each early morning?
Where is the one whose sorrow has uprooted us?
No surprise that the soul of souls is so restless,
    searching within us for a cup of wine.

I gave up on desire, but this pained heart could not.
Everyone departed and resettled, but the soul could not,
    for even a moment.
Everyone masters something, then turns their back,
    but the authentic are always searching.
Whoever has seen your disheveled hair
    is forever restless at heart.
Whoever dreamed of your smile found sleep impossible.
Neverending dreams of your smile.

I abandoned the heart.
You are my heart.
I abandoned the soul.
You are my soul.
Blood on my face could explain my story.
Now my life is out of control.
No explanation.
A tragic death is better than life without you.
Splendorous is the life of anyone who dies in front of you.

Blissful it is to serve you so attentively day and night.
Blissful is the sweet singing bird in your sweet home.
Nighttime slumber steals our thoughts.
Blissful are those eyes that see the face of the shining sun.
Your feet, like those of idolaters, mired in mud.
Unaware are you of how blissful it can be,
    walking beneath the sheltering sky.

I am not me.
You are not you.
You are not me.
I am me.
You are you.
You are me.
O beautiful beloved, the way I feel today means
    I know not if I am you or you are me.

When you seek a gem you are a gem.
When you desire bread you are bread.
Good to know the secret:
You are what you seek.

To know a lover, be in love.
To find someone loyal, be loyal.

"I flee from sorrow," you claimed.
"I am happy," you said.
Let your soul be happy.
Walk away even from claims such as these.

Silence!
No stories.
A gesture is all we need.

My thirst for wine is limitless.
Oceans are required.

What is to be done when love takes hold?

Travel from yourself to yourself upon the path of love.

In all six directions are we enriched by love.
Yet to stray from these six is more blissful still.

Speak in silence and the enemy cannot claim
    that your words are stolen from books.

I told you not to sit with sorrowful companions.
Sit only beside sweet beauties.
Enter the garden but stay away from the thorn.
Sit nowhere, except with flowers.

Upon the path to union there is no difference
    between prayer and sin.
In the tavern there is no difference
    between dervish and king.
For a roguish face there is no difference
    between brightness and darkness.
Atop castles in the sky there is no difference
    between sun and moon.

Walk around a Kaaba of the heart if you have a heart.
The heart is the real Kaaba.
Do not think of it as stone.
God ordered you to walk around the Kaaba
     and thereby soothe a heart.
Even if you walk around the Kaaba one thousand times,
     God will be unhappy if you break a heart.

The master of love gave me advice:
Be afraid of who you love.
She who toasts you will bleed you.
Become a slave to the drunken eye
     and never will you be free.

How unnecessary is the beautiful garden!
Instead we have your face.
How unnecessary are these wines!
Instead we have your eyes.
We have given our house as insurance.
We live on your estate.
We have destroyed our shop and have no job.
To claim love can lead to honour or dishonour.
We, who disdain honour, prefer dishonour.
The lesson of love shall not be forgotten.
We are free of debate, argument, repetition.

Your face like a flower, your hair like a box tree.
When sorrowful for you, my soul is happy.
Riches not earned from your sorrow are dust.
Desiring anything but you is meaningless.
The dust on your feet crowns all kings.
Whoever loves you is like Farhad in love with Shirin.
My heart invites you not to speak.
This is no time for noise.

I saw the mortal imagination in the mirror.
"What are you?" I asked.
"I am the rust of life," came the reply.
In eternal life you see living people.
Everyone else is missing out on life.
The harmonious are life's winners.
The rascals keep fighting.

O love, you emerge gentle, beautiful!
You take the skirt of the soul,
    pulling it towards the beloved.
Despite bandits, you secure the soul.
You take to the gallows those who steal the heart's riches.
You reveal the garden to those excluded from life,
    to those burdened by thorns.
You reveal thorns to those who pretend to be flowers
    but are actually thorns.

So cruel you were to me.
No beloved has ever treated her lover this way.
"I am innocent, but still you want to shed my blood?"
"Yes," she replied.

Me, injured by her love.
I am like a harp.
I am not empty.
I am full of tears.
Your desire is like a cup.
Your love is like wine.
Such wine.
Such wine.
What bliss!

You are all one.
Seek not duality.
Loyalty asks not to be disloyal.

O friends!
O friends, do not seek separation!
Put aside your desire to flee.

The perfection of love is achieved in union.
Come!

People of this world are spiders.
They hunt only insects.

Silence!
Do not tell an ocean tale to a bird from the dust.

Thank God.
We were burnt.
We learned how to burn.

She came to me like this because she was like that.
I welcomed her like this because I was not like that.

They told me that the pain of love is soothed
    by reading the heart of the Koran.
My soul touches my lips, so what use is reading?

Why seek treatment if you are healthy?
Why look upon this healthy body as if it were ill?
Share desire only with companions.
He is someone else.
You are someone else.

In some ways you have achieved perfection.
Move only in those directions along the path.
The guilty forsake such things.
The bird so perfect is miserable when in the dust,
     dishonoured and wet when in the ocean.

Solitude.
The beloved.
Dancing.
You asleep.
You should be ashamed of the beloved's disheveled hair.
From now on just me, nighttime walks,
     and the beloved's labyrinthine hair.
A long feverous night.
Unrevealed secrets.
Beauties, outwardly arrogant and fiery.
Seek their tenderness, hidden within the night.

You are poor.
You are poor.
You are poor, son of the poor.
You are great.
You are great.
You are great, son of the great.
You are the principles.
You are the principles.
You are the principles, son of the principles.
You are wise.
You are wise.
You are wise, son of the wise.
You are kind.
You are kind.
You are kind, son of the kind.
You are the world.
For you, both worlds are less than hay.

To steal hearts and be in love is our secret.
Our work is the real work.
She is our beloved.
The time of bric-a-brac merchants has passed.
We sell new things.
This is our bazaar.
We turn away from ourselves and relatives.
Whoever was our relative is now a stranger.
Selfishness is an infelicitous condition.
It turns faith into denial.

Our work is being in love and being disloyal.
Our work is the real work.
She is our beloved.
We intend to shed the blood of our relatives.
Whoever was our relative is now a stranger.
If logic rules this land,
     like a thief we will hang them by the neck.
Selfishness and selflessness cannot exist at the same time.
Every flower that grows from selfishness is a thorn.

O Muslims!
O Muslims, I have a bandit beloved who singlehandedly
     crushed armies of lions!
She touches the bow and the heart of the sky trembles.
Moon and Venus crash to earth.
People know her as love, but I know her as
     the affliction of my soul.
Suffering and a sweet affliction.
Without, restless am I.

Destroy the harp of my wisdom.
One string for me, one for you.
Play the heart's music for me, for you.
In union of passion are we as one.
We break the silence.
I am one beloved, you are one beloved.
Whoever seeks me should search your estate.
Leila and Majnun are you and me.

You are the soul.
You are seeing eyes.
How are you?
Moon and sheltering sky are envious of you.
How are you?
We and one hundred people like us are drunk, broken.
We seek you.
Without you we are weary.
How are you without us?

Have you ever seen someone drink
    and not suffer a hangover?
Have you ever seen a flower not injured by a thorn?
Have you ever seen spring without autumn
    in the garden of this world of water and clay?

There are no pearls to be found in a spring.
The seeker of pearls must explore the ocean floor.

To open this lock a key from almighty grace is needed.

Love and shame.
Opposites.

O Joseph of our time, we are Jacob!

Kings are we.
But still we thirst for wine.

Free yourself from everything.
Turn away from the game of conversation.

You know not your own value.
You ask for a feather as your price.
Never sell yourself short.

Me, a slave to all beauties, even those who insult me.
I would never sit with the ugly even if they treat me well.

Everything blissful is forever forbidden.
Ordinary people have no excuse.
Wine, music, beauty, dancing.
Halal for the special, haram for the ordinary.

O untarnished heart!
From whom do you plead justice?
Love can kill.
Justice for lovers goes beyond the soul.
Not worth thinking about.

Stones split in desire of union with you.
The soul soars with passion when thinking of you.
Fire is turned to water.
Drunken logic.
My eyes become the enemies of sleep.
Do not hold back the traveller.
Do not allow the smile to become a frown.
Do not be cruel to your slaves.
You, so irreplaceable.

Again love enveloped my door and walls.
Again my revengeful camel tore its bridle.
Again the lion of love attacked with bloody paws.
Again my unclean heart is thirsty for blood.
Again the moon is full.
Madness, despite my deep knowledge of things.

My religion is to become lost in being lost.
My ritual is non-existence in existence.
I walk the estate of the beloved
        and ride the world like a horse.
In one breath I turn my back on one hundred worlds.
This is the first step of my life.
Why do I need to explore the world?
The beloved is within my sweet soul.

Who can be this bound to the soul?
We have lost control over ourselves.
Whose cold hands are these?
The sun moves like a golden ball.
Whose mallet has struck it?
O sun, the bandit did not block your way!
Even if he had,
        he would understand that this is your path.
Moses smelled the apple and lost his life.
Seek that smell.
From which orchard does it come?

Place your hand
      upon the head of whoever arrives headless.
Stab with a dagger whoever arrives with a head.
The soul on fire burns because of your love.
Place it within this divine lake to keep it alive.
Such lips of yours!
Get the world drunk, make it blissful.
Steal the harp of Venus.
Play it while drinking.

The desire for you that dances in my heart
      is accompanied by many other drunken thoughts.
My intoxcated talk.
One hundred times do my words move
      from tongue to heart and heart to tongue.
My words, drunk.
My heart, drunk.
My drunken thoughts of you.
Everything together, entwined.

Enter a heart and you are like God.
You reveal the burning bush on Mount Sinai.
Wherever you go you are like wine.
Your beauty induces two thousand
      disturbances and rebellions.

Arise!
Around us the world.
Soul and youth.
The sun rose.
Behold the light!
Those created can find in all directions
      the signs of a creator.
The lover in love is dissatisfied with such signs.

The lover, most definitely not Muslim.
In the religion of love there is no faith or blasphemy.

Lovers lose both worlds in one breath.
In one single moment they lose one hundred years of life.

The direction followed by most people should be avoided.

Lovers, broken-hearted, sit upon the heart's throne.

Do not let the jealousies and vanities of others offend you.
Be offended by your own.

Promise of union with you is nothing.
Nothing.
For how long will this sorrow of separation last?

Good deeds are remembered.
Life does not stop good people from doing good.

O beloved, my roisterousness is not all I am!
Think about that wine you gave me.
O my beautiful, you are Simorgh of the soul!
Your house is the magical mount.
No need to ask whence you came.

You can never be at rest when a companion of someone.
I shall turn you upside down.
I own you.
Unless you are dishonoured,
     the secret shall remain hidden.
No one, except the dishonoured lover,
     will drink from that cup.

From birth have I been a devoted slave.
I found heart and soul in you.
I gave you my heart and soul.
I neither rip nor sew nor make nor burn.
I am no prisoner of night and day.
I am not in decline.
A blissful day when you build me up.
If you burn me I will become incense.
I weep because of you.
I smile because of you.
I am sorrowful because of you.
I am happy because of you.

Bring wine.
I am thirsty for wine.
God accused me.
I am afflicted.
Bring a cup of wine that the sun is envious of.
I swear to love
     that I turn my back on everything but love.
I awake each morning despite those who cannot see.
For them there is neither sunrise nor sunset.

People beat carpets.
But this is not for punishment.
They are made clean.
A carpenter carves a piece of wood.
But this is not to break it apart.
He has a reason.
A piece of skin is scrubbed one thousand times.
Dirt removed.
The leather itself is unaware.

Seeking the beloved is a religious duty.
Lovers flow like water to reach her.
She is the seeker, we are shadows.
All our words are hers.
The beloved is like a river.
Sometimes we are in bliss, flowing.
Sometime we are trapped in her pitcher.
We, sitting with the beloved.
O beloved!
Where is the beloved?
On her estate we wail like drunkards.

Bring wine.
For a long time have I thirsted for you.
Poor am I, yet still your close companion.
You must obey when I thirst for you.
When I am drunk I will obey you.
The cup broke, but no wine spilled out.
I am with you.

I am dead.
You blow the horn on the day of reckoning.
You are the soul of spring.
I am cypress and lily.
I told half the tale, you tell the rest.
You are the logic of logic of logic.
I am stupid.
I drew a face.
You give life to it.
You, the soul of soul of soul.
Me, the body.

Although I am with relatives,
      I never feel at rest when you are far away.
God!
Let no one be so anxious as this.
What can I bind to your feet that will stop you fleeing?
Such a disloyal soul are you, fleeing as does our beloved.

My heart is a turbulent ocean
      to which all divers are invited.
My words are pearls.
Most minds are undeserving of them.
I close my mind and silence myself.
I am filled with sorrow and pain.
God, I am on fire!
Bestow patience upon me.
Hide my misdeeds.

Morning arrived.
Time for brightness.
For those awake at night it is time for separation.

Everyone desires words.
I am a slave to the one who knows silence.

O logic, you were copper, transformed by love into gold!

Moon.
Night.
Beloved.
Cup of wine.

Alas!
You long for someone else.

Do not escape the fire.
You will be cooked.

We want.
Others too.
Fate will decide who is given access.

No invitations for the narrow-minded.
The garden is being decorated for lovers.

The poet praises the king.
If he were aware of himself,
    the king would praise the poet.
Silence!
Poetry remains, but its meaning disappears.
If this were not the case,
    the world would be filled with meaning.

A physician saw a blind man
    and gave him ointment for his condition.
"Apply this and your eyes will be healed," he said.
"If you could see who I can see," said the man,
    "you would remove your eyes and make yourself
blind."

In this world exist good things and bad.
O brother, neither good nor bad are we!
In our one existence were one hundred versions of
    "I" and "We."
Things changed and that one existence fell away.
We became one hundred different people.
Without turning one's back on selfishness,
    arrival is impossible.
We detached from ourselves and arrived.

O beloved!
Our duty is prayer.
Do not deceive us with prayer.
"Accept divine judgment," you said.
Do not deceive us with divine judgment.
Silence!
We desire no one but you.
Do not deceive us with gifts.

Sorrow does not consume me.
I move towards the beloved, towards Heaven and garden,
    dissatisfied with the autumn of separation.
I move towards the garden of eternity
    and the everlasting cypress.
A fish cannot avoid water.
I flow like water.
I am in prayer.
I move towards the river.
Sorrow of love will eventually take me by force.
Better that I move of my own volition towards the
beloved.

When I open my eyes, your beauty is all I see.
When I open my mouth, your wine is all I drink.
I will not talk to anyone, but when I am supposed
    to tell your tale I will speak of everything.
When you turn your back on flirtation,
    the only thing I need is you.
My existence will become only about my need of you.
Silence.
Say nothing for a while.
I will play music while you dance.

Last year I drank wine.
This year I am drunk, broken.
Do not ask about my pain.
Just look at the colour of my face.
That should answer any questions.
My soul drunk, my body broken.
The drunkard sits in a ramshackle house.

The soul is orphaned without you.
The moon splits into two without you.
The garden is filled with cruelty
        when you spread seeds of cruelty.
You are logic and soul.
You are this and that.
You are water and bread.
You are beloved and companion.
I silence myself to prevent the fleeing of the heart,
        not because I had much to say.

You make my mouth bitter.
You give sugar to others.
You give no rain to my farm.
You give water to others.
You are my soul, my beloved.
You are my everlasting fortune.
You are my garden, my springtime.
You bring autumn to my garden.

You are not as I am.
I am not as you are.
You are not going to be me.
I am not going to be you.
I am what you decide.
You are in my blood.
Even if I become moon and sun,
        compared to you I am still nothing.

Love was born before this world and will forever remain.
Countless are the seekers of love.

Silence!
I became silent.
I found peace.
Listen to me.
Become silent and you will find peace.

Love just happens.
It cannot be learned.

Turn your back on flirtation.
Avoid loneliness.

You are a quarry full of pain.
Be patient and find treasure within.

A pure rogue avoids the ignorant.

Blissful am I if you are loyal to me.
Blissful am I if you are cruel to me.
Let me not travel without you,
        whether you are loyal or cruel.

Time for wine.
We are drowning.
We thirst for wine.
No!
No!
Forgo wine.
Drunkards over there have no wine.

Enter the garden of the heart
    and become fragrant as a flower.
You grow beautiful as an angel
    while flying through the sky.
You become light when burnt like oil.
You become more blissful than anyone
    when sorrow makes you thinner than a strand of hair.

O God, give her a cruel lover!
A lover flirtatious like no other.
A lover angry, who sheds blood,
    who understands our dark nights.
Give her the sorrow of love.
Give her love.
Give her too much.

This world has six directions.
You will find nothing worthwhile in any of them.
Stray from them all, turn your back on all six.
The gazelle is in this trap.
Why search the desert?
You lost the gem at home
    so why seek it within these ruins?
Everyday you find a new room in this house.
O soul, you are not just one thing!
Seek and you will see that you are one hundred.

O cupbearer, how untimely you arrived!
Enter as would a man
    and drink five cups of wine in one cup.
O cupbearer, you up in the sky!
Crush all you see down below, seek treasure amid ruins.
O cupbearer, do not blame me if a cup is broken
    or festivities bring chaos!
I am in love.
O cupbearer, all-knowing are you!

I am in love.
For me there is nothing else.
No deception growing inside me.
I prefer poverty.
My back turned on greed, I am a cloud filled with rain.
Let this gem-like world be dedicated to me.
I rain life down upon the thirsty of the earth.
I live a wondrous life, hidden in the fist of a flower.
I am like day in every night, like spring in every autumn.
When with the bird of night, I am night.
When with myself, I am free of both.

I meet you and am confused.
Me, like a dream among your dreams.
You, so compassionate, soothe my heart
    and draw in my love.
By your breath are my existence and mind established.
I am your words and expressions.
Sometimes I was king, sometimes slave.
Now I am neither.
You perplex me.

Shining moon.
Dog howling.
No fault of the moon.
This is simply what a dog does.
The ruins of either world on this path are palatial.
Turning your back on all advantages
    when on this path of love is beneficial.
"Do not ask these women for advice," told the prophet.
The ego pretends to be pious, but is like a woman.

Tonight are all things hunted.
Do not remove saddle from horse.
Walk around the night of Leila.
You, Majnun, do not give up.
Cease your prayer!
You have prayed too much.
Bring your ears closer and hear the amen.

What happened to promises you made me last night?
May your promises, your breaking of those promises,
        and your beauty all be eternal.
What happened to providence?
What happened to those stories?
What happened to those solutions?
What happened to the saviour?

He beheaded by you became big-headed.
He whose farm was burnt by you acquired a larger one.
He whose head you split found fame in the sky.
He abandoned by you in a dark well
        found a world of brightness.

At every hour comes from the sky a wondrous voice,
        heard only by those of passion and love.

When the sun emerges from the depths of dark waters
        you can hear from each and every particle:
"There is no God but Allah."

My mind took me to a garden at dawn.

You are the soul if you seek the soul.

Do not talk about the secrets of others.
Look at the one who knows hidden secrets.

Bathe in tears before prayer.
Pray when in need.

Whoever can make peace with the beloved
    will always have a beloved.
Whoever can make peace with the customer
    will always have money.

It is not my body that is ill.
There is illness in my heart.
What medicine is this?
Bring me wine.

Change the rhythm.
Play new music.
Fresh songs heard from the sky.
Mind and ears will not come to life
    unless wisdom yields new secrets.

My heart, my heart.
My heart beside you.
Your face, your face.
Your majestic face.
Beloved, beloved.
If you want my life, I will give it.
I will give it.
I swear to you.

O how last night you howled with me in drunkenness!
So happy together were we.
O soul!
For the sake of sweet union last night
    do not now be angry with me.
If they said bad things of me, let me hear them.

O beloved, please, no accusations!
Think about a cure for our pain.
O beloved, do not separate from us!
Separate us from affliction and sorrow.
Find happiness amid sorrow.
Be loyal in this disloyal world.

Come, let us make peace together.
If happiness diminishes, make peace with sorrow.
Worry not if every child of Adam disappears.
We will make peace with Adam.
And even if Adam abandons us
     I swear we can achieve peace without him.
If fire becomes an ocean, we will drink it.
If an injury is suffered, we will remedy it.

Come, let us appreciate each other
     so we shall not suddenly miss each other.
Deception blackens friendship.
Eliminate all deception from the heart.
You will make peace after our death.
Our entire life you test us with sorrow.
Imagine my death.
Make peace.
We are like the dead, in submission.

One thing you should know is that
     two things are impossible in either world:
Escaping God's love and gaining something from nothing.
Your heart will find no happiness within a somber chest.
Your chest is either a prison or an open field.
You should know.
In a mother's womb a baby happily drinks blood.
That blood, better than wine.
That womb, better than a garden.

My soul finds happiness as I grovel before my beloved.
My soul grovels before me.
Were I to make a mistake while serving the beloved,
    the soul will become an enemy of my cup.
The heart punishes me.
Early morning I prayed that my soul would become dust
    under the feet of the beloved.
I heard the cry of amen within my soul.

We start shouting only once night arrives.
No one hears the silent noises we make.
We keep our loyalty secret, like placing a lid upon a pot.
No one smells its scent.

A slave to the moon am I.
Speak of nothing but the moon.
Speak to me of nothing but candle and sugar.
Speak not of suffering.
Speak of nothing but treasure.
Those unaware of it should not bother themselves.
Silence!

The religion of the lover tells us it is unfair to see
    the world through you but not actually see you.

Upon the path of the beloved is absolute poverty
    ever more blissful.

Hunt like hunting dogs.
Silence!

All night solitary people drink wine and eat sweets.

A smiling pomegranate am I.
How to conceal the smile?

We worry about everything when conscious.
Not so much when drunk.

Look at my yellow face and say nothing.
Look at the limitless pain
      and for the sake of God say nothing.
Look at the bloody heart.
Look at the eyes full of tears like a river.
Walk past it all.
Do not ask how and why.

Eyes, logic, wisdom, soul.
All gone.
You must stay.
Seeing you is better.
You must stay.
Sun and sky are under your shadow.
Sky and this shining star are gone.
You must stay.

O loss! O loss!
O loss! O loss!
Sober amid drunkards and the selfless.
O cupbearer!
Be careless, again and again, as you hand over wine,
      so neither the conscious nor logical
         remain in this world.
The beloved claims that if you are in love, be crazed.
Impossible to be logical in the circle of the crazed.

O new spring, you are our soul!
Make our souls fresh.
Make bloom the gardens and freshen the harvests.
All flowers are peaceful.
The thorn is an ill-natured fighter.
O Vameq, arise and make fresh
     the promise you made to Azra!
Thunder speaks.
The arrival of clouds.
Fragrance spreads over dust.
O garden, wash your face!
Make fresh your body.

Out of everyone, that one there is the soul.
But I do not call it the soul.
That one is a world.
Water flows over dust because of her love.
That one is a walking cypress in the garden of love.
The heart is passionate about her but keeps quiet.
That one is beyond expression and explanation.
On the day she was born no earth and time existed.
That one is beyond earth and time.

Any soul that does not seek real love is better off dead.
Its existence is shameful.
Be drunk in love.
Love is whatever exists.
Without the business of love
     we have no business with the beloved.
"What is love?" it is asked.
Tell them:
"Turning your back on free will."
Whoever is not free of free will has no free will.
It is love and lover who remain eternal.
Bind not your heart to anything else.
Anything else is a mirage.

O lover, open your eyes!
See those four creeks that flow through you.
One each of water, wine, milk and honey.
O lover, contemplate yourself!
Do not allow them to make fun of you.
Prevent one from saying this about you,
        another saying that.
From now on keep your eyes open.
Do not follow other people's eyes.
Prevent one from claiming you as an unbeliever,
        another that you are religious.

Help me, half drunk, to another cup of wine.
With a good companion at your side
        turn your back on good and bad.
Search neither for those made tearful by cruelty
        nor those naked in the world.
You are not responsible for everyone.
Sit and focus on your own work.
Take a look at wine.
Take a look at this harp and flute music.
Take another look at this statuesque beloved's face.

O morning breeze, welcome!
On your return to the beloved tell my tale
        – mine, the stolen one – to her compassionate ears.
A lily can tell her my tale through one hundred tongues.
You, tongueless, so like a daffodil,
        must utter secrets with your eyes.

O Sanai!
Love requires pain.
Where is that pain?
Beauties are cruel.
Only a real man can bear the burden.
Where is that man?
The cruelty of beauties
      is beyond yesterday and tomorrow.
Reveal the soul of someone from yesterday or tomorrow.
Where is that person?

You, placeless, like a soul.
I am like a body.
I search for you everywhere.

Us.
The dream of the beloved.
This furnace of a heart.

Trees raise up their hands, as do those who pray.

Whoever passes by my grave will become drunk.

The sun is unconcerned when the laundryman is angry.

Swear to God!
When my beloved enters, so blissful it is.
Swear to God!
When she embraces me, so blissful it is.

God brought forth a remedy for every pain.
Aged is the pain of love.
There is no remedy.

All anger is born of pride.
Cleanse yourself of pride.
If you do not want to feel pride, lie down in the dust.
Anger is born only from pride, my pride, our pride.
Step upon both, like a ladder, and ascend to the sky.

O soul, so beautifully you walk away!
Do not leave without me.
O life of lovers, do not visit the garden without me!
O sky, do not rotate without me!
O moon, do not shine without me!
O earth, do not grow without me!
O time, do not move forward without me!

She smiled sweetly, turning the world into Heaven.
She taught me to smile just as flames smile.
I was born, from non-existence, smiling, into bliss.
Love taught me to smile in a different way.
O astrologist!
If you believe in the miracle of splitting the moon,
	you should smile at yourself, at sun and moon.

Three days since my beloved has changed.
Sugar cannot sour.
How can my sweet beloved be sour?
The spring flows with the water of life.
I brought a pitcher.
The spring filled with blood.
Ancient furies between her eyebrows.
Leila's brow, furrowed.
Dead Majnun.

If the world and all its work is so meaningless,
     why complain about retribution?
Words breeze by but their meaning lingers.
Morning winds breeze by but the garden stays happy.
The world, fearful of wind, trembles like a leaf.
You don't know.
The wind can carry a sword of steel.
If I weep too hard, you will not hear.
Weeping beats hard within my heart.

Sufis arrived left and right, everywhere wandering,
     searching for wine.
The cupbearer brought out the pitcher.
All those in love, follow me!
In all religions such drunkenness, such wine, is halal.
Turn your back on atonement.
Here at these festivities
     is atonement equal to one hundred thousand sins.

What will happen if for a moment
     the beloved caresses me?
What will happen to spring if this tree smiles?
I am exhausted, hunted.
She aims her arrow of magical flirtation in my direction.
What will happen if kindly she speaks my name?
Me, so passionate, full of love,
     like a bowl brimming with water.
What will happen if I, a jug of water,
     reach the lips of the beloved?

You said that divine judgement should be embraced.
Why try to deceive us by calling on divine judgement?
There is no remedy for my pain.
Why try to deceive us by offering one?

I have come to hate the bazaar of the world.
You are the businessman.
Go to the bazaar.
This is my job until death.
You have your own job.
Go do your own job.

Poor.
Mystic.
Dervish.
Conscious.
Think about it.
All false names.

Your heart, struck by lightning, made restless.
Seek that lightning within the rain of your tears.

Plant seeds of generosity and loyalty in your own soil.

Those near drunkards themselves
     become ever more drunk.

Do not weep because of the beloved.
There is no love without cruelty.

Spending without earning is for God.
It is not of this world.
But some people have good fortune.
How that happens I wish I knew.

The scale could not measure the value of the gem.
Me, drunk, I broke the scale.

O you thing of beauty!
How happily you arrived!
You, soul's happiness, come forth with joy.
Until it is like this, let it be.
O heart, how beautiful you are!
Become like Shirin for that Khosrow.
If you are Shirin for Khosrow, be in love with Farhad.

I am no needy lover who flees the beloved.
Nor have I a dagger that will enable me
    to survive this battle.
Thousands of centuries are needed
    to again encounter this fortune.
Where will I find her if this time I flee?

When you see flowing water, turn your back on dust.
When the day of union arrives, turn your back on
austerity.
If you flirt, no mature lover are you.
If you wheedle, you are tamed.
You will find beauty and attraction
    when bearing the burden.
Silence!
Better to be silent than to consume honey.
Set fire to words.
Point to nothing.

O beloved, your face like a moon!
O musician, such sweet music!
Your song nurtures the soul.
Stop only once dawn is here.
The king arrived.
The king arrived.
That shining moon arrived.
That milk and sugar arrived.
Stop only once dawn is here.
How blessed are these festivities by your presence.
Bliss pulsates through your breath.
Like a gleaming candle, do not stop until morning.

Wine made from grapes for the nation of Jesus.
Wine made from victory for the nation of Muhammad.
Some pitchers full of this wine, some pitchers full of that.
You will never taste this wine
        unless you break the pitcher of that wine.
That wine will eliminate sorrow from the heart
        for the length of a single breath.
It cannot kill sorrow or uproot enmity.
A drop from this cup makes everything gold.
Let my life be sacrificed for this gold cup.

O how colourless and traceless am I!
When can I see myself as I actually am?
"Reveal secrets between us," you said.
But for me now "between" has no meaning.
When will my soul become immobile?
Me, immobile, yet in motion.
My ocean was drawn into itself.
Such a wondrous and limitless ocean am I.

You are your own shadow.
Become nothing under the sun.
For how long do you want to watch your shadow?
Look also at the light.
Whoever lives in darkness
      is fearful of his own imagination.
In darkness everything frightens.
"What is this darkness?" asks the bird of night
      when it sees day.
It has become a companion of night.

I am like an afflicted hawk,
      on this earth because of illness.
I am unlike people on this earth, and nor can I fly.
As the hands of kings caress me, fire embraces my soul.
No feathers to flee or wings to help.
Eternal sweetness is found within the souls of lovers.
Such tears, such weeping.
All to avoid evil eyes.

Last night I described separation as cruel.
Me, so furious at life.
Life always seems to bring forth separation.
In my imagination I was with you.
With these images in mind, I lay down to bed.

Someone's charm is making me twist like a snake.
A maze am I, like the beloved's labyrinthine hair.
I swear to God that I know nothing of all this twisting.
The only thing I know is that if I stop twisting
      I shall become nothing.

God has created us for this.
We are logic's enemy.
We are a foe of consciousness.

Sit with the unaware and you have won.
Sit with the conscious and death will come for you.

Water a sapling and it is as if you youself had planted it.

Do not reach out for those who flee from hands.

No place for hypocrites among lovers.

I took a piece of wood and in my hands it became incense.

When you sleep this way and that I become a slave
    to your intoxicated eyes, to your sleepy gaze.

You want goodness.
It comes from the beloved.
But for those unaware of this, all is vanity.

The moment I am filled with sorrow, happiness arrives.
The moment I am destroyed, prosperity arrives.
The moment I am static and silent like earth,
    my thunderous shouting reaches the sky.

So close to you am I that I am far away.
So fused with you am I that I am in isolation.
So exposed am I that I am hidden.
So healthy am I that I feel ill.

Embrace us and bear not your burden.
Swear to God that the caresses of a lover are not shameful.
Since the night you showed your moon to lovers,
    we all are restless as the sky.
We experienced the workings of your love.
Since then, in such a wonder are we
    that our work has become of no concern to us.

I give an example of burning love:
A fire burns within me.
Either I weep or not.
Fire rages night and day.
Logic dresses us in religious robes.
The hearts of lovers burn them.

Your treatment of slaves is never just.
Delicate is my face, your personality too.
The secret in your heart must also be so.
Why should the one who dies tomorrow be cruel today?
Why should he test on other people the things he dislikes?

O harp, I long for melodies of Isfahan!
O flute, I long for blissful burning tears!
Sing a song with the melody of Hejaz.
Me, a hoopoe, longing to be an ambassador of Solomon.
Give the lover a gift of Iraqi melodies.
I long for new, tuneful melodies.
Begin a new melody.
As the old one said,
    "I long for a melody containing short, flat notes."

Your love is all goodness.
You, a foe of dishonour and fame.
Your drunkenness complete, madness is your fate.
Tell me, I ask you:
Have you ever seen such an immature person
    with a burnt heart?

Where is that compassionate lover, she who slays?
Where is that Khosrow of Shirin, our sweet one?
Without her face our festivities are joyless.
Where is she, so full of joy, so artful, compassionate?
With his staff can Moses in the desert make flow
        one hundred springs.
Why not from our hard stone?

The garden of your face became a tableau
        observed by my heart.
Bitterness of your cruelty became sweetness for my heart.
We do not complain about your sorrow,
        although there is bliss in listening
        to the sighs of my heart.

Night shows I am a companion of drinkers.
I am a soul for those with a burnt heart.
For the loveless I am an angel of death.

O tears, depart the sleepless eye!
O fire, depart the restless chest!

My lips, desirous of your ocean.
Not even one thousand rivers can quench my thirst.

I am not drunk.
My words devoid of any wit.

So blissful you are.
Let evil stares avoid you.

Hallaj was pointing out the secret of love.

Cherish Ramadan.
Its final day is not yet upon you.

I lose my heart whenever I describe my beloved.
How to find it when I am so lost from myself?

As many lives as there is sand in the desert
    would be insufficient payment for a kiss from you.

The ego is like a wild dog.
I wanted to tame it, to place around its neck
    a chain of atonement.
But upon seeing a carcass
    such a chain would be ripped apart.
What is to be done with this creature?

Me, roaring.
"I want you silent," said she.
Me, silent.
"I want you roaring," said she.
Me, gushing.
"No," she said, "be still."
Me, motionless.
"I want you gushing," said she.

From the heart of the sky comes
    a garden of flowers and jasmine.
Autumn winds on watch.
How can it be?
Why?
O drunken nightingale, tell me!
For how long will you weep because of winter?
Enough talk of cruelty.
Be thankful and speak of loyalty.
Turn away from every fragment and speak of the whole.
Turn away from the thorn and speak of the flower.
Forget her qualities.
Look into her essence and speak of God.

Forget everything else.
What do you do?
What kind of life do you lead?
Even if either world were a temple full of beauties,
    the question remains:
Where is your compassionate beloved?
Suppose there is famine in this world, no food anywhere.
O you, king of things hidden and revealed!
Where are your provisions and savings?
Suppose the world is like a thorn, a snake, a scorpion.
O you, happiness and bliss of the world!
Where is your garden?

O sorrow!
Become as thin as a strand of hair
    and I will care nothing for you.
This world, filled with sweetness.
Nothing here for you.
Sorrow enters those hearts empty of desire for her.
Grief goes where the compassionate beloved does not.
O sorrow!
If you become gold, if you become sugar,
    I close my mouth and to you I say:
"The king dislikes sugar."
The homesick heart longs for her sweetness.
The heart that longs to travel will take us only
    towards the beloved.

Me, so sad, in a bad mood.
But it isn't my fault.
O my beloved!
How can I experience bliss without your beautiful face?
Without you I am winter.
I share my pain with unwilling people.
With you I am a garden.
My springtime mood.
Without you I am sad, crazed.
Whatever I say is wrong.
Me, so ashamed of wisdom.
Wisdom is ashamed of the light beaming from your face.
O heart, avert your eyes from the beloved as best you can!
Either she abandons or embraces you.

My body, a vast city.
On one side resides sorrow, on the other is me.
On one side I am like water because of her,
	on the other I am like fire because of her.
With bitter people I am bitter,
	with sweet people I am sweet.
In front of me is she, behind me is she.
So blissful am I because of her.
The flower, bestowed with a smile.
The flower never weeps.
What does the flower do but smile?
The lily blossoms.
She makes conscious my heart.

You, in love with me.
I make you unhappy.
Listen to me.
Build less, for I will destroy whatever you build.
Listen to me.
If you build two hundred homes, like ants and bees,
    I will make you homeless.
Listen to me.
If you are Luqman and Plato, full of knowledge
    and reputation, I will transform you into a fool.

For some time as children we went to school.
For some time we were happy meeting friends.
Listen to the end of our story.
We emerged like a cloud.
The wind carried us.

I tried hard to escape.
My shadow did not detach.
Even if I become as thin as a strand of hair,
    the shadow takes care of me.
If you run after the shadow for two thousand years,
    in the end you see it ahead of you.

We travel neither east nor west.
We walk, until the end of time, towards eternal sun.

You hoped that separation would make my enemy happy.
My enemy is now happy.
Time to come home.

Medicine for the world are we,
    but still wracked with illness
    when standing before you.

Blissful is the one unaware of all.

Your conscious mind obliterates all consciousness.

Today's kings hang enemies by the neck.

Wind is the soul that carries the body as dust.
The wind ceases at night.
Dust settles.

I have many friends outside.
Inside are my many companions.

Important to be an individual upon the path of poverty.
Important at all times to be a companion of pain.
To be a man means not to embrace union.
Important to be a man on the day of separation.

O companion of life!
What kind of life is yours without me?
O compassionate one!
What kind of life is yours without me?
My face is like autumn.
Broken am I without you.
Your face, like springtime.
What kind of life is yours without me?

Selfless am I.
Selfless are you.
Who will take us home?
Many times have I told you to drink less.
Too many pitchers.
I see no one sober in this city.
This one more crazed and ecstatic than the next.
O friend!
Come to the tavern and see the blissful soul.
No blissful soul without the beloved.

Today is for you the day of reckoning.
Arise and ascend to the sky.
Make a ladder from the fire of love.
Place the ladder upon the dome of the sky.
Seal our lips.
You speak through your eyes.

If it could be just the two of us,
     I would be completely satisfied.
With no rival at hand I could kiss her
     and be completely satisfied.
Many sins have I committed in secret.
I long to sin with her lips one day
     and so be completely satisfied.
Shake off all strangers one by one so I might be embraced
     by someone familiar.
That would make me completely satisfied.
Such a blissful day it is when piece by piece she disrobes
     and I embrace that naked body.
That would make me completely satisfied.

In this cold and rain is the beloved even more blissful.
The beloved beside you.
Love in your mind, the beloved beside you.
Delicate, beautiful, alert, fresh is she.
In this snow we kiss her lips.
Snow and sugar make a fresh heart.
My desire for her shoots into the heart.
How startling!
O God!

Send a remedy for my pain.
Send rain for my harvest.
Send the cupbearer of lovers' souls to sit with drunkards.
All to no effect.
But send my soul to the beloved
     and every particle of the world comes alive.

You come here to reveal my secret to all,
     and expose and exhibit that traceless king.
Last night a drunken dream, cup in hand, came to me.
"I do not drink," I said.
"Drink," it said, "or suffer the consequences."
"I am afraid that if I drink," I explained,
     "all shyness will fall away.
I will touch your labyrinthine hair
     and again you will abandon me."

Throw me your gaze and receive back a love poem
     in which your poetic beauty is illuminated.
Impossible to compose poetry while thirsty for wine.
Quench my thirst with wine found
     neither on earth nor in the sky.

Both gourd and owner are full.
My burning heart!
The only thing I enjoy is water.
I break the jug and tear open the gourd.
I turn my face to the ocean.
For me there is no other path.

Without this restless love no one would know me.

Without "I" and "you"
     we both are you and we both are me.
Are you my soul?
Are you mine?
Are you me?

For both thief and lover is the night long.

How fortunate that the soul knows of your nights.

One stalk can contain the wheat of one thousand farms.

I am a slave of the beloved, she who feels no pain.

How immature to speak of
     what is mine and what is yours.
"I" and "you" do not exist for you and I.

For a long time we wept and our separation smiled.
Today it is time for our separation to weep
     and for us to smile.

Midway down the path you have abandoned us.
Stop!
You are angry with us.
Stop!
You seek profit for yourself and loss for us.
But there is nothing to be gained by such activity.
You will suffer loss.
Stop!

You are clear water.
Do not muddy this water or conceal the heart.
Do not upset it.
Saints in contemplation encircle the heart.
Beware of any shameful action.
Keep yourself, and your heart, pure.

The ocean of generosity
    does not diminish if one takes a sip.
The grace of God does not diminish
    if he forgives an unbeliever.
Bring rest to this restless heart with a cup of wine.
Bring the shell of existence a pearl.
Either free me from logic or let me follow my instinct.
Either construct a ladder or open a door to the sky.

"Give me your life," the hidden beloved secretly tells me.
"Give me your life."
Such cruelty.
Be roguish.
Or at least hire a rogue.
Be a salamander.
Be a salamander.
Enter happily into the fire.
Enter into the fire.
Enter into the fire.
Walk with bliss through our embers.
Fire is transformed into a garden for our Abraham.

Look at the cupbearer.
Ignore the drunkard.
Look at Joseph.
Ignore your hands.
Look at the original,
        in existence since the beginning of time.
Ignore the copy, newly created.
Look at that limitless garden.
Ignore the thorn, which pricks your foot.
Be like the cypress and hyacinth.
Grow towards the sky.
Ignore the violet, which grows downwards.

Until the day of reckoning this is my beloved.
Broken and drunk am I.
This is my job.
I failed in business.
My business is love.
O face, be yellow gold, as valuable as a gold coin!
No more logic, an ability to discern.
No heart.
The solution for all?
These three are consequences of meeting the beloved.
Do not sit with your ego.
Sit with anyone else.
Detach from your ego.
It is estranged from you.

Appearing from nowhere came every direction.
Of the missing person a trace was found.
The return path disappeared.
Logic lives and breathes because of the empowered God.
A dog, under a shepherd's care, on watch.
When the dog sees what belongs to the shepherd,
    all his losses are gains.
When the dog sees himself as a shepherd,
    all his gains are losses.

Look carefully at my face.
I am not the same person each time.
See the ocean of sweetness, the waves of pearls.
If you smile like Jesus, you will see the smile on her face.
If you prepare yourself like Moses,
    you will climb mountains.
Like a lily you have one hundred tongues.
Silence!
Listen to the news from the tight-lipped blossoms.
They speak of silent ones.

The beloved brought a cup of poison for us.
It came from her hand, so happily we drank.
In our heart we float above the earth.
Our body is underground.
Our body is dead.
Our soul lives on.

You enslave us and enthrone the ego.
Enthrone us and enslave the ego.
You bestowed indulgences prepared for common people
    upon the uncommon.
Today bestow indulgences prepared for the uncommon
    upon the common.

There are many happy enemies.
You need to find a compassionate friend.

Follow logic and forever feel homesick.
Follow love and forever feel drunk.

Turn your back on everyone.
Sit with their creator.

Touch the sun's skirt with all your hands.

Walk and the path will be open.

I collapsed and lay down.

Cupbearer!
Cupbearer!
Is it fair that our days are spent in consciousness?

For us are you both eyes and light,
    both affliction and relief.
Weep!
Weeping is the remedy for the wound of separation.

My soul follows my heart.
What else can it do when encased within a human frame?
How empty is the heart of the world without you.
How leafless is the flower in the garden without you.

Garden, springtime, statuesque cypress.
We do not intend to leave this neighbourhood.
Unveil yourself and close the door.
A house empty, except for the two of us.
Today we are the special companion of love.
Fearless cup in hand.

O musician, begin your joyousness, your drinking!
Play the stringed instrument.
Forget dishonour and make peace with the rival.
Forget war and take the cup and pitcher.
See the flower's tenderness and ignore crimes of the thorn.
Open your labyrinthine hair.
Spread the scent.

Drunk, joyful, happy am I, all because of you.
I am pregnant in expectation of your justice.
If a pregnant woman gives birth,
       do not consider it a crime.
Will the day ever come when the universe moves no more
       and earthquakes cease their shaking?
The world is a book, all rules hidden within.
Understand that your soul is the introduction.
Be happy, be angry.
Carry the water yourself.
Silence!
Unchain the donkey.

I failed to reach you.
When hunting you,
       sometimes I am on the roof of your house,
       sometimes I am walking towards the desert.
The disheartened trap knows nothing
       about how to trick a wandering bird.
Joseph of Egypt knows nothing about where
       the calamitous life might lead.
I am destroyed like Sodom and roam as did Lot.
I want to know the reason, but lack courage and power.
Attar was in love, Sanai was a victorious king.
I am neither this nor that.
I am lost.

Are you well?
O beloved, tell me how you are!
How are you in these times of cruelty?
I think about you day and night.
How are you in these days and nights of death?
Me, ill.
You, the physician.
Ask the ill how they are.

You, a mere drawing.
How can you know anything about
     how you were created?
You are a shape, a body.
How can you know anything about the soul?
You do not hear the sound of the drum,
     so how can you understand its hidden secrets?
You remain a beginner in blasphemy.
How can you know the realities of faith?

Take peacefulness from the hearts of drunkards.
Take from the flower in the garden.
Take the moon's hat.
Take this flower's treasure from the garden.

Now it is morning.
Get up!
You, young man!
Pack, and join the caravan.
The caravan has departed.
You, unaware, still asleep.
You are missing out.
You are missing out.
Missing out!

You!
Your life is outside time.
I spent my life loyal to you.

The world of love, ruled by a queen.
I am a servant of love.
I will go to the land of love.

Look closely at these people.
You will close your eyes to them.

We are beautiful.
Make yourself beautiful.

How can a thirsty fish live without water?

My fire is dead.
What smoke is this around me?

You broke our thorns, then our heads.
You took my close friend, then all my companions.

They all contemplated what was going on around them.
I contemplated what was going around in my head.

My soul is your soul.
Your soul is mine.
Have you ever seen two souls in one body?
O body!
You think you are alive with your one hundred souls,
    but none of these are her.
Seek that genuine soul.
Never boast about this body.

Blood eventually dries and darkens,
     but the blood of lovers is forever fresh.
Never tell me that this blood here is old.
It is the blood of lovers.
Always alive, it will be forever so.

"Why expect tenderness from a thorn?" asked the flower.
"How can you expect anyone to be conscious
     in all this madness?" I replied.
"Why is there no scent in this garden?" asked the flower.
"If you cannot smell such things," I said,
     "do not search for the garden."
"Loyalty is but a dream," explained the flower.
"Why expect a dream when you are awake?" I said.

I long for that happy day when you return from the path
     and shine through the door of the soul,
     as does the moon from above.
You are water, I am the creek.
I seek nothing but union with you.
A creek without flowing water is dead.
Your happiness is imperative.
It empowers you to be greater than anyone else.
Swear to God!
When you are with yourself you will never be at peace.

Arise, for today the world is ours!
Soul and world are our cupbearer and guest.
Rostam and thousands like him are within our grasp.
Arise!
Generous is the commander of soul and world
     who follows our commands.
There is no one to represent her.
She is the only thing that exists.
She is ours, so nothing but us exists.

This is my job.
I have no job.
I am in love, unembarrassed about my devotion to you.
I am a resident of your ocean beach.
I live there.
Intoxicated by lips am I,
       although I have embraced no one.
I was born of love.
No identity more joyful for me than this.
What is more valuable than both worlds?
The city of love.
For me there can be no better place.

Us.
Desire for you.
Your eyes quench our thirst.
For us you are the water of life.
How are you?
Bitter is my separation from you.
Bitter it is to be far from home.
Let no one be far from you.
How are you?
You, a horse in the field.
How are you when so caged?
You, nightingale of the garden,
       how do you cope with the deaf?

O beloved!
Your mistake was to go with another lover.
You turned away from your life,
     involving yourself in that of another.
One hundred times did I forgive you.
I did my best for you.
You, my favourite companion, left me again.
One hundred times I made magic.
I removed the thorn from you.
You did not value the garden.
You, once again, caught on a thorn.

My heart needs you as fish need water.
Leave me and my soul will die as would a fish.
Fish have no patience outside water.
Lovers have no patience
     when separated from the beloved.

O heart!
Turn away from honour when in the realm of love.
The first step of love is dishonour.
To cover the soul
     when in the ocean of love means trouble.
Seeking honour and riches when in love is immature.

When in love, days and nights feel different.
I am beyond night and day.

Close your mouth like a blossom.
Smile like a flower, but without your lips,
     so no one will know your true wealth.

Look at my face and see yourself.

Two thousand ways to define myself.
I chose the most wondrous.

Greed is the cause of all suffering.

When it comes to love, knowledge is ignorance.
How easy to be honoured because of great knowledge.
The ignorant belong to love.
Those full of knowledge are oblivious to it.

It is the duty of fire to be angry.
It is the duty of a candle to weep.
Our duty is to loyalty and service.
The beloved's is to disloyalty.

Slowly blew the wind across her hair.
Scent spread from every strand.
The wind became drunk,
        stealing hair from the face of the beloved.
Light uncovered.

My tears are witness enough.
Witness enough.
Witness enough.
My colour is indication enough.
Indication enough.
Indication enough.
Signs of the beloved, face like a tulip.
Like a tulip.
Like a tulip.
My face like saffron.
Saffron.
Saffron.

O soul!
For how long will you remain in that foreign land?
Why stay there?
Come home from exile.
For how long will you be so upset?
I sent you one hundred letters
        and showed you one hundred paths.
Either you do not understand the path
        or you never read my letters.
Come home!
No one values you in that prison.
Do not sit with the stone-hearted.
You, the gem.

Every tearful eye for the beloved will one day
        receive good news, a message of union with her.
Jacob from Canaan was weeping for Joseph.
Suddenly he received good news from honoured Joseph!
In love, tears like a ladder.
When trying to ascend, one will reach the roof.

It is untimely.
It is untimely.
The sun entered the water well.
The sun of the lovers' soul entered the solitude of Allah.
Day hidden in night.
A Turk among the Hindus.
Nighttime rampage.
The beloved entered the pavilion.
If you are made aware of this light,
        your sleep will burn away.
Venus, in service, awake all night,
        becomes a companion of the moon.
Every seed looks the same before the harvest.
Half become succulent, half hay.

Every dawn, flowing tears bring news from my heart.
No one is made aware of my heart.
Your sorrow, each piece as thin as a single strand of hair,
    transformed into the water of life, even a gem,
    all inside me.
Even with twenty burning suns in my night,
    no dawn will come unless you show yourself.
The heart is a plant.
You harvested its seed in water and dust.
It will not grow and become a tree unless
    you embrace it like springtime.

You arrived, then sat on the corner,
    preventing us from sleeping.
You entered my heart like a fish,
    but as soon as my heart looked at you,
    you jumped away.
With our separation the pillars of this house cracked.
Never again can it be a home.

Tell no one what you know about me
    on the day you take me from me.
For how long should I shed tears about death
    when you are the water of life?
If she brings forth death, let me die.
Death is better than the breath of youth.

Lovers weep like a flute.
Love is the flute player.
What love blows through our flute!
Sometimes it plays the flute, sometimes it chews the flute.
Alas!
This sweet flute player who plays sweet music.

If you are in love, turn your back on sorrow.
Bear witness to the wedding,
    turn your back on mourning.
Be the ocean and turn the ship upside down.
Turn your back on the world.
Be the world.

Do not knock on every door like a beggar.
You, with long arm, knock upon the door of the sky.

Silence, even if every beloved used gold ink
    to record your every word.

If I am a wrong word, you are the pen.

Yesterday departed.
The story of yesterday departed like yesterday.

I am neither with you nor have I the patience
    to be without you.

Love.
Half dependent, half independent.

I had a dream last night, but forgot it.
The only thing I know is that I awoke drunk.

You became old, worn out.
Flee from aged logic and spring will reveal
    fresh flowers and gardens.

You cannot flee from us.
No one can destroy the trap of power.
You are powerless to flee from us.
Submit.
Scorn rebellion.

So crazed am I, in love!
I collapse on your path.
I swear to God that I know of no other place.
O beloved, I broke your cup because I was drunk!
Me, drunk.
Do not ignore me.
I am in danger.

"Why are you like this?" I asked the heart.
    "For how long do you hope to be
    a companion of love?"
"Why not join with me and witness the joy of love?"
    replied the heart.
"If you are aware of the water of life, never choose
anything
    but the fires of love."

The heart like a butterfly,
    floating around the soul's burning candle.
It has landed in the glow of the beloved's candle.
You, proud and powerful, drunk on love.
You are chaos.
You are alert when standing before the beloved,
    crazed when with yourself.
Your shape angry.
Your soul peaceful.
Your face bitter.
You are sugar.
Never have I met someone so alien yet so familiar.

Wash the road, for the beloved is coming.
Give good news to the garden.
Springtime scent is coming.
Let the beloved come,
        that beloved as beautiful as the full moon.
Her shining face spreads light.
The splendour of the garden is coming.
Eyes and light are coming.
Sorrow departs.
The moon embraces.
As you arrive on our land
        you see that our custom is silence.
When we talk the air fills with dust.

Without everyone else life goes on.
But not without you.
My heart, which will never abandon you,
        was burnt for you.
You intoxicate the eyes of logic.
Skies descend in front of you.
Happiness follows you.
Life ends without you.
You, my wine, my hangover.
You, my garden, my springtime.
You, my sleep, my rest.
Life ends without you.
Alive without you, I feel no joy.
Dead without you, I am joyful.
I cannot pull my mind out of sorrow.
Life ends without you.

My beloved became a little more considerate.
Yesterday she seemed a little happier.
Yesterday, springtime of beauties,
     she smiled and my life became a little better.
My flower, with one hundred leaves, appeared joyful.
My garden became a little more verdant.

O gardener!
O gardener, autumn is here!
Autumn is here.
Look at those branches
     and leaves for signs of a pained heart.
O garden, listen!
Hear the trees in every direction weeping, mourning.
One hundred tongueless trees.
There is always a reason for wet eyes and dry lips.
A face yellow as saffron always brings with it
     a pained heart.

A self-absorbed bird has no courage
     to enter the garden of the selfless.
No Majnun ever became a lover of Leila
     except whoever was a Leila for one hundred Majnuns.
O soul!
No one can reach the sun on his own.
The sun must rise over a desert.

We worship the sun.
We ascend this roof.
No wall can block the sun from us.

I am like the rider of a wild horse with a ripped bridle
     in a terrifying land.

You, the cause of autumn.
Because of you spring turns bitter and sweet.

Me, in tears because of bad manners and all I have to bear.

The dervish was emptied of himself.

Today, as with all other days, we are destroyed.
Destroyed.

Under the wall of your existence
    you are a treasure trove of gems.
Remove yourself and all treasure is revealed.

Silence.
Just listen.
Be neither preacher nor chanter.

Life once again brings springtime,
    full of parties that will remedy hangovers.
I empowered the courageous, those with patience.
Desire for a beloved stole my heart and restfulness.

"Do not go there.
I am your companion."
Did I not say that to you?
"In this mirage of death, I am the spring of life.
If angrily you leave me, eventually you will return,
    for I am your destiny."

Pour love's water of life into our vessels.
Translate morning's mirror at night.
You are the father of new happiness.
Enter the vessel of our soul, become the crystal ball.
Turn your back on both worlds.
This land, with its six directions.
Search not for the *qibla* of this world,
    for only the dispossessed will find it.
Non-existence is your refuge.

You are the beloved, my splendour.
You are my garden, my springtime.
My life is yours.
You have stolen my nightly sleep.
You have been my companion.
You caused me pain.
I benefit from nothing but you.
I was a soul before I was created,
     living with you in the sky.
We, free of language, speaking to each other without
words.

O heart, she is aware of you!
Sit with her in the shadow of the blossoming tree.
Stop your aimless wandering from stall to stall
     in this bazaar of perfume.
Head directly to the one with sugar.
Not every cane contains sugar.
Not every down has an up.
Not every eye can see.
Not every ocean contains pearls.
With a fresh heart you become like a blossoming tree.
At every hour you offer fruit, you travel into your heart.

For me the lover is the one who, when ascending,
     brings about days of reckoning, full of fire,
        in every direction.
I want a heart full of fire, a heart that can burn Hell,
     make chaos in two hundred oceans,
        that never escapes ocean waves.
With a heart like a whale, the lover, as does the lion,
     welcomes battle, allowing nothing but itself to exist.
It battles with itself.
When it turns from ocean towards mountain,
     lakes of gems are created on this earth.

Break the jug, tear the gourd.
I move towards the ocean.
Clear the path.
Sudden floods swept away my farm.
Smoke rose from my heart.
All seeds and hay scorched.
My farm gone, but I am unconcerned.
Why worry?
I have another farm.
Moonlight from the shining face of my beloved
        is enough for me and one hundred others.

God!
I know the aim of my beloved.
She has blocked the path of my escape.
My heart and restfulness, stolen by her.
God!
I know the aim of my beloved.
I know how far she takes me and why she blocks
        every direction to captivate me.
She is my blasphemy and my religion.
She is my eyes which see the light.
She is this for me, she is that.
Never can I turn my back on her.

Here am I, there is the pride of the kingdom.
I am poorest of the poor, lowest of the low.
I am the one unaware of the name you have given me.
I am your slave.
I am king of kings.

I embrace you, I free you from everything
        as together we joyously contemplate joy.
I give you special wine and make you drunk
        until the end of time.
You will believe that you are my eternal joy.

Morning.
Create light between night and day.
Create something that is neither moon nor sun.

My heart is the house of happiness.
I am free of sorrow.
I am disconnected from everything angry.

In love, silence is joy.

O soul!
If your arm is broken, take the bow.

We atoned for our entire being.

One cup of wine.
Better than one hundred thousand souls.

Your face, like the moon.
Never shroud it.
Men and women everywhere, envious of your face.

Silence!
Silence!
Silence contains thousands of languages and words.

You, my beloved, nourish my soul.
My thirst for you is endless.
Be not cruel.
Be not cruel.
I deserve no cruelty.
O my queen!
Amid fire am I, but still happy with this cruelty.
I am in your shadow.

For a moment does confusion reign in my soul.
"O joyful beloved!
You are beauty, made from fire and water.
Your face nourishes my soul.
For the sake of God, you are mine.
You, my gorgeous musician.
For the sake of God, this is all I have."

O heart!
What did you drink last night?
Tell me the truth, hide nothing.
Do not turn your face towards the sky as do innocents.
Do not become bitter.
Do not conceal your secret.
Do not do this again.
Do not do this again.
You, a drinker of special wine.
You, a drinker from the cup of freedom.
Do not keep the scent in your mouth.
The scent of wine.

When my beloved is with me I fear no one.
I have a sword.
No fear of needles have I.
My lips will never be dry.
The river seeks me.
My heart will never be sorrowful.
The sympathetic beloved is with me.
I am drowned in sweetness.
For me there is no bitterness.
Winter never consumes me.
Springtime is with me.

O sorrow, remove yourself from my heart!
Tenderness from the beloved comes forth.
O heart, leave me!
The beloved arrives.
I would never describe her as happy.
She is beyond happy.
Happiness is for me dishonour.
I am in love with her.
O all you faces, leave!
New faces arrived.
Your flags are taken down.
She, equal of so many, arrives.
The walls and doors of my chest exploded.
Too much inside.
The beloved, unable to enter through the door,
    scales the wall.

The crazed heart departed
    for a madness better than this one.
Both heart and madness lost.
If the lover has no feet, he can fly with eternal wings.
If the lover has no head, he has many other heads.
While in love, I turned the world upside down.
Do not look for the beloved here.
She lives elsewhere.
Today, love in my heart.
Tomorrow, the beloved in my heart.
Today my heart has another tomorrow in its heart.

O beloved, bring wine and make me fortunate!
Hunt my heart with the lasso of your hair.
Joyous festivities.
We and everyone happy.
Bring fire and burn incense.
Pour from that infinite cup into the cup of wisdom.
Punish the self-absorbed heart by being selfless.

Go sleep.
Leave me alone.
Abandon me, the destroyed and afflicted night walker.
We, waves of madness, solitude from night until morning.
You can either forgive us or be cruel to us.
Pain.
No remedy, only death.
How should I ask for a remedy?

You are the new moon.
Announcement of the feast.
O my hidden moon, punish the moon!
You, my life, my death.
You, my fury, my happiness.
You, my truth, my hypocrisy.
You, my lock, my key.

The fire of you in my mouth.
I remain silent, not knowing whether
     the drunkenness of love is for me good or bad.

Ears hear my words.
No one hears the cries of my soul.

You are wine.
You are hangover.
You are enemy.
You are friend.
Let me sacrifice one thousand holy lives to this enemy.

Wine concealed.
But not its scent.

I would never trade the pain you inflict for any remedy.

Logic searches for everything by finding its location.

Ignore the bitterness of wine.
See the drunkard's joy.

My mischievous beloved arrived.
Again she wants to fight.

This poem has no beginning and no end,
    but can bear you from beginning to end.

My tight chest overwhelmed the sky.
My yellow face more delicate than the moon.
I want the work of every physician ended.
I am salvation for patients and a remedy of all pain.

We agree with no one in this world.
We build no house under the sheltering sky.
We are drunk, hungover, thirsty.
All others are done.
We do not stop.

The world is a trap.
Desire is a seed.
Do not follow the seed and so become trapped.
Do not desire sun and moon.
Be pure.
Desire only the beloved.
Life becomes bright, dark, warm, cold.
Make your home at the origin of life.

Who's that knocking at my door?
My soul.
My world.
My desire.
If she does not knock on my door, I will suffer.
Misery if she does not remember me.
On entering the ocean a drop of water becomes a gem.
An ocean becomes a drop on entering my ocean.

O heart, in love are you!
Best wishes on your madness.
You freed yourself from every location.
Best wishes on your new place.
Ignore both worlds.
Be alone, and every angel and person will wish you
        the very best on your solitude.
Deep within the heart's sanctuary
        is the turmoil of the poor.
O pure heart, best wishes with your turmoil!
O hidden lover, best wishes on joining with the beloved!
O seeker of sky above, best wishes on your ascension!

Take my bread.
My soul remains intact.
Our love's wanderer will never be dispossessed.
The one whose body I cover will never be naked.
The one for whom I am the solution will never be
miserable.
The one I hire will never be fired.
The stone that becomes a gem will never again be a stone.
The lover might become ill, but never dies.
The moon becomes thin but never a star.

O lover, turn your back on deception!
Become crazed.
Become crazed.
Enter the heart of fire.
Become a butterfly.
Become a butterfly.
Make yourself a stranger.
Destroy your home.
Come live with lovers.
To deserve the beloved one must be pure,
    of nothing but the soul.
As you move towards the drunkard, be drunk yourself.
Be drunk yourself.

You wanted to hunt, you yourself were hunted.
You wanted to find restfulness, you yourself grew restless.
I can call you Khidr because you drank the water of life.
I can sacrifice myself in front of you
    because you fell in love with the beloved.
You were sorrow's prey.
You had no creator.
You reached union with the creator
    because you toil upon the path of love.

Bring wine that burns wisdom and inflates the heart.
We will ignore our existence
    as does the heart after drinking.
Come joyfully.
Bring the beginnings of joyfulness to the festivities.
We are joyful with everyone, but even more so with you.

I am dark night, angry with the moon.
I am the naked beggar, angry with the king.
I have turned my back on sighing.
I never sigh, even if the beloved is angry
    or sorrow steals my peace.

This year is our year.
Fortune is for Venus and the moon.
O heart, such infinite joy and happiness!
Get yourself involved.

Tender love made my soul so fragile.
I want no heart.
I want no soul.
Where is the one I own?
Where is mine?

Death is life.
Life is death.

Every day I bear a new burden.
A new one.

The story of lovers is neverending.

Ship.
Night.
Clouds.
We sail.

We set fire to our job, trade and business.
We learned about poetry, lyrics and couplets.

You ask how I am.
See how I am.
Broken, selfless, dazed with madness.

You are contrition cracked.
I cannot escape you.
You reside in my heart.
I cannot escape you.
You, light of my eyes.
I cannot see without you.
You chained my neck.
I cannot escape you.

O musician, sing this poem!
O beloved, I atoned!
I turned my back on every flower and atoned the thorn.
My heart, ripped apart by thoughts,
    searching for a solution.
A solution would be misery.
I had no option.
I atoned.

Never search for warmth.
The only place to find it is within, where fires burn.
The heart is never set alight by those fires without.
The hidden king appears only to those most in pain.
He enters the heart and kindly asks, "How are you?"
See the beloved at every moment, despite your pain.
Why are you seaching for a magical remedy?
Poor you.

Do not blame me.
You have not seen her face.
You will regret expressing judgment upon something
    to which you have never been witness.
Amid the day of reckoning, if that moon rises,
    another day of reckoning will arise.
Real beauty is her beauty.
It destroys all.
Her fiery flirtation burns away our wellbeing.

Only the passionless remain in the house of sorrow.
Your secrets are not to be found in passionless hearts.
You deserve only what you do not fear.
The heart of a lover fears nothing.
It reaches beyond the sky.
Your pain comes from the one you think has a remedy.
What you call loyalty are lies and trickery.
Where love resides, there is no place for the soul.
Where there is madness, logic cannot fly.

O soul, do not be disappointed!
Hope emerged.
The hope of all souls came from the hidden world.
O soul, do not be disappointed!
In darkness of prison arrived the king
        who purchased Joseph and set him free.
Jacob unveiled himself.
Joseph arrived.
Whoever broke the chastity of Potiphar's wife arrived.
O aged pain, blessed are you!
Finally, a remedy!
O locked lock, open up!
Finally, a key!

O beloved, your lips smile!
Good news.
From now on you long to be loyal.
Our prayer is meaningless if you are not with us.
There is nothing to be gained.
It is accepted when you fulfill our needs.
When a cruel person tortures,
        the prisoner asks him to be afraid of you.
You are cruel to us.
We, in hope of justice, take refuge in God.

My job is being jobless.
My heart is upset with life.
Me, who saw nothing but darkness in the dark of the dust,
    nothing but trickery from the aged world.
You let the heart's net drop into the ocean.
You neither fish nor quit.

I will not leave this house of light
    nor voyage from this blessed city.
Me, the beloved and being in love,
    all for the rest of my life.
Slay me and still I would never turn my back on her.

I am a flower, but have thorns in my feet.
I am Joseph, but am in prison.
I am full of thorns from head to toe,
    but still a smiling flower.

Worry not.
Any happiness you lose will undoubtedly return to you
    in another form.

A thorn in the garden of the beloved is better than
    one thousand cypress trees and lilies.

The ocean cannot quench my thirst,
    so how could a creek?

A lover, humble.
How else could he be?

Give me the cup and I will be happy.
Curse me and I will be happy.

Do not believe it when someone tells you the fire is cold.

Ascend the roof and watch the new moon.
Enter the garden and pick apples.

Impossible to depart without her.
Impossible to speak without her.
Impossible to sit without her.
Impossible to sleep without her.

I follow an invisible hand that leads me.
Whose visible and invisible hand is this?
I follow it while I am visible and invisible.

I remedy this pain with dregs.
I make this work easy by being patient.
Either I remove my soul from this world
        or sacrifice my heart and fate to the beloved.

If you have no beloved, why not seek one out?
If you reach your beloved, why not be joyful?
You consider such things as strange.
Your inertia prevents you from involving yourself.
How strange that you have no desire
        to do such strange things.
Waves of words emerge, but better to utter them
        through your heart and soul, not lips.

If you are drunk on wine,
        why not live a day of reckoning?
If you have no wine, why not ask for some?
Why are you separated
        from the one who makes you drunk?
Why not turn your back
        on the one who gives you a hangover?
For the dervish, this world is worthless.
Why not enjoy this celebration of poverty?

The one who has love and desire in his heart,
	but whose heart does not reveal such things, is ill.
Go sit before the heart's door.
The hidden beloved comes at dawn or midnight.
Whoever does this is a companion of the soul
	and joyful at the moment of death.
When a stone hits his feet, he finds a gem.
When his soul departs, he is with a sweet-lipped beloved.

My sun and moon arrived.
My ears and eyes arrived.
My beloved arrived.
My goldmine arrived.
Drunkenness arrived.
Light of my mind arrived.
If you think of something else,
	that something else arrived.
You gave me the ring and today I am Solomon.
Majestic crown upon my head.
My pain absolute, I travelled in love.
God!
What good fortune I achieved along the way.

There is no excuse, and even if there were,
	there is no tongue and heart.
There is no path to escape,
	and even if there is I have no feet.
The world was created.
We flow and dance like a flood,
	from the tip of the mountain down to the ocean.
He sits there dreaming of tomorrow doing this and that,
	unaware that there is no tomorrow.

O stranger of the sky!
You deserve more than this earth.
O world of beauty!
What are you doing in this world?
No one asks the sun why it moves
        or the garden how it feels.
A yellow face is asked about heartache.
No one asks the Judas Tree how it feels.

We are your ears.
Silence for how long?
Drunk and selfless for how long?
We are burnt.
You are not thirsty.
For how long must it be like this?

You have travelled the world and seen nothing but shapes.
Wash your face with water.
You are most definitely asleep.
Take the cup of joy and escape prison.
You, awake to this world,
        held captive by questions and answers.

If you want to place us upon a throne,
        place it at the heart of the ocean.
If you want to hang us, do it from the great dome.

O soul!
At the heart of each particle shines a sun.
One hundred flowing rivers in every drop.

I choose no one but you.
What else is there?

I am a soul with one hundred thousand bodies.

New stories unheard by aged ears.

Speaking is sin.
Atonement will do me no good.

O God, such a beloved have I!
I have a beautiful beloved.
One hundred meadows have grown
      from the seed she planted in my heart.

If our beloved wants more, so do we.
If our beloved seeks less, so do we.

You never left my heart.
Enter!
Welcome!
You, a candle shining in the night.
Bravo!
Welcome!
O night, take care of the curtains!
The moon wants privacy.
O musician, change the music!
Welcome!

Today there is a dance.
A dance.
A dance.
There is light.
A beam.
A beam.
A beam.
This love is common.
Common.
Common.
Goodbye to logic.
Goodbye.
Goodbye.

Because of the great soul who created my soul,
    you embrace me with your soul.
Because of the concealed treasure buried in our ruins,
    you hide me from everyone.
Close the door you have never closed on us
    if our gain is your loss.

If, while weeping for the flower, you are with the
    nightingale in the garden, consider the thorn a flower.
Inside the thorn is a flower.
Outside the thorn is a flower.
Be careful whom you serve.
The bitterness of medicine is joyful,
    as is a slap from your teacher.
What a gift it is to experience cruelty
    from the loyal beloved.

O tribe that travelled to the Haj!
Where are you?
Where are you?
The beloved is here.
Come back.
Come back.
Your beloved is your neighbour.
Why search while wandering in the desert?
The face of the beloved transcends form.
Observe her face and be enriched.
You become a home.
You become Kaaba.
Ten times you walked that path to reach that home.
Ascend, one time, from this home to the roof.

Tell the heart not to befriend sorrow.
Sorrow will never diminish if all you feel is sorrow.
O bird of heart, do not fly sorrowful!
Sorrow will not strengthen your feet and wings.
The heart flies when free of sorrow.
It flies beyond this world.
O heart, be stubborn and less sorrowful!
Secrets are kept hidden from the sorrowful.

Come! Come!
I will become crazed by your sorrow.
Alas! Alas!
Loneliness is killing me.
Wonder! Wonder!
You came to ask how I am.
See.
See how impatient I am in love.
Give.
Give the gift you have brought for me.
Sit with me and rest awhile.

You know that separation has devastated me.
You know I long for union.
A hidden flower.
A nightingale flew from my garden.
You know I am tired of the pain of the thorn.
Your secret remained concealed in my heart.
You know I never tell it to anyone.

The one drunk on love is shameless.
The wine of love is priceless.
I am warmed by the first cup.
Surrender to divine judgement.
There is no way to avoid it.

O bird of the sky, time to fly!
O gazelle of wisdom, time to graze!
O lonely lover, you are chosen for all lovers!
Ignore the creatures and bear witness to creation.

Pour poison into my cup and joyfully will I drink.
If I do not accept everything from you,
	either mature or immature, I will be immature.

In front of the mirror of love we speak not of ourselves.
When we are destroyed your treasure
	will be buried within us.

Your beauty deserves flirtation.
Do not ignore desire.

Like a cloud.
Time to weep.
Like a mountain.
Time to bear the burden.

Ask the lover for the story of love.

If you are not in love, be a slave.

O heart, caught in her trap, free of one thousand traps!

Be like a fish in the ocean of wisdom.
Never be a companion of anything but pure water.

No need to protect your beauty from evil eyes.
Your form is shifting.
You are not what you were.
If I say you are the same old beloved, my heart will burn.
If I say you are the same old soul, my soul will burn.

To be free of shadows, flee from your neighbour.
Do not contemplate yourself.
You see yourself as a strand of hair.
If you are drowning in the ocean, why walk on land?
If you are upon the seashore, why not wash your face?

Look not outside yourself for sorrow's cure.
You are cure and antidote for every sorrow.
You are not fragmented.
You are free of everything and everyone.
You are with people.
You are without people.
You are alone.
You have no need of a remedy if you suffer no headaches.
You direct chaos on the day of reckoning.

For how long will you be here amid this chaos?
Get used to it.
Tear up loneliness.
If you want good fortune, if you want not to be bound
    to every shadow, wherever you are turn inwards
    your face, or be forever shamed.

One can make garden and flowers from your face.
One can make incense from your hair.
You are the Khidr.
Your water of life can turn every beggar
    into an Alexander.
You intend to ask how I am.
One can make something impossible possible.
O heart, return to yourself!
One can find within the heart concealed paths
    to the beloved.

Even if all around are thorns,
    the lover's heart will be a garden.
Even if the sky stops moving, the world of lovers goes on.
Even if everyone is made sorrowful, the souls of lovers
    will be delicate, happy, compassionate.
Even if the lover seems lonely, he will not be lonely,
    for a hidden beloved has he.

Either I should abide by or tolerate sorrow
    from the beloved.
You have many judgmental enemies.
A sympathetic beloved is preferable.
A companion, disloyal, limps upon the path.
One must seek a competent companion.

You are dear, generous and tender, but also conscious.
Leave here now.
Lovers do not deserve conscious companions.
No one should be in love with such people.
Bring me wine.
How hateful I consider logic.
For how long will you allow logic to own me?

You will never be at rest, no matter whom you befriend.
I turn you upside down because you are ours.
Only your disgrace will reveal the secret.
No one but the disgraced lover
	will drink that cup of wine.

You have seen wonders.
Look here.
This is the true wonder.
The beloved beside the lover, with him, without him.
Contemplate the faithful and the unbeliever.
You see only weeping, wailing, prayer.

Morning.
Let us get up.
For how long should we sleep?
Let us take the water of grace and pour it on the fire.

To left and right
	are many people unaware of left and right.
Many people who speak of "I am..." and "We are..."
	are unaware of who they really are.

Only a foolish flower would fight the wind.

Me, in the heart of a mirror.
In my heart, a mirror.

You are raw fruit that deserves to hang from the branch.

Cruelty fuels the lover's soul.

O love!
Because of you both worlds are broken and drunk.
Who has broken you?
Who has made you drunk?

Contemplate non-existence and observe wonders.
Such hope there is in disappointment.

O beloved!
You, a sudden departure from our city for a trip.
We, embittered.
You went to the warehouse of sugar.
Send news of you and your blessed soul.
Your departure was big news.

O sky!
For how long should I complain about the beloved?
There is no single night when I can come
    and speak of being with her.
Only the cries of crows amid winter ruins.
If I get through these hard times,
    I will praise springtime like a nightingale.

If your sun is missing, the sun does not shine.
If I do not contemplate you,
    there is nothing to be gained in contemplation.
If I am not with you, life is wasted.
If you do not protect us, a shield is of no use.
Stars are meaningless on a moonless night.
If a bird is headless, two wings are of no use.

I fear the eyes of day, those magical eyes.
I fear the hair of night.
Chaotic night is ready to give birth.
I am told not to be afraid.
Suffering brings glory.
The remedy, crushed in a mortar, brings light to the eyes.
All fear is born of existence.
Go, be less desirous!
All fear is born of failure.
Fail, and find safety.

The drunken one who sells his donkey
        worries not about bridle and saddle.
He walks barefoot through the thornless garden.
For him a donkey is worthless.
Tear down every curtain.
A lover is unafraid of being shameless.

Nor for one single moment should she be far away.
Separation brings on destruction.
Many carefree people.
Many difficult tasks seem easy.
No matter how you are, be with her.
Being close leads to love.
Never test separation.
No one tests poison.

O cupbearer!
From heavenly sky we fell to earth.
Our ears fell upon joyful music.
We were in the tavern, now we are drunk.
Here are we born.
We know no other place.
Outwardly we seem tired of the beloved.
Inwardly how blessed we feel because she is in our heart.
We are drunk, joyful, powerful.

I heard, in my heart, nonsense spoken by my enemy.
I could see his thoughts.
My feet bitten by his cruel dog.
I never bite him as would a dog.
I bit my lips.
All flaws are mine.
This is my art.
I deliberately pulled a scorpion towards myself.

You are king.
Such a fine day it will be for me
    when I die in front of you.
I die scattering sugar in your warehouse of sugar.
I die in the shadow of the cypress tree in the garden.
One hundred thousand flowers with one hundred leaves
    grow from my dust.

It is in your hands whether or not I leave you alone.
It is in your hands whether you want me to be
    your Vameq at every moment, and not Azra.
Break no promises.
You are the wrong man doing wrong.
Do no wrong.
Me, I do no wrong.

The one you embrace will turn his back
    on the people of the world.

Move!
Moving is the key to receiving daily bread.
Maybe you are unaware of just how beautifully you
move.

Do not teach the eyes of a priest how to contemplate.

I am grapes trampled underfoot.

Wings of the butterfly search to understand
    the warmth of the candle.

What is shame?
When in love, shame has no meaning.

Blessed is that moment when gracefully you caress lovers.
Blessed is that moment when spring winds blow
    in autumn.

I wonder how valid is the prayer of a drunkard.
He is unaware of where he is, of when it is.

Today is the day to embrace the beloved,
    to contemplate so deeply her beautiful face.
We can grasp the beloved's hair and follow her,
    as does Jupiter the moon.
We can make chaos in the bazaar.

Today, a happy day.
Come, be each other's companions.
Let us take each other's hands
    and move towards the beloved.
Today is the day for every beloved to dance.
We close our shops.
We are without work.

I am slave to the sun.
I speak only of the sun.
I am no night, no worshipper of night.
I tell no tales of dreams.
I walk like a sun.
I shine on ruins.
I flee from the palace.
I speak only of ruins.
I was born of sunshine.
I swear to God that I am Kay Qobád.
I do not rise at night.
I never speak of moonlight.

I am in love with you.
I have no other job.
I turn away from everyone not in love.
I am never sorrowful.
I am never sorrowful.
I do not complain of suffering.
I have no gold.
Look instead upon my yellow face as gold.
The heart is Khosrow, sorrowless but for Shirin.
I have no sympathetic companion.
My heart bears no sorrow.

We departed.
Let others live long.
Whoever is born will someday depart.
The sheltering sky has seen everything fall to earth.
Never work too hard.
No student can ever outdo his teacher.
If we were bad, we achieved badness.
If we were good, remember us.

My day turns to night.
At the last moment of life my soul came to visit my lips.
I prayed so much that the sky heard
        and itself began to pray.
The beloved arrived, cup of wine in hand,
        a wine hostile to religion.
Just a single sip will make me drunk, but this cup is full.

Time for me to break promises, to tear apart chains,
        to ignore all advice, to shatter this evil sky.
Death is like a sword, cutting all bonds.
I will do the same.
For how long should I worry about everything?
I should be ashamed before love.
When will I be beyond caring?

We are like water at the door of a house.
We know not why.
We are unaware of how ecstatic we are.
At every moment are we ever more intoxicated
        by unknown wine.
We know not why.
Your love has chained our feet.
We wander without feet and hands.
We know not why.

For a time we used eyes to look at each other.
Today we used eyes to see each other.
Fearful of the rival,
        our eyebrows uttered secrets of the heart.
We listened with our eyes.

Yesterday gone.
The day before yesterday gone.
Today's soul waits to see what you will bring.
You, spring wind, carry love and madness.
You can be no companion of anyone
        with a sorrowful heart.

For artful Khosrows, creating chaos is an art.
Give your heart and life to this life of souls.

O soul!
There is no joy in my words when I am conscious.
Please, bring two cups of wine and hear my words.

We were your harvest.
You harvested us with the sickle of love.

Because of separation I choose the fiery coffin.

They said that our story was told without words.

I see your face.
What blasphemy it is not to believe in beauty.

O beloved, you lion!
I am a gazelle, held captive.
Who has ever seen a prisoner like me,
    so fearful of freedom?

Sacrifice your head like a pencil.
Walk through your heart upon the path of love.
In non-existence can be found many advantages.

Love hands you a cup of wine.
Seize hold of it blissfully, joyously.
Wine calls out to sorrow.
Whoever hears a greeting from you
    will tire of salutes from kings.

You have lost all interest in us, yet still we search for you.
You have stopped walking the path,
    forgetting the promise you made
    to be our companion.
When sun departs, dark night remains.
When wisdom departs, stupidity remains.

We want no silver, gold or riches.
We ask of you tenderness to deliver us wings.
We want no judge and no judgment.
We want your judgment.
You are precious life.
Be our life.
We want no week, month, year.

So dishonoured am I.
No one calls out for me.
A man like me
     has nothing to do with honour and dishonour.
Sometimes they call me piteous, sometimes roguish.
Poor me, for I know not which I am.
I am like a candle.
I will burn until only a piece of me remains.
Fire is my land.

Handsome Joseph arrived.
Our Jesus arrived.
The flag of one hundred thousand victories arrived,
    carried on springtime's horse.
Your job is to enliven the dead.
Arise, time to work.
The lion that hunts the lion arrived, joyful,
    in the meadow.

Today our beloved never appeared.
Our beloved never arrived.
Tonight the flower in the garden of our soul
    did not come to embrace us.
We run towards the desert like the gazelle.
The scent of the beloved never arrived.
The cupbearer of the soul never appeared.
The remedy for our hangover never arrived.

Me, the moon, I live nowhere.
Do not look for me outside, for I am within the soul.
Everyone asks that you come to them.
I ask that you return to yourself.
Paint me any colour, either honourable or dishonourable.
I do not care.

I am the slave who freed my master.
I am the one who made the teacher a teacher.
I am the newborn soul that brought about the old world.
I am soft wax which claims to make steel hard.

Like a bird, you escape the hawk of death.
What is it like to fly burdened with such fear?
Death is your life, although it seems destructive.
You are unaware.
You escape it.

I want a fool who contemplates the beloved,
    not an artist who contemplates art.
I want a heart like a seashell that will embrace the pearl.
I want no delusional heavy heart
    that thinks it owns a pearl.

Although I am sour, I am no jar of vinegar.
Although I go everywhere, I am no gadabout.

Standing before you, the sun prays at dusk.
When will you emerge from the sun's heart?

Happy am I, free of the world's happiness.

The restfulness of love is haram, haram.

I am not unaware of you.
Always I think of you.

Logic appears as a preacher.
I offered advice.
You are like Plato.
Get out of here.
You spoiled our festivities.

Shame on you!
After witnessing the joy of the crazed
    you became logical again.

As you see the sun, remember the beloved's face.
As you see the cloud, remember the tears of slaves.
As you see the new moon like me inflamed,
    for the sake of your soul, remember my poor soul.

Nightingales bring good news this year.
O God!
Much sugar is given to parrots.
Enter the gardens this year and explore.
Such wondrous fruit offered by brittle branches.

O beloved!
Today we cannot recognise ourselves from strangers.
So drunk are we that the path home is unknown to us.
We are freed from the caravan of logic.
We know only how to be crazed.
"In this trap is a seed," they said.
Trapped, we cannot recognise the seed.

Flow! Flow!
We are the ocean of poetry.
We have no work but love.
Love!
In this dust, in this dust, on this clean farm,
    we plant nothing but love and tenderness.
We know nothing.
We know nothing about what we drank last night.
Today, all day, we are exhausted, hungover.

Last night the cups of the cupbearer were all full.
I wish our whole life, until the day of reckoning,
    was like tonight.
The sounds of drunkards drinking reached the sky.
Wine was in our cup and wind in our head.
In the sky were one hundred thousand upheavals.
One hundred thousand Kay Qobáds were praying.
O Muslim, begin your life again!
The beloved turned non-existence into existence.
She gave justice to lovers.

You are the glory of all cupbearers.
Let your cup be at work.
Let your eyes be drunk.
May our soul be thirsty for wine.
Clarity became drunkenness at your festivities.
Let logic lose its turban amid your flowing love.
Let the hands and heart of the soul be injured
    like the women of Egypt.
Let splendour be for Joseph of Egypt.
O cupbearer!
Many hands were lost by your hands.
Let your drunkard forever have your hand.

Who do I look like?
One moment an angel,
    the next a human searching for an angel.
In the fire of passion I am present like a candle.
I am both smoke and light.
I am both fragmented and unfragmented.
What kind of bird am I?
Neither partridge nor hawk.
Neither beautiful nor ugly.
Neither this nor that.

I saw the fire, the tree.
"O my dear!" someone calls out to me.
The fire was calling me.
Was I Moses?
Ask not about ships and ocean.
Come, see the wonders!
For years have I steered a ship through this land.
Sometimes I am stone, sometimes iron, sometimes fire.
Sometimes I am scales without a stone,
     sometimes both scales and a stone.

Wind blows through the willow and makes it dance.
God only knows what the tree will tell the wind.
If you seek secrets, move among drunkards.
Secrets revealed by a shameless drunkard.

O beloved!
Let me not be without a beloved.
Forgive me.
Let me not be alone.
Let me not be alone.
Your warnings killed me.
Do not deprive me of your warnings during separation.

You are a candle.
You are the beloved.
You are wine.
You are springtime in winter.

"For how long do you want to blow?"
     asked a tree of the wind.
"Wind brings springtime," replied the wind,
     "although you are ailing."

Beware!
Never battle with the unaware.

I am not in your eyes.
You are in my eyes.

May he be shamed who is discouraged.

Whoever faces down cruelty longs for one day of loyalty.

All others are like autumn wind.
They make the garden yellow, locking away into the dust
     the goodness of every seed.

Without a cup no house can be bright and beautiful.
You, mountain of grace.
You, ocean of generosity.

To make the flame smile, the candle must weep.
To expand the soul, the body must be made thin.
Be like angels.
Enslave the demon.
When your cow is sacrificed, you step into the sky.

If you want a heart that will not weep,
     seek it beside the beloved.
If you want a flower that never fades,
     seek it in springtime.
The seeker of restfulness is saddened.
Expect a joyful soul in love to be restless.

I run fast.
I run fast to reach those horse riders.
I become nothing.
I become nothing and reach the beloved.
This world is only dust and air.
The gem is blasphemy and non-existence.
I enter the heart of blasphemy and reach faith.
No physician offers medicine when there is no illness.
To reach the remedy, I become every pain.

I can be two thousand different people
    and still wondrous me.
Listen to that shouting.
Do not place your hands over my mouth.
If I become crazed, never place glass on my path.
I will break everything in my way.
At every moment I reach out my hand
    to touch a beloved.
She scratches my face and tears my shirt.

O lovers!
Do your best to fly into the sky
    when body and soul are dead.
Use water of wisdom to wash dust from heart and soul.
Beware!
Never let eyes look with regret at this world.
Your non-existence is the east, your death the west,
    both in a sky different from this one.
The path to Heaven is within you.
Beat the wings of love.
When wings of love are empowered,
    there is no need to worry about the ladder.

Alas!
All my companions gave up.
The wine of love did its work.
They all fell to the ground, distressed by love's pulsations.
They put down their hats and stopped.
O cupbearer, here is my hand, there your skirt!
I am thirsty for wine.
Deliver justice to my heart.
All other people are cruel.
I can no longer be repaired.
You obliterated me.
Those drinking your wine will be obliterated.

I was dead, I came alive.
I was a tear, I became a smile.
Love's fortune arrived and I became everlasting fortune.
My eyes have seen everything.
My soul is courageous.
I have the courage of a lion.
I became shining Venus.
"You are far from joy," she said, "not one of the joyful."
I became joyful, full of happiness.

There is no serious work in this world.
Whatever I do is like beating clay with my feet.
My beloved needs no help from me.
I am no dark dust carried by the wind,
     no indigo sky causing my clothes to rust.
My head is not broken, so why use a bandage?
Because I am a physician of the world I will never be ill.

O soul!
If my sorrow makes you happy
    I will give my heart to sorrow and make you happy.
What is the soul?
From the garden of your beauty half a leaf.
What is the heart?
From you a blossom.

If your face is as cloaked as your soul,
    there is nothing to lose should you hide away.
Why force yourself to send a message?
O close companion, come take this joyful cup!
Become so drunk that nothing is recognisable.

Grass, lily, tulip, hyacinth.
It is said that whatever you plant will grow.

You, sunshine of the world, will become dark cloud.
If you are fresh spring, you will follow autumn's religion.

Better that I fall in love with what you desire.

Asking questions will not reveal the secrets of life.

The ship of fools is always drowned in the storm.

The madness of love is better than
    one hundred thousand pieces of wisdom.

Two pains within the soul of Majnun.
Being with gypsies.
Separation from Leila.

Winter crow and desert stork have no understanding
    of songs sung by a drunken nightingale.

Moon and Jupiter envy you.
You are with us, but hidden like an angel.
Joyfully you carry me.
Where to?
Wherever you go, you are with me.
You are eyes and light.
You carry me anywhere you want,
      either towards drunkenness or into non-existence.

I am like an arrow.
I do not fly unless you release me.
Come, place this arrow in the bow.
The sky, so miserable because of your love.
Send down the ladder from the roof.

O friends, spring has arrived!
Let us move towards the garden.
Arise and come together
      around those strangers in the garden.
Today we fly like bees, from one flower to the next,
      bringing splendour to the honeycomb of the world.
We dance in every corner of the field,
      with no control over ourselves to do this or that.

My life, spent in search of heart's desire.
No fear of a sorrowful heart.
The heart wants to end my life.
I wait to see what the heart decides.
At dawn I deprived my eyes of sleep
      so I might bear witness to the face of love.

Whoever flees from our circle
    flees from hearing and seeing.
The heart is a parrot.
The beloved's cruelty is sugar.
All parrots love sugar.
Whoever surrenders when confronted by winds
    is an insect.
Whoever flees from moonlight is a thief of the night.
Stop!
Do not hunt what does not deserve to be hunted.
Dreams of the night flee dawn.
Night flees dawn.

Shame on the heart for knowing nothing about you.
The body with no good news of the soul must perish.
How worthless are those words of love
    that merely comfort.
These are useless words, uttered by tongues,
    heard only by ears.
Shame on the heart in love which avoids fire.
A heart spent like gold coins will never become treasure.
At this time, do your best to rid yourself of time
    before the time when there is no time for anything.

Your beauty turns me into incense.
My land at the heart of fire.
This fire from you.
The lover accepts it as an arrow released from your bow.
The sorrow of your fiery love turned me into a dead tree.
A dead tree deserves to burn.
The ears of my soul heard the dawn call of your love.
"Enter our fire and free yourself from the world of fire."

I saw Jonah sitting beside the ocean of love.
"How are you?" I asked.
"I live for myself," he replied.
From now on ask not how we are.
Leave that question alone.
Whoever is selfless cannot speak of how he is.
Shedding our blood is haram for sorrow.
Shedding the blood of sorrow is for us halal.
We shed the blood of every sorrow that came near.

Everyone seeks victory over the enemy.
Seeing the beloved of our enemy is for us victory enough.
Everyone seeks treasure.
We seek love, which for us means suffering.

If you are incense, come celebrate with us.
If they do not let you in from the roof,
    enter through the door.
You are Joseph.
There is no way to avoid both water well and prison.
Come embrace the poison of cruelty as if it were sugar.

Words of love rain down.
Flowers blossom from flowers.
Thorns are born of thorns.

You are allowed to be cruel.
We are forbidden to expect from you any loyalty.
Occupy our bloody souls.

Roaring call.
Tired throat.

No death for my love and my beloved.

If Heaven becomes a seashore, no fish there will be at rest.

A cup of wine is better for a hangover than
     one hundred houses filled with gold.

Without you there is no remedy in this world
     for our pain.
Let us die without you.

Whoever has love and passion in his heart and soul
     will live like a salamander amid fire.

O queen!
Come here for a moment and open the door of joy.
I care not what happens to this or that.

A blessed place is non-existence.
Existence is nurtured by non-existence.
Every heart contemplates non-existence.
The garden of Heaven is non-existence.

Come, the seed is valuable.
Do not fear this trap.
Enter the house of gambling.
Do not fear dishonour.
You have heard that upon the path of love
     one should be worried about losing life and head.
The beloved is the water of life.
Do not fear these words.
Desire for the beloved brought me a cup.
"Drink this wine and fear no one."

Learn alchemy from the prophet.
Be happy with whatever God gives you.
If the messenger of sorrow comes to you,
     embrace him as you would someone familiar.
If the beloved is cruel to you, bless her.

So joyful are you on this corner.
Cherish it.
O friends, such good fortune you have!
Cherish it.
How unfair it is to beg for seeds.
Do not do it.
You own two hundred harvests and warehouses.
You are angels born of angels,
     although you now weep like beggars.
Everyone seeks art to rid themselves of flaws.
Flawed are you because you celebrate
     in the company of souls, yet remain conscious.

O lovers, good news!
Good news!
Clap your hands!
The lost one returns joyous.
There is nothing more joyous than the soul.
Even if the soul departs worry not,
     for something better will arrive.
Everyone wonders about something.
I wonder how something that cannot be spoken
     can reveal itself.
I silence myself.
I speak not of secrets.
When the souls of words appear, I cannot stop speaking.

When a lover sighs, the sheltering sky cracks.
The tears of lovers are precious.
The sky rotates thanks to lovers.
It exists thanks to love.
It rotates around love.
Arise!
Let us also rotate.

If with its feet or wings a tree could move,
    the saw would inflict no pain and the ax no wounds.
Through the night the sun does move,
    ending with the erasure of dawn's darkness.
If you cannot travel by foot,
    take a journey within yourself.
Be like a gem and let light beams impact upon you.

My house is dark but seems good enough
    for handsome Joseph.
A beloved at the bottom of a water well
    looks beautiful from above.
A beloved that towers over you
    is beautiful from below.

My cupbearer arises.
With no words from me she brings precious wine.
She hears words from my heart.
No need to utter them with lips.

Quit your work, open the wine.
This cup is a horse, ridden by wine.
O cupbearer, open it!
Your splendour surpasses that of Saturn.

Here, the house made of water and clay.
There, the house made of soul and heart.
O God, I miss my city, my land!

Strike with a stone the pitcher
    full of words from the ignorant.

The world is a corpse.
Most people are like wild dogs.

Time for every beloved to dance.

Among people of the heart is room only for the heart.

With endless kisses did honest, sweet-lipped beauties
     close the moving lips.

You know nothing about love.
Just ask the night.
Ask the yellow face and dry lips.

If you are thirsty for wine, enter.
If you are looking for bread, leave.
No bread here.
Whoever worships bread cannot be among these beauties.

Everyone drank and slept.
No one remained in this land.
Time to enter the garden with joy.
Everyone drank and departed.
Let us live forever!
We are heart and soul of life.
We, king of the earth.

One thousand fires.
Smoke and sorrow.
They call it love.
One thousand pains.
Regret and affliction.
They call it the beloved.
For those enemies of their own lives, time to do
something.
A call to give life.
A call to the slayer.
Silence!
Silence!
Love always means the opposite.
Words become meaningless if too often spoken.

No one remains alone.
Beware.
If you do not make peace with the beloved,
    someone else will.
If I depart and this house becomes empty,
    someone else will show up.
That someone will be like me, or worse still.
This world, one thousand centuries old,
    was inherited by us.
Father is buried in the dust.
The son becomes a father.

Milk and sugar mixed again.
Lovers mixed.
Night and day removed, sun mixed with moon.
The colours of beauties and lovers,
    mixed like silver and gold.
Good, evil.
Dry, wet.
All found in nature.
Good and evil mix.

Every day life moves on, longing for tomorrow, unaware,
    towards chaos.
Sometimes rich, sometimes poor, life moves on.
With every breath we lose life.
Death, upon the path, watching.
A man walks, exploring.
Death is closer to us than is our mind.
Only an ignorant mind ignores it.

You, the queen who has hunted me.
Without you there is neither joy nor sleep.
You are my beloved, my splendour.
Do not be so cruel to poor old me.
Every day so much is achieved
        with just a glance of your eyes.
Look at me and make my problems disappear.

Sorrow is the shadow of happiness.
Sorrow runs after happiness.
Turn your back on happiness.
These two are together forever.
Night comes after day.
Sorrow comes after happiness.
Once you see day, you can never avoid night.
As you run after sorrow, happiness runs after you.
As you run after happiness, sorrow is on watch.

The beloved, whose face is unfamiliar, hides all tenderness.
Her tongue bitter, but in her mouth sugar.
Inwardly she is familiar, outwardly a stranger.
Never before have I seen such a kindly enemy.

When the beloved becomes angry, love speaks to me.
"Be no artless lover.
Beware, do not turn your face!"
The beloved's bitterness is like bitter wine.
Sweet to the soul, bitter to the tongue.

Love teaches the soul one thousand arts
        not found in school.

Either I speak of the shadow, or not.
My shadow never leaves me.

We move from garden to garden, like flowing water.

Like a mosquito we are drunk on our own blood.

I do not bind my heart to good fortune
    which lasts only two days.

We long to be neither king nor beggar.

Day of union.
Here, the beloved.
Think not of the future.
Cherish today.

What is the relationship between love and joy?
The mirror reflecting creation.
What is the relationship between love and jealousy?
The mirror reflecting flaws.

Our fires cannot be understood in words.
The secrets of the heart cannot be spoken.
No sighing can remedy our pains.
There exists no soul to listen to our sighs.

Life without you is haram.
No life exists without you.
To live without your beautiful face is death,
    although we call it life.

You are ours.
Be happy like us.
Be like the cypress, free in the garden.
If sorrow arrives, do not let it bother you.
Demand justice.
Be the king of justice.
Be like a hedgehog amid all those thorns.
Head hidden, happy, splendorous.

Today I seem to be born of kindness.
Delicate and tender am I.
The beloved, too proud to let me kiss her, asked for a kiss.
I turned away.
A strange dream I had last night.
Today I am fortunate indeed.

O God, be content with lovers!
Let them be victorious.
Let them celebrate your beauty.
Let their soul be like incense in your fire.
O beloved, you shed our blood!
Let the soul be for this bloody hand.
If someone prays for relief from love,
        let that prayer be rejected in the heavens.

Let me be drunk on love, with never a hangover.
I need no wine to become intoxicated.
We are lands covered in sugar cane.
Love is the fire.
We wait to see when fire will enflame us.
Our lands watered by fire, refreshed by fire.
We are fresh forever because of the beloved.
She, winterless springtime.

O nightingale!
Speak of springtime beauties.
Today we want wine.
Be a cupbearer and bring it.
We wait for you.
Hurry!
End our expectation.
Speak.

If you do not find me, seek beside the beloved.
Look for me in Heaven, in garden and meadow.
I sleep like a shadow.
Seek me in the shadow of that tall cypress.
If you want to see me broken and drunk,
        look for me near eyes thirsty for wine.

The thoughtful use two kinds of words,
        those concise and long-winded.
The superficial use two kinds of words,
        those long-winded and concise.
Better if many poems are written.
Better if the ocean is filled with pearls.
Even a camel can enjoy poetry.

You, unaware of being a queen.
You, the Azrael of lions.
You, the distressed lion.
You broke your cage.
No surprise if a cage is broken by a lion.
Such a surprise that a lion like you sits in the cage.

If you are in love, love is proof.
If you are not in love, why search for proof?

The seeker upon the path seeks not the queen.
The queen has a heart but is not our beloved.

You will never see her as long as you see yourself.

"Stop!" I said.
"Stop, and I will stop," she replied.

Advice makes us no better.

Sometimes I am short, sometimes long,
    like a shadow before a light.

Poor am I, but still I cannot accept a gem so small.
I long for a gem both rare and priceless.

All these people complaining, weeping.
They upset me.
I long for the shouts and howls of drunkards.

I need to be with special people, non-existent people.
I do not drink from the cup that most people drink from,
    even if delivered from Heaven.
If a man is a jeweller, he knows his own value.
To be a guard does not make anyone Kay Qobád
    and King Sanjar.

Love, poverty, service.
Signs of life all three.
Revelation, contemplation, visibility.
You seek the water of life, you wash your clothes in water,
    you sit beside the heart,
        all so that a door is open to you.

My joyful head, your joyful heart.
Better that sorrow has no heart and head.
Falling in love and drinking wine is better
    than a beloved and love.
The world is like an ocean, the body like a seashell.
The soul speaks of the pearl's beauties.
The pearl is better than all these.
Make your face yellow as gold.
Talk to the yellow face of gold.
With gold comes sorrow.
Without gold comes sorrow.
But sorrow with gold is better.

You intend to leave.
God bless you.
You will return victorious.
God bless you.
Everywhere you make every heart happy.
Your unique beauty and loyalty.
God bless you.
You make everything better.
You remove sorrow from the heart.
You remove yellow from the face.
God bless you.

Sugar is nothing but kind and sweet.
The moon does nothing but shine.
The garden brings forth nothing but beautiful colour.
The fresh branch brings forth nothing but
    leaves and blossoms.
We and the passion of drunkenness.
Drunkenness and idolatry.
We can do nothing more than this.
We explore like flowers in colourful clothing.
We become Majnun.
Eating and sleeping will end in nothing.

My eyes blink.
A sign of the beloved's arrival.
The heart shudders.
A sign of the beloved's arrival.
This lapwing comes from the army of Solomon.
This nightingale comes from the garden.
The city is safe.
Every thief has fled, in fear of the powerful guard.
O those poor in the garden!
Autumn robbed you.
The king of springtime arrives to make sacrifices.

This face is not that of my beloved.
My garden has no such trees, leaves and fruits.
Everyone broke their promises.
But in this city, the custom is different.
She spread seeds and hid the trap.
Unaware were we that she hid her enmity.

Logic holds us back, us walking the path, and you lovers.
O young man!
Tear apart this chain.
The path appears in front of you.
Ask me not about love.
Ask no one about love.
Ask only love about love.
O young man!
Love speaks like a cloud raining down,
    spreading words like gems.
O young man!
Love is not the work of delicate, sleeping people.
Love is the work of heroes, of the courageous.

Your soul has made my soul aware of itself.
Your thoughts have affected my every moment.
Whatever you think or imagine will at the same time
    be on my mind.

You have wasted the water of life to save your honour.
You have taken poison and discarded sugar and sweets.
So broken and drunk are you
    that you cannot distinguish sky from earth.
You have polluted the river with sewage.

I sing better than the nightingale.
Jealousy from others means my mouth remains closed.
I long to weep.

I swear to God
        that without you the city is for me a prison.
I long to be uprooted.
I love being in the desert.

A lonely Joseph.
One hundred wolves.

At every dawn ask the wind about my heart.

Love has no logic.
Logic is a walking stick.

You said so much that you transcended words.

It is said that this was impossible to find.
"I long to find what is impossible to find," he said.

Like Jacob, I weep.
I long for the beautiful face of Joseph of Canaan.

Make peace with the beloved and avoid loneliness.
Know the secret of making peace
        and reach the water of life.

Go become one with the beloved's shadow.
Let no footprint of yours remain.
If a big cup of wine is offered, drink.
O soul, be carefree!

O lovers, arise and ascend to the sky!
We have seen this world.
Let us see the other.
All these paintings are signs of an unknown painter.
O let us hide from evil eyes and become unknown!
This path is filled with danger, but love will lead us.
Love teaches us to walk the path.

Her job is to flirt, our duty is to weep.
We have no job other than weeping.
We go into the garden to pick flowers
    and hand them to lovers.
If you are our companion and keeper of secrets,
    to you will we reveal our secret.

On the day of my death, when my coffin is borne,
    do not think that I suffer pain in this world.
Do not weep for me when you catch sight of my corpse.
Union with the beloved is finally here.
Do not bid me farewell when you place me in the grave.
The grave is a door to Heaven.
When you see the sun setting, expect it to rise soon.
There is no loss when sun and moon set.

Come, the drunk cupbearer has arrived.
Give good news to the miserable.
Arrival of the solution.
The king of love arrived and opened the tavern.
His gemlike wine touched even the most hardened.
From him flowed one thousand springs of milk and sugar.
He opened up, handing cradles to children.
Turn your back on tongues and become only ears.
Hurry, for the earrings have arrived.

I was freed from poetry.
O king of eternity, the rhythm of poetry killed me!
Let the flood take away all rhythm, all misleading words.
The heads of poets are brainless, nothing but a shell.
I am a mirror.
I am a mirror.
I am no man of letters.
Turn your ears to eyes and all will be made clear.

If you are no seeker, joining with us will make you one.
If you are no musician, joining with us will make you one.
One candle from our festivities
    can light one hundred other candles.
You are either dead or alive.
Joining with us will make you alive.
When a seed falls to the ground
    it will grow and become a tree.
If you understand this secret
    you will join with us and fall to the ground.

We detach from ourselves.
Selfishness is our destination, our goal.
Being with the self is just words.
Join in these special festivities.
Discriminate between special people and everyone else.
Inside your heart for special people,
    outside for everyone else.

O lovers, the beautiful beloved has arrived!
Begin your bliss.
The beloved is embarrassed.
See the day of reckoning on this day of reckoning.
See the statuesque beloved
    who turned the world into Heaven.
The arrival of one thousand new springtimes.

Cup of wine in one hand, hair of beloved in the other.
I long for such a dance in this city square.

At every moment are songs of love heard left and right.
We travel up into the sky.
Who wants to explore?

O soul!
You are Joseph.
Ask how Jacob is.

Do not expect sourness in this warehouse of sugar.

Hidden truths will appear.

In each and every painting I see the painter.

My heart in pain.
Do not allow enemies to be happy.
My heart happy only when you are content.

Parrots brought news of sugar from the beloved.
In mountains and deserts
        grew one hundred thousand sweets.

The month of fasting is over.
The beginning of a new year.
The beginning of a new year.
The night of separation is over.
The beloved appeared.
When morning emerged, your Azra became Vameq.
When the beloved became a lover,
        your guide became your follower.

Climb onto the horse of love.
Do not worry about the path.
Ride this graceful horse.
Even on an uneven path the horse will carry you home
    in one go.

O soul!
If day is over, be a guest of nighttime drunkards.
From dusk to dawn be the guest of selfless relatives.
O Joseph of beauties!
Do not stray from Jacob's vision.
Make this night divine.
Be light in the house of sorrow.
How blissful it is to host the moon in darkness.
O soul!
Arise and become a moon for those who travel at night.

Can you not see this day of reckoning?
Can you not see this statuesque beloved?
Crazed and mad are the walls and doors of this house.
I sit atop the wall as a sign.
O how pure you are!
Is it you who is crazed, or me?
Drink a cup of wine with me.
Ignore all accusations.

Here we are.
Heart, love, body.
Broken, drunk, joyful.
All with you.
You decide whether others will weep or smile.
We are tree branches, love is the wind.
Your love is like a wind which makes us
     both yellow and green.
You own this land.
You have everything.
Stones and clods know nothing of springtime.
Ask grass, flowers and trees about springtime.

Sugar does nothing for me.
I need your gem.
The moon does nothing for me.
I need your beauty.
Your eyes make everything drunk.
Without them wine has no spirit.
This journey is worthless if you are not with me.
Treasure does nothing for me.
I need your tithe.
Your body does nothing for me.
I must embrace you.
I am artless, save my contemplation of you.
Art for me is worthless if you ignore me.

Logic tells us there are only six directions.
Beyond this there are no other paths.
Love tells us there are other paths.
"I have walked them," says love.
Logic tells us not to step into non-existence,
      for there exist only thorns.
"Every thorn is inside you," love tells logic.
Silence!
Remove the thorn of existence from the heart's foot.
You will see gardens within yourself.

Become sour.
All people here are sour.
Become blind.
All people here are blind.
Limp.
All people here are limping.
Fasten something to your foot and walk as do the injured.
Apply saffron to your face if you are beautiful.
Show your beautiful face and you will be stabbed from
behind.

Everyone slept.
Me, in love, unable to sleep.
All through the night my eyes counted stars up above.
Sleep departed my eyes, never to return.
My sleep drank the poison of separation, then died.

Look at the nightingale moving towards the garden.
Look at the rouge upon the face
      of that pomegrante flower.
The fruit is ripe, outside itself.
Blissfully it moves, like Mansour, towards the cross.

The city dog unable to hunt.
The hunter must inhabit mountains, forests, deserts.

Our beloved never leaves us.

Whatever is made plentiful loses value.

You need no proof.
You are drowned in the world of senses.

The nightingale praises the one who taught it words.

You, Joseph, full of miracles.
Your beautiful face is all we need as proof.

Better to keep an immature brain inside its shell.
A ripe brain needs no shell.

How unfair.
Never give my heart to separation.
O beloved, this is not to your advantage!
Do not slay the one who was slain for you.
You, a source of sugar and sweetness,
      how beautiful you are.
Never speak of bitterness.

New year.
Two moons together.
The beloved's beautiful face.
Shining moon in the sky.
Both share secrets.
This new year they are the cause of one thousand desires.

If you are in love with love, seek love.
Take the sharp dagger and cut life's throat.
Honour upon the path of love is an enormous obstacle.
I am telling you the truth.
Accept it gracefully.
You pull up your clothes to avoid getting wet.
There are one thousand ducks in the ocean for you.

The affairs between love and my heart are all in the past.
Little by little I remember them.
Love, it seems, was born of me.
But the truth is that I was born of love.
Life has made me a master.
Such bliss when I receive curses instead of kisses.

After becoming dust, either profit or loss will follow.
For the time being I become dust and see what happens.
Becoming dust even before death arrives
    is done only by lovers.
God showed them how to tear apart the chain.
One moment becoming dust.
One moment becoming water.
One moment becoming fire.
One moment becoming smoke.
One moment becoming the beloved.
One moment becoming a companion.
One moment becoming warp.
One moment becoming weft.

Remove the world's sorrow from your heart
     and forever live blissfully in the garden of life.
You can wash all dust from your heart
     with the water of suffering.
If you toil to find a place beyond dust,
     you will find it in almighty Heaven.
If you think deeply, you can compensate
     for what in the past you have lost.

I implore you:
Do not stop working, do not sleep.
Do not sleep for one single night.
For one thousand nights your selfish desires
     benefitted from sleep.
For the benefit of the beloved, do not sleep this one night.
Give your heart to the delicate beloved
     who never sleeps at night.
Do not sleep.

Call out to truthfulness.
Stop playing in the dust.
I have one life and now long to sacrifice it.
When this fire appears, the whole world weeps.
Give me a moment.
Give me a moment to die now.
The world, ripped apart because of fear.
The soul flies because of love.
I will make every bird jealous when I fly.

Hurry towards that heart, free of questions and answers.
That heart is the sun of the world.
Pour dust into greedy eyes.
Pour tears into burning jealous eyes.

When I teach two thousand books,
    even if no one is happy, I feel no upset.
No flower smiles, no tree dances.
No garden spreads its scent without a morning breeze.

O wind!
Make branches dance in remembrance of days of union.

O flower, you fled from separation!
Why are you not smiling?
O cloud, you left your beloved!
Why are you not weeping?

You sell your beauty through flirtation.
Keep your customers happy.

Arrival of crazed winter.
Arrival of long nights.

The heart's window is a joyful window.

I saw the red flower.
My face turned yellow.

Silence!
Speak in another language.
You have been following this olden custom.
Follow another.

Sometimes are you happy, sometimes sad.
Turn away forever from sadness
    by abandoning this hive of hardship.

Without you life is haram.
Without you good fortune sleeps forever.
You are good fortune.
You are life.
All other things are only names, lies, torture.

You intend to depart, taking with you my life of joy.
Remember me.
Despite us, you ride the horse of separation.
Remember me.
You will find trustworthy companions on this earth
    and in the sky.
But remember promises made to your old lover.

Inadvisable to turn your back on companions.
Inadvisable to travel without light.
Inadvisable to become a beggar after having been a king.
The beloved urges you to leave behind your ego.
Inadvisable to hold your ego so close.

Today, a new madness has arrived.
One thousand hearts unchained.
Today flowers grow on clod and stones.
It seems that God has created a new world
    in the old world.

Eyes filled with blood.
Sleeplessness.
My heart filled with madness.
Sleeplessness.
Birds and fish wonder why I do not sleep day and night.
Before this I wondered why the sky never sleeps.
Now the sky wonders why I, so miserable, do not sleep.

Eyes should be closed at night, open during the day.
Wherever our beloved rides the horse,
    quickly should we follow.
The kitchen of the soul is nowhere to be found.
Our nose should be turned towards it.
Truth, concealed in anger.
Silence, golden.

An expert physician giving bitter medicine to a patient
    might seem cruel.
But no, he is just doing his job.
Even in darkness the foot recognises its shoe.
Desire guides homewards the heart.
If you seek union,
    sit with people already with the beloved,
    those in union.

The joy of poverty, like wine.
Kneeling in prayer, joyful and humble.
Both flow downwards.
To be proud is nasty.
The proud deserve a head empty of desire.
O fish, seek in the ocean whatever your heart desires!
Reject greed or else be caught in the net.

Midnight.
Crazed drunkards.
We.
Night.
Candle.
Wine.
The beloved.
Our sleeping ego.
No trouble.
We are with our own beloved.
Embraced.

Close the door.
We love festivities where for a moment
    we can talk to the sweet-lipped beloved.
The rope of your trap freed us from the water well.
From that day on we have played with rope.
We, companions of rope.

Either fulfill my desire or free me from desire.
Do not promise tomorrow.
Do either this or that.

Leave this seashore of water and mud.
Travel to the gem.
You are the ocean.

You, a baby fish, cannot live without water.

I slept in the shadow of good fortune.

The soul does not have the strength
    to see your face unveiled.

Whoever escapes love will shed his blood.

Sometimes you lie.
Sometimes you are disloyal.
Yes.
As long as you are like that, I shall be like this.

Sometimes I graze here.
Sometimes I am grass for others.
Sometimes I am a wolf.
Sometimes I am a ewe.
Sometimes I am a shepherd.

We are empowered from beyond this life.
Our splendour comes not from Saturn.
We are held captive in the water well of this world.
We bless the bucket that comes to free us.
Many Jacobs await us in Canaan.

For a moment she makes me joyful as a garden.
For a moment she makes me like winter.
For a moment she makes me a man of letters, a teacher.
For a moment she makes me a schoolboy.

O cupbearer!
From which grape is this wine made?
It brings a hangover to the hearts and souls
    of my companions.
Open the old pitcher and close this one,
    which like poison has erased everyone's joy.
Give us that old wine, which is blessed.
Do not break the old promise, which is blessed.

What burns beneath these festivities?
A desire for art gives off smoke.
Where is the fire?
I have lost my way.
What is it that breeds such enmity?
We are connected like a chain,
    so why are the doors closed?

Loving you has made me drunk, blissful.
I, drunk and selfless, know of nothing else.
People say it is best to avoid being like that.
It wasn't really me.
Love made me do it.
I appreciate sky and earth too much.
I was earth, love made me sky.
O heart, stop!
What my beloved did to me cannot be explained in words.

With good fortune comes love.
Loveless days do not count as life.
Time spent without love
      brings shame upon us before God.
Whoever does not become drunk on love
      will forever be hungover.

O cupbearer, bring wine, for these are indeed joyful days!
Today is the day of wine, exploration, fire-making.
The cupbearer is beautiful, the wine delicate, time blessed.
These festivities are bright as the sky,
      the beloved's face bright as the moon.
Listen to songs of the flute.
The flute is inspired by the breath of the beloved.
Drink red wine.
Here is sorrow.

The surfaces of things have no power.
They are temporary.
The true nature of things is of no use.
They are hidden.
When I was poor I decided to talk less,
      but all flowers have thorns.
We are thorns of this flower.
Brother, be my witness.
To be like this thorn is honour, not dishonour.
Your intention is cruelty.
Stop.
You intend to accuse us, to separate from us.
Stop.
You are an angry lion in the meadow of passion.
Why do you shed my blood?

Your smiling face is like one hundred gardens.
Enter the almighty garden.
Trade thorn with flower.
Remove your clothes and contemplate the naked soul.
The soul is joyful when naked.
You do not need to keep its clothes.

Almighty grace is like flowing water.
It moves downwards.
To reach almighty grace I must be dust.
I must be drowned.

Me, like a nightingale in the garden of the heart.
Shame on me if I behave like an owl.
Me, like a flower in the beloved's garden.
A pity if I behave like a thorn.

The less we have in hand and heart, the better.

Whatever you deserve will be born of fate.

No one remains conscious under the sheltering sky.

Joseph sang.
Jacob danced.

O brother!
Words of wisdom:
Become new, as does the sky, in this old world.

Love.
Union and separation.
Ups and downs upon the path.

My Khosrow returned again from the mountain.
The beloved is my soul, my love, my religion.
Again she remembered me.
Love and passion pushed me to recite
     the heart of the Koran.
My beloved is the heart of the Koran.
She calls out to me.

Come! Come!
Separation from you erased all wisdom and faith.
Poor winter am I.
Restfulness abandoned me.
Ask not about my yellow face, my pained burnt heart.
Words cannot explain.
Come see all with your eyes.

Today is the day for a meeting with the beloved,
    for the powerful sun's good fortune.
How beautiful you are!
A glance from you is like a tithe.
My eyes filled with pearls, my face yellow as gold.
"The door is slightly open," she said.
    "Look at me through the crack."
One of my hands on your door, the other on my head.

O flower, delicate is your face!
Do not place your face upon the beloved's.
Delicate is she.
Think not about it, even within your heart.
She sees every secret in every heart.
Delicate is she.
Remove all sorrow from the heart.
The heart is a house where my desire for her resides.
Delicate is my desire for the beloved.

May this feast be a blessing on lovers.
O lovers, a happy feast, with the scent of our soul!
May it be happy, like souls throughout the world.
O moon of sky and earth!
A joyous feast to you in all seven skies.
The feast arrived with the sign of union in hand.
O lovers, bless this sign!

Beware!
The time for patience is here.
The time for hardships and challenges is here.
When the knife reaches the bone, promises are broken.
Promises become fragile when, because of hardship,
    a man is close to death.
O heart, be not fragile!
Time to be strong.

Do not hide away.
Blessed is your face.
Contemplating you is a blessing for every soul.
Tonight every heart desirous of you
     will tomorrow surely be blessed.
Give us more silent wine.
Make us silent.
Blessed it is to keep words in the heart.

O Solomon, bring the ring!
Make every angel and demon bow down to you.
I am tired of the well and its water.
Make flow almighty springs.
Worship not gold and woman.
Blasphemous has God dubbed such things.

Assign me the task to kiss you again and again.
Make me happy with a smile.
I wish God would make soft your heart.
Such a joyful prayer!
Amen.

To be in love means nothing
     but turning away from desire.
It means to become bloody, to suffer, to be loyal as a dog.

You still have thorns in your feet.
Sit.
To you is the verdant garden unknowable.

Nothing more blessed than sorrow.
Endless are its rewards.

Whatever a drunkard does is only because of wine.

My madness equals the riches of one hundred wise men.

Blessed is that person who became as we are,
    happy and submissive.

A house filled with drunkards.
Yet new drunkards arrived.

O musician!
You sing joyfully and play beautifully.
You should sing beautifully.

I am treasure from the heart of this earth.
Do not search on earth.
I am the *qibla* of the sky.
Do not turn your face upwards.

O cypress, listen!
The lily beside the river
    is like a tongue that speaks of you.
Your kindness can open closed blossoms.
You open them.
To you are they dedicated.

Great sorrow for you.
My heart became the house of madness.
Seeking you, my heart travelled everywhere.
Give no mercy to my heart, my poor heart.
Alas, my poor heart!
Alas, my poor heart!

In union of passion, we all are one.
When we start talking, a beloved for me,
    a beloved for you.
I travelled widely in the world of thorns.
Now I remove them from my feet.
A thorn for me, a thorn for you.
Whoever seeks me should search your estate.
There, Leila and Majnun.
One is me, one is you.

You emerged from my soul.
Where is your home?
You, my shining moon.
Where is your home?
Moon and shadow together.
Moon takes care of shadow.
O moon, tell me, where is your home?
Me, looking for the moon.
I searched one hundred houses.
Free me from this search.
Where is your home?

Whoever waits for you will hunt good fortune.
The farm waits for rain and is made verdant,
    full of flowers.
Waiting for the sun turns a stone into a gem.
Long is the story of those awaiting the beloved.
It will last beyond the day of reckoning.

Better for a lover to suffer, for incense to catch fire.
Drinking from the cup of cruelty is difficult,
    but in the hands of the beloved becomes bliss.
Drink poison from the cup painted
    by generosity and kindness.
Be like a ball in her polo game.
The sky will become your carpet.

I want a beloved the soul can follow.
I want a musician better than Venus.
I have a cup bigger than the ocean.
I have a crazed heart that cannot be chained,
     that heeds no advice.
Such a life you have.
So drunk am I.
You deserve that, I deserve this.

Two houses in this world.
One of good fortune, one of suffering.
I swear to God that the lover resides in neither.
He seeks neither the day of joy nor nightly rest.
His heart, like dawn, hidden between day and night.
Neither anguish nor sadness are the cause of his tears.
At every moment he longs to be ever more sorrowful.

"How are you?" you asked.
"Look at my face," you said.
"Are you happy without me?" you asked.
Enough sarcasm.
"Have a joyful life," said smiling you.
No one can be joyful without you.
Go tell another tale.

Drunkenness, love, youth.
Arrival of joyful springtime.
All became companions.
A willow tree beside the river.
It sees through a mirror,
     wondering why new branches are dancing.

Do not leave! Do not leave!
Why so often do you leave?
Tell me.
Tell me.
Why so rarely do you return?

O sorrow, depart!
No work for you beside the drunkard.
Find a conscious man and sting him.

A conscious man is like a wild dog
     that knows nothing but how to fight.

I, so poor, wail against knowledge and awareness.

We escaped divine judgement into the hands of the one
     who satisfies our needs.

It has become a proverb:
Eat grapes and ask not about the vineyard.

Loyalty is unnecessary for the queen of beauties.
You are a lover with yellow face.
Be patient, loyal.

The weeping flood journeys along this uneven path,
     yet step by step it explores.

Finally you became drunk and emerged.
When you make yourself drunk,
     no one else remains in this world.
Is it you or me who is the body?
Do you embrace us or do we you?
Whatever you are, I want no life without you.

One glimpse of the early morning beloved
    and all enemies are slain.
Her face is good news, a sign of a life blessed.
Suddenly are you awakened!
Suddenly you behold the face of the beloved!
Such prosperity, good fortune, happiness.

If wheat grows from my dust and bread is made from it,
    that bread will make you ever more drunk.
The dough and baker become crazed
    while the oven sings a drunken song.
One visit to my grave and you will be dancing.

When will this cage turn into a garden fit for my desire,
    for my life?
At that time the full moon will embrace us
    and the jealous will suffer hardship.
Everyone who has fallen into the water well of separation
    will find their way as a companion of rope.

Go, go.
You passed through this world,
    through suffering and trials.
O painting, you travelled towards the painter!
O soul, you moved towards the soul of souls!
Eat from the tree of faith.
You passed by the fearless house.
Enter the water of life, as would a fish.
You passed through exile in this world of dust.

Again you became cruel.
Remember.
You did not do what you said.
Remember.
You said you would be my companion until
        the day of reckoning, but now you are
        a companion of cruelty.
Remember.
You slept, then left me awake and alone these dark nights.
Remember.
Many times you fell and I took your hand.
Next time you fall, remember.

Every heart without a beloved
        is like a man without a head.
Whoever is far from the trap of love
        is like a bird without wings.
Whoever is unaware of the awakened is aware of nothing.

O beloved, you are like a statuesque cypress!
When sorrow for you arises in my heart, my body arises
        like a cypress devoid of heart and soul.
If your beauty attacks the sheltering sky,
        the residents of Heaven will seek harmony.
Springtime envies you.
Pass by the garden of this world early one morning.
Autumn customs will leave the garden.

Do not ask about restfulness.
Seek rest under her good fortune.
No restfulness in my heart because of her face.
You, trapped by her.
Do not seek freedom.

Alas! Alas!
The beloved packed for a journey.
Alas!
I did not accompany her.
Alas!
I have no control over travel.
If so, I would wipe away all journeys.

Remove yourself from poetry.
Contemplate the world before this world.
My sorrowful desire was born there.

Where there is a candle,
    the butterfly cannot avoid being burnt.
Impossible to avoid kneeling
    before such a statuesque beloved.

A beloved at home is of no use.

Today the beloved asks us to become crazed.

No ladder can reach the roof of poverty and faith.

Invite this crazed man to be chained for one night.

If you do not want to hunt, place no traps upon the path.
If you fail to blossom, do not claim to be a garden.

Yesterday my cloud sat upon the seashore.
"Become dust and I will rain down on you."

Look into the mirror.
It arrived from its journey.
Look kindly upon it.
Dirty from its journey.
Ignore the dust.
Like a blossom, I am always on watch, so long as
      the cypress of the soul travels through springtime.

Your beloved has no lover.
Do not take another beloved.
Endless is the beauty of her face.
Never leave her.
The world is a place for hunting.
At every moment something to hunt.
Appear as would a lion.
Hunt nothing but a lion.

Nights and days we spent
      in sorrow and happiness for you.
We reached light of day.
Now is night in many cities of this world, but here is day.
The world of ignorant people is dark as night.
They sleep.
To us did the sun of love bring day.

Let there be more tricks of the beloved to fool lovers.
Love sees me weeping and begins to smile.
Let the world be filled with smiles because of love's smile.
When confronted by her gem, stones melt out of shame.
Let shame be ashamed of shame for her.

The beloved settled down.
Let it be like this forever.
All her blasphemy turned to religion.
Let it be like this forever.
Land destroyed was destroyed by evil.
The hawk becomes Solomon's.
Let it be like this forever.
The beloved who attacked my heart
    and veiled herself for us is now a companion of lovers.
Let it be like this forever.
Time for the feast.
Time for the feast.
The beloved who fled has arrived.
Many gifts surround us.
Let it be like this forever.

Do not flee from fire, otherwise you will remain raw.
Step away from this circle and still you remain trapped.
Do not flee like rain from your companions.
If you become angry, forever will you wander.
Be loyal to the beloved.
Loyalty comes from non-existence.
I worry that you will die while still unloyal.
Time to make peace with us.
Like kings, you will remain happy to the end.

Wherever you see a poor man, sit with him.
Wherever you see a man weeping, move away.
Escape the poor man, whoever searches for daily bread.
For us, the real man in poverty is Bayazid.
Most people celebrate twice a year.
We, Sufis of the soul, celebrate twice in every breath.

Look!
Today the Kaaba follows pilgrims.
One thousand caravans are blessed by it.
Look!
Today the sour grape is made sweet because of joy.
Look!
Today salt is growing like a plant.
Sorrow dies, tears depart.
May you and I live forever.
Today wherever there is sorrow will be full of smiles.

O musician of lovers!
Begin your playing.
Light a fire in believers and unbelievers.
Inadvisable for love to be silent.
Unveil the good purpose.

Blame us not if we are good or bad.
We are a harp, our hearts the strings.
You play such harps.
But if not, better to put down the harp.

The world is like a pot.
Many other immature people have been boiled in it.
But you were not here.
They could not escape it.
Acceptance was the only remedy.

O heart!
Speak less about the scent of love.
The real lover will smell it himself.

Our joyful beloved will never experience joylessness.

The shadow appears, although it is nothing.

I arrived at the prison of this world with good purpose.

Night departed.
Our story did not end.

Night
Poetry from the Classical Persian Canon

Selected and adapted by
Abbas Kiarostami

Conversations with kings are darkness
    on the longest night.
Seek light from the sun, which hopefully will rise.

                        Hafez

No night was as dark as this night.
Tonight it seems there was neither light nor moon.

                        Helali Jagata'i

Ignorant as you are,
night and day,
of day and night,
how do you expect
day and night's secret
to bring you joy?

                        Attar

The mystery is one of respecting love's rituals.
At night, birds leave the flying to butterflies.

                        Saib Tabrizi

Day is for business and trade.
Desire for night is something else.

                        Rumi

Her lips, words, hair and face
are wine and sugar and night and moonlight.

Khwaju Kermani

Half your life is day.
The other is night with shining stars.

Jami

She allowed no one's night to darken.
In every heart does light burn with longing for her.

Iqbal

This is the night of separation.
What will tomorrow bring?
I long for the morning of my hope to be filled with light.

Iraqi

"You do not know what this dark night
will give birth to,"
I said.
Be patient.
Let it deliver.

Farrukhi Sistani

Each day until night
do I live with one thousand sorrows.
I will see what divine judgment unveils behind the curtain.

Abusa'id Abolkhayr

I longed for a day of joy
to be delivered from fate.
I had no idea that
fate is pregnant
with the longest night of the year,
which brings with it for me
one thousand sorrows.

Vahshi Bafqi

Dark night.
Fear of waves.
Fearsome whirlpool.
How can those who rest upon the seashore
    understand us?

Hafez

Night.
Desert.
Wind.
I am lost.
Only a hidden fortune can guide me.

Salman Savoji

Bound to the hair of the beloved.
We expect some resolution to this dark night.

Iraqi

There is for me every week
one night of solitude
for which I would not trade
the other six days.

Khaqani

Night dark as tar.
Hidden moon.
Birds and animals sleeping.

Ferdowsi

Dark night.
Desert.
I will get nowhere
unless the candle of your face shines upon the path.

Hafez

You are unaware of the story of night.
No ear is as deaf as yours.

Vahshi Bafqi

Not a night passes
without pleading to the sky.
But what can I do?
There is no saviour.

Khwaju Kermani

Day and night
rush and roar
as they travel through
narrow curtains
of the mind.

Attar

For us
there is no difference
between night and day.
No difference if the sun rises or sets.

Rumi

Ask those awake how long is the night.
It seems short to those sleeping.

Saadi

Wakefulness,
nights
and me.
Calling on God
from night until morning.
God!
Let no one see such nights even when dreaming.

Helali Jagata'i

For others, days of joy and happiness.
For me, dark nights and tears.

Fayz Kashani

Our soul howls through the day.
A heart filled with pain.
Tears from night until morning.

Iraqi

As dark night arrived
tears were shed
by the heart of the dervish.

Helali Jagata'i

Those asleep are unaware of night.
Angels host divine guests.

Rumi

The moon is cold, wet, colourful.
It walks through night.
Restless.
Wandering.

Anvari

Every night
I have another thought
and a different conclusion.
Should I depart tomorrow because of you?

Saadi

Endless night and day saddened me.
How joyful is that place free of day and night.

Fayz Kashani

Wherever is your hair is night.
Wherever is your face is sunshine.

Anvari

No wonder your dark hair sits on either side of your face.
Each day between two nights.

Helali Jagata'i

The candle and I burn at night.
My flames inside.

Saadi

Nightwatchman
of heart's sanctuary am I.
Night after night
I think only about her behind this curtain.

Hafez

Tonight is my feverish sorrow
more intense
than other nights.
Look after me this night.

Vahshi Bafqi

O heart!
Stay away from her dimple,
        concealed behind beautiful hair.
This night is dark.
Watch out for a water well upon the path.

Foroughi Bastami

"I will shed your blood some other night,"
she told me yesterday.
I hope tonight she remembers those words.

Hatef Esfehani

I sit at night
in remembrance of your eyebrows.
I turn my back on sleep.
I turn my face to sanctuary.

Fayz Kashani

The night of impatient lovers is a long night.
Come!
From the start of night is the door of morning open.

Saadi

Dark night of separation.
Me, near death.
Time for you to rise like a shining moon.

Hafez

Every night, without you.
Me and my corner of solitude.
My feet buried in sorrow.
My heavy head.

Helali Jagata'i

Impossible this dark night
to hide on your estate.
Such light from your face!

Iraqi

No wonder my heart was blind to daylight.
Your hair encloses
the one hundred longest nights
of the year.

Fayz Kashani

Union with the beloved is like a sun
    that for me never rises.
This dark night of separation for me has no end.

Fayz Kashani

Separation.
Every night I weep to God.
God weeps because of my tears.

Khaqani

Last night there was no hope for morning,
so pained by your love was I.
The prisoner of love cannot tolerate long nights.

Saadi

Let my night be long.
Dawn is there.
I am here.

Orfi Shirazi

The pain of the heart
tells a story.
Sorrow of long nights.
Not a story that can readily see light of day.

Ubayd Zakani

Leave out the story of the night of separation
and so appreciate her unveiling on the day of union.

Hafez

O Foroughi!
On this night of separation
let there be patience until dawn.

Foroughi Bastami

Being with you
turns everyone else's night into day.
Sorrow of separation turns my day to night.

Fayz Kashani

All night
just me
and a light.
My companion until daytime.

Khaqani

I resolved to be close to your face and hair
from morning until night.
Eventual separation turned my day into dark night.

Salman Savoji

Life is gone.
Dark night of separation did not end.
Either my night should have been shorter or my life
longer.

Helali Jagata'i

Night of separation.
Sorrow upon sorrow.
Day of union with you.
Happiness and joy.

Fayz Kashani

Night.
I go to bed with the sorrow of separation
if that day I have not embraced you.

Saadi

Glimpse her beauty
and you will understand
why day and night of separation
are so dark.

Foroughi Bastami

My morning of union cannot transcend
the mountain of separation.
The day of my hope is dark as night.

Iraqi

Too long is the night of separation.
Especially tonight.
I long for day after this night of separation.

Vahshi Bafqi

Ask the night of separation how I am.
See how I burn in flames of desire.

Khaqani

Every night I think:
God!
If this is separation,
what would union be like?

Roudaki

If the entire surface of the earth were a notebook,
the story of the night of separation would not fit.

Fayz Kashani

Who can tell the story of the night of separation?
Only whoever counts stars like Saadi.

Saadi

Alas!
Life consumed by nights of separation.
I still do not know what the day of union is.

Helali Jagata'i

Impossible for the world to be filled with light
in your absence.
Sun and night cannot come together.

Anvari

If every morning you cannot hear me weeping,
who then will rescue me from nights of separation?

Khwaju Kermani

The night of separation has an unforgettable effect.
It is the morning of union of which one can find no trace.

Salman Savoji

You are aware of my suffering this night of separation.
Are you aware of my daytime suffering?

Abusa'id Abolkhayr

The heart, afraid of separation.
It seems that the day of union
is the same as the night of separation.

Anvari

The night of separation
is the longest night of the year.
God!
Free them all, those in captivity.

Saadi

As you reveal your face
from behind your hair
the sun rises on the longest night of the year.

Gha'ani

I do not mean to complain,
but you, so kind,
should you not be doing something to help?
"Every night a tired man sheds tears upon my door."

Iraqi

Many nights did I spend longing for you.
Why withhold your dawn breeze from me?

Khaqani

Do not turn your face from us.
Our midnight sighs
have turned many bright mornings
into night.

Saib Tabrizi

My life without you is dark, no?
Nights of longing for union are restless, yes?

Sanai

Ever since that night
when you revealed your moon to lovers,
everyone has been restless,
just as the world is restless.

Rumi

If every night
you burn like a candle,
at dawn
will you be rewarded.

Attar

The heart that tonight longs for union with you
will tomorrow surely be blessed.

Rumi

Thinking at night
about sorrow of day
destroys me.
Daytime thinking about
nighttime suffering destroys me.

Vahshi Bafqi

Every day
I burnt in your love
from morning until night.
Burn me
like a miserable candle
every night
until dawn.

Attar

The tears of the candle
are not for the butterfly.
Dawn closes in.
The candle worries
about its own dark night.

Saib Tabrizi

What else can the lover do
but be humble?
What else can he do
but come every night to your door?

Abusa'id Abolkhayr

Day.
Night.
I know neither.
What is there to know?
Who is there to know?
O beloved!
You count the days.

Rumi

We are love itself.
Our heart is restless night and day.

Shah Nematollah Vali

Every night
comes affliction
from the cruelty of life.
Every moment of life spent in pain.

Attar

We enter into the turmoil of night
and make waves in night's ocean.

Rumi

At night,
desirous of her,
I make happy my heart
by hoping for tomorrow.
But I am afraid that this night of longing
may have no tomorrow.

Salman Savoji

Divine night.
If you were men of wisdom,
you would see moon and sun both.

Shah Nematollah Vali

I cannot live a day without you.
I cannot sleep a night without you.

Sanai

On the night of union, my night turns to day.
I swear to God, how good it will be!
No more counting days and nights.

Rumi

Saadi!
Tell the story of the sorrow she brought forth
and night will end before your story does.

Saadi

All night have I wept too much because of life.
Every night two hundred of my tears touch the sky.

Helali Jagata'i

My nightly cries and sighs
are those of joy
when standing on your doorstep.

Iraqi

Ask the morning breeze.
It knows that the scent of your hair
is our soul's companion
from night until dawn.

Hafez

Because of her, my night of joy was filled with daylight.
Alas! Alas!
She departed and my day became dark as night.

Helali Jagata'i

Your hair dark as night.
The shining sun hides,
waiting to rise
on the day of reckoning.

Fayz Kashani

Day.
I see you.
Night.
Sorrow of separation.
O beloved!
You turn night to day.

Rumi

In my mind,
nights without you
are dark as the grave.
Should dawn arrive without you,
it will be the day of reckoning.

Saadi

Your beauty makes the world beautiful.
Without it, my day is like night.
In your absence my tears burn the world like a candle.

Hafez

Darkness of night descended.
The dervish, tormented by separation.

Helali Jagata'i

Whoever separated me from you
and so turned day into night,
may his day be as dark as my life.

Helali Jagata'i

Good fortune upon you.
Sleep joyously.
If you need a guard,
at midnight I will pray
and fill the world
with an army.

Vahshi Bafqi

"Morning breeze will bring you news from me,"
you said.
Tell this to someone
who expects morning to follow night.

Salman Savoji

To spend night until morning with you
I would need a night longer than the day of reckoning.

Helali Jagata'i

516

The night you become nothing brings forth light.
Progress upon the path to mysticism.
Seek the value of a candle
on the longest night of the year.

Vahshi Bafqi

Hafez!
Turn your back on every myth.
Drink wine for a moment.
Last night we did not sleep.
The candle burnt like a myth.

Hafez

You ask why all night I never sleep.
The eyes of lovers must never sleep.

Saadi

No rest for me this night of separation.
No patience from me this day of union.

Saadi

Bring no candle to this gathering.
At our nighttime festivities the face of the beloved
shines as does the moon,
a full moon.

Hafez

A night spent with restless heart,
longing for you,
shall by day shine brightly upon the world.

Rumi

No one asks you how long is the night.
Whoever knows is last night's sleepless one.

Saadi

Your face, a full moon.
Tonight, divine night.
O queen of beauties!
Sleep not tonight.

Rumi

He turned his back on every impurity.
He neither slept at night
nor rested during the day.

Jami

He neither slept at night
nor rested during the day,
so reached the point of self-sacrifice.

Attar

All night we fail to sleep.
O you who have been sleeping your entire life!
Beware!

Saadi

I was unaware of the day of reckoning.
The night of separation
was created as the longest night of the year.

Foroughi Bastami

We did not appreciate the day of union.
On the night of separation
our worries kept us awake.

Saadi

Whoever is not awake to your love
through the night
will never deserve good fortune.

Foroughi Bastami

Thinking about you
keeps me sleepless
every night.
I want sleep, but worries frustrate it.

Mohtasham Kashani

Day of separation.
"Good night," I said to sleep.

Saadi

For how long, each night,
should the sanctuary candle and I burn?
For how long, each night,
should we spend our lives
restless, wandering?

Khwaju Kermani

Be mine,
for just one night,
amid one thousand nights.

Nezami

Me, awake all night until morning,
trailed by your sorrow.

Anvari

On the night of separation
the heart is split into one thousand pieces.
Where are those joyful moments of union?

Helali Jagata'i

I died awaiting day of union with you.
Is there an end to this night of separation?

Iraqi

Day and night,
remind the one beside the beloved:
"Think about the pains of those with hearts
burnt in separation."

Fayz Kashani

Night of separation.
Darkness,
even if one thousand moons arise.

Saadi

Alas!
My life.
Nights.
Nights of separation.
Days.
Days of separation.

Hatef Esfehani

Complaining about the night of separation
    is no simple tale.
Describing one single glance requires one hundred books.

Hafez

Darkness of night.
We departed towards moonlight.

Vahshi Bafqi

Moonlit night.
Springtime.

Ubayd Zakani

O heart!
For how long will you beg for moonlight?
Inflame the night with your breath.

Iqbal

Night of union.
Me, free of moonlight.

Helali Jagata'i

Night of separation.
No shining stars.
Go to the roof of the palace and light up the moon.

Hafez

Night of separation.
Creator of all darkness.
Day of union.
Bringer of morning.

Fayz Kashani

Contemplate dark night in the beloved's hair.

Fayz Kashani

We wander through the beloved's hair.
Divine night.
Divine we become.

Rumi

Not a day turns to night
when desire for your hair
does not send armies of affliction
from all four directions
into my heart.

Attar

Night.
The world as dark as your hair.
No seeker.
No seeking.

Attar

Reveal your face.
In the dark night of your hair
is my heart,
lost,
seeking moonlight.

Salman Savoji

The story of the night of separation
and our predicament
is as long as the hair of beauties.

Ubayd Zakani

Every night a vision of your face comes to me,
turning my day to night as dark as your hair.

Anvari

No one knows how long is the night of separation,
save the one held captive in the prison of love.

Saadi

The night of separation visits us all,
bringing with it the longest night of the year.

Vahshi Bafqi

On my knees, I declare union with you.
Is there an end to this night of separation?

Fayz Kashani

Night.
Desert.
The heart is lost.
Left.
Right.
Front.
Back.
There are water wells upon the path.

Salman Savoji

Dark night.
I have lost the path of desire.
O guiding star!
Arise from anywhere!

Hafez

My day became night.
The moon did not pass by.
Such a futile life.
A year spent, but no moon passed by.

Helali Jagata'i

The road is long.
We run quickly across and alongside night.

Rumi

Night is dark.
The path to safety lies before us.
Where is the fire of Sinai?
When is our meeting?

Hafez

Alas!
I walk upon the path of love,
alone,
joined only by nightly tears and morning sighs.

Foroughi Bastami

The day of my fortune once again darkened
as does night.
The morning of my hope again darkened.

Iraqi

Day and night
I am restless
in my desire for you.
Day and night my head upon your feet.

Rumi

Time for separation.
For how long do I await union?
Day of union never arrived.
Night of separation never departs.

Fayz Kashani

Scatter my ashes at dawn.
Give me at least one night of joy.

Iqbal

My day died.
Come to me at night.
I am the wanderer.
Find a solution to my life.

Attar

I am in exile.
I am in love.
Take a look at me.
Honour lovers with a visit one night.

Sanai

Long night of separation.
Clinging tightly
to the vessel of my soul.

Mohtasham Kashani

Without you my day is night.
Even if it is day,
it is night
when the sun is hidden.

Khwaju Kermani

Should the day of union with beauties
be the lot of others,
let the nights of separation
cast their shadow upon us.

Mohtasham Kashani

Except for the day of union, all life is wasted.
Such a waste.
My whole life spent in nights of separation.

Helali Jagata'i

Cherish nights together.
After we are gone
the sky will forever rotate
and many nights and days
will pass.

Hafez

From night until morning
only the anguished nightingale
is here to weep with me
in desire of your beautiful face.

Khwaju Kermani

You have spent not one single night waiting.
You know nothing about the night spent
by those who wait impatiently for you.

Saadi

Night of separation.
Burn like a candle,
enflamed by sorrow,
until morning union.

Attar

Today is the day of union.
Happy are you.
Prepare yourself for sorrow
on the night of separation.

Hatef Esfehani

Tonight, for me, weeping and wailing.
Tonight, patience is hidden.
There is no consciousness.

Abū-Sa'īd Abul-Khayr

Come,
and I will tell the tale
of nights of separation.
Were I to keep such things to myself,
there would be one thousand of them.

Fayz Kashani

Who will bear witness
to my sleepless nights?
My dreams of you,
forever companions of those who are awake.

Salman Savoji

My pain is beyond description.
Do not ask me.
It is a secret.
Many feverish nights do I lie awake.

Khaqani

Our night of solitude
is the curtain
of the day of reckoning.

Foroughi Bastami

Saadi does not light a lantern
this night of separation.
He fears opening his eyes to someone
other than the beloved.

Saadi

O captive bird!
Do not wail in desire of the garden.
Night is long.
For a while sleep engaged.

Khaqani

Only dreams of you and my sorrowful soul
know what I do with my heart each night.

Hafez

Only one piece of me remained
on the night of separation.
That piece burnt on the fire of separation.

Helali Jagata'i

Every night
my bloody heart
waits at your door.
It longs for morning,
when you might pass by.

Iraqi

Everyone who came,
like a candle,
to my bed this night of sorrow,
was burnt
and like me fell ill.

Mohtasham Kashani

Every night,
all night,
I write a letter
which will never be acknowledged.

Mohtasham Kashani

Me, abandoned.
Ask me not about the night of separation.
No talking.
It is a long story.

Khwaju Kermani

Until morning you are drunk on sweet sleep.
For me there are nights
that seem free of dawn.

Saadi

It is told that dawn prayer is effective.
Yes, but a lover's night has no dawn.

Vahshi Bafqi

Do not ask me
how I have spent
these months and years.
My life passed as quickly
as the night of union.

Saib Tabrizi

Ask me what happens in the world.
I count stars from night until morning.

Hafez

You sleep.
Every night I wrap you
in the solitude of my soul.
I watch over the heart.
I contemplate myself.

Vahshi Bafqi

Not unusual for both my eyes
to be wide open on a long night.
How cruel you are!
Would you find it unusual if I slept?

Saadi

My head forever drunk.
My dawnless night.

Fayz Kashani

My night of sorrow
is the longest night of the year.
No dawn in sight.

Mohtasham Kashani

A life that lasts forever is not enough.
I take delight in my torment
on the longest night of the year.

Vahshi Bafqi

Many stories in the heart have I
to tell the morning breeze.
How unlucky I am
that this night has no dawn.

Hafez

Past midnight.
All eyes resting,
save mine and Parvin's.

Saadi

Every night I sleep beside sorrow.
Far am I from your arms.

Anvari

Keep hidden
your nightly sorrow and daily suffering.
Let patience summon hope.

Jami

Drunk from being awake all night.
Pen in hand, like a sword.

Nezami

Night after night
people kept awake
because of my wailing.
Alas!
The one I hope might hear me
sleeps soundly.

Hatef Esfehani

Days of sorrow.
Nights of sighs and tears.

Fayze Kashani

All night you slept.
Nothing for you from dawn's nightingale.

Saadi

Neither day nor night
did I ever see her.
But my days and nights were spent
longing for her.

Foroughi Bastami

Such nights are not for sleeping.
Tonight, all night,
is the time for solitude.

Saadi

Night binds my hands, keeping me from work.
My hands dedicated all night to night.

Rumi

Night of separation.
I have no need of the silk blanket.
For a lonely man, the night is long.

Saadi

Whenever at night
I mentioned the flame of my scorched heart,
I lit a candle and burnt the butterfly.

Helali Jagata'i

Those with no experience of separation,
not even for a night,
can never understand the sorrow of my nights
when the beloved is far from me.

Attar

Night.
Dark.
Beloved.
Far away.
No companion.
O separation!
Kill me.
I am lonely.

Abū-Sa'īd Abul-Khayr

Weeping.
Tears.
Every night.
She captivated me.
She freed herself.
O God!
How can anyone treat the wretched so badly?

Vahshi Bafqi

Ask the physician about my suffering and pain.
Ask the patient how long is the night.

Baba Tahir

Extreme are my nightly tears.
For how long can someone weep nightly tears?

Attar

Endless night.
I am awake.
I long for morning.
I hope your scent brings me morning breeze.

Saadi

Night, all night,
I pray that you stand in my shoes.
I long for you to fall in love with someone cruel.
He will punish you.

Vahshi Bafqi

Every day you curse me one thousand times.
For one thousand nights
I prayed for you.

Anvari

Tonight, a night with no dawn.
My useless prayers.

Vahshi Bafqi

Every night like a burning flame.
Dead at dawn.
O beloved!
Today I cannot tell night from dawn.

Rumi

Every night with my drum and harp
I deviate from the path of piety,
a path I now long to follow.
Such a strange story!

Hafez

No words, save those in remembrance of God.
Conceal nightly prayers from all.

Abū-Sa'īd Abul-Khayr

My night of solitude.
She planned to slay me.
She thought she was doing me a favour.

Hafez

Not for a single night
is dust from your estate far from me,
even if guards are everywhere.

Khaqani

Through the days of my life
I have woven no hope
into the dark night of your hair.
My desire to kiss your mouth is abandoned.

Hafez

If you have no desire for us,
grant us your vision
so at night I can share with it my hidden secrets.

Saadi

My life is all night.
No candles needed.
No light required.
You breathe and the morning unsheathes its sword.

Saib Tabrizi

Midnight.
Dreams of you attacked like an army.
Without those dreams
my soul would have left the encampment long before
night.

Abū-Saʾīd Abul-Khayr

Not a night goes by
without your image
in my eye.

Salman Savoji

Water your vines
with midnight tears
and from them sunbeams will emerge.

Iqbal

Night arrived.
I embraced the sorrow of separation.
Tears, the companions of my weeping eyes.

Abū-Saʾīd Abul-Khayr

One night the spring cloud wept.
Life, a neverending stream of tears.

Iqbal

Night of separation.
Embers of fire,
not tears,
issue from my eyes.

Baba Tahir

Night.
I returned from your estate with wet eyes,
thinking about the day
your skirt was in my hand.

Vahshi Bafqi

Deepest night.
Whoever does not shed gemlike tears
will never attain the gem of union.

Foroughi Bastami

If my weeping during the day has no effect,
what say you to the force of nightly tears?

Vahshi Bafqi

I hoped tears might be a solution.
Alas! Alas!
On that night of union they would not flow.

Rudaki

On the day of separation
I understood how valuable was
the night of union.
I was ignorant of its value.
That night was divine night.

Saadi

Every night I await her call.
Not a single night passed when my ears were not alert,
awaiting her call.

Vahshi Bafqi

Night of separation.
Last day of my life.
Tears are my companions.

Foroughi Bastami

The laughter and tears of lovers come from another place.
I write poetry at night.
At dawn I weep.

Hafez

543

Nothing for us this night of union.
By the time you teasingly begin to undress,
morning has arrived.

Saib Tabrizi

She is not here.
But night's full moon
resembles her beauty.

Ubayd Zakani

Night.
All night until morning
you are my companion.
Day.
I work.
You are my business.

Fayz Kashani

Contemplating you tonight
is more joyful than sleep.
In the lover's house, sleeping beside the beloved.

Saadi

Every night I ask you for union.
No request more joyful.

Khaqani

544

Night began.
You abandoned me.
You belittled me.
Dawn.
I returned alone
and apologised.

Vahshi Bafqi

At night all doors are closed.
Access only for lovers.

Abū-Saʾīd Abul-Khayr

Yesterday at dawn she promised to meet us.
I worry that dark fortune
will keep night from becoming day.

Foroughi Bastami

Do not miss tonight.
Do not postpone things until tomorrow.
There is no tomorrow for the dark night of a crazed man.

Khwaju Kermani

The more difficult dark night is for you,
the more important it is
to ask morning for a remedy.

Fayz Kashani

Night,
all night,
hoping for a beloved
whose face shines like the morning.
No morning can make the world as bright
as does the beloved.

Saadi

All day have I worried.
What will be delivered from my pregnant night?

Fayz Kashani

I sigh in remembrance of the candle of your face.
It spreads light across dark night.

Foroughi Bastami

You are with me.
I fear your departure.
Day.
I count moments.
Night.
I count stars.

Roudaki

Day and night
do guides of the path
contemplate your grandeur.

Attar

Key to the treasure of desire
are nightly weeping, morning prayer.
Take this path and join with the beloved.

Hafez

Night.
Awake.
Night.
Lovers reveal secrets.
Night.
They fly around the beloved's estate.

Abū-Sa'īd Abul-Khayr

O friends!
Awake at night.
Candle and wine and the lonely beloved await.

Rumi

Alas!
Long nights without you.
Alas!
Without you!
Your alluring sleep.

Abū-Sa'īd Abul-Khayr

The ignorant man complains that life is short.
Night seems long to those who are awake.

Saib Tabrizi

Whoever has seen those nighttime beauties
will not want to sleep.
He runs from sleep.

Rumi

Sun rises.
Night departs.
The beloved's attention arrives upon us like an army.
The suffering depart.

Rumi

Caravan of night, what news of morning?
Bird of Solomon, what news from Sheba?

Saadi

Night departed.
The moon disappeared.
Hopefully morning will arrive.
Sunrise.

Shah Nematollah Vali

Unaware of awakened eyes are the ignorant.
Their hearts have stopped.
The value of dark night is unknown to them.

Saib Tabrizi

Night after night
the soul runs in one direction.
Morning brings it back.

Rumi

O young man!
Night so dark.
But morning
brings brightness
and shining sun.

Shah Nematollah Vali

Morning overtakes night.
Night veils its face.

Attar

We see the sun at night.
How unexpected it is to see the sun at night.

Shah Nematollah Vali

You are the sun.
How surprising that you appear at night.
You show yourself and night turns to day.

Khaqani

Those who breath like fire through the night
give their lives,
like candles,
to reach the morning breeze.

Said Tabrizi

Our moon emerged
like a sun
at midnight.

Shah Nematollah Vali

Hiding itself from view,
thus did divine night become all light.

Shaykh Bahai

Blame me not
if this divine night
I have drunk a cup of wine.
The beloved arrived joyfully.
A cup sat on the shelf.

Hafez

Divine night.
Every angel present.
O cupbearer!
Do not let me stay sober tonight.

Fayz Kashani

If one day the wine I drink is impure,
my hangover will mean ten nights of sleeplessness.

Ubayd Zakani

A night of wine-drinking
is not worth
a morning hangover.

Saadi

A night of wine-drinking will wreck my sleep.
If I complain to sunshine, the day will fall asleep.

Hafez

Before sunrise
your companions tell the tale
of nighttime wine-drinking
and the journey made by the moon.

Vahshi Bafqi

Me, drunk.
Love like a pickpocket.
Midnight.
My willpower taken from me.

Attar

If Khwaju drinks wine in the darkness of night,
let him drink.
Even Khidr finds the water of life amid darkness.

Khwaju Kermani

Night.
Penetrating moonlight.
Drink wine.
There can be no better moment than this.

Khayyam

You spent the day,
until night,
in a dark mood.
Spend your night with the light of wine.

Khaqani

Night passed.
You,
pious one,
drank no wine.
The rogues' festivities do not befit your station.

Orfi Shirazi

O cupbearer!
Worry not about our tomorrow.
Bring the cup.
Night will pass.

Khayyam

On the night of union
not once did Helali
put down the cup of wine.
Was it the cup of your lips that made him so drunk?

Helali Jagata'i

Dark night.
Stony ground.
Me, drunk.
The cup fell from my hand but was unbroken.

Baba Taher

Eventually,
one night,
I shall complain to morning tears.
I shall demand justice from this cruel beloved.

Foroughi Bastami

Smelling good news of union,
every night until dawn
I place the burning light of morning
into the path of the wind.

Hafez

The night of separation is dark as your hair.
Hopeful am I
that morning nears.

Salman Savoji

Dew reached the sun by being beside the flower.
The eyes of those awake
through the night
are near union.

Saib Tabrizi

I no longer worry about dark night.
For every night there is day.

Saadi

These burning tears make a difference.
Dark night followed by sunlit dawn.

Foroughi Bastami

Our joyous nights of union are over.
Our separation will also end.

Hafez

Eventually this dark night of separation will end.
Eventually will come relief from my pain.

Iraqi

Stars carried dark night into the sun.
I have hope for my mourning heart.

Saib Tabrizi

O novice musician!
Play simply.
Tonight is the night for the festivities of lovers.

Attar

For years has my joy
been in dark night.
Much needed dawn.

Anvari

Unveil your face in darkest of night
and even a blind man will find his way.

Abū-Sa'īd Abul-Khayr

The cruel cannot defeat your followers.
The army of night dies
when attacked by the sun.

Anvari

O God, such a night is tonight!
A star has risen.
No longer am I in love with sun or moon.

Saadi

Hafez!
Gone is the night of separation.
The good scent of union is here.
Congratulations on your happiness, you lover of
madness.

Hafez

Her face turns every night of the world into day.
At morning she contemplates every sky.

Saadi

May those hearts
toiling all night,
seeking your union,
be joyous at night.

Attar

Every night is for us a night of union.
Every day is for us a day of joy.

Shah Nematollah Vali

Such a blessed dawn and joyous night it was
on the divine night when this promise of a gift
was made to me.

Hafez

Night departed.
Morning arrived.
Sorrow departed.
Victory arrived.
Sun shining.
Let it be like this forever.

Rumi

Day ruled over night.
The cup paid a visit to the lips.

Khaqani

Day and night of separation ended.
I read my fortune in the book.
The star passed over.
Culmination of bad fortune.

Hafez

558

Thank God.
The night of separation is now over.
The sun of union rose over the horizon of fortune.

Vahshi Bafqi

Worries of long nights
and sorrows of the heart
ended beneath the shadow
of the beloved's hair.

Hafez

A beloved at our home tonight.
To us she is kind.
So blessed is her arrival
that the moon sits under our feet.

Foroughi Bastami

All treasure given by God to Hafez
was given because of nightly prayer
and dawn incantations.

Hafez

A blessed and dear divine night.
I long for such a night,
sleeping beside you until morning.

Hafez

Tonight is divine night
of which people of solitude speak.
O God!
Which star has been affected by fortune?

Hafez

Such a strange thing.
Sunlight entered my eyes at night.

Attar

At the heart of night
I became aware
of the world
beyond this world.
With this knowledge I lost consciousness.

Fayz Kashani

The beloved has arrived.
Make space for her beside you.
Night of separation
became morning union.

Fayz Kashani

Without nights of fear,
Saadi would not appreciate
the value of this day.

Saadi

Tonight is not just a night of union.
Tonight is my divine night.
Tonight is better than one thousand days of spring.

Helali Jagata'i

Every night has a day.
Every day has an end.
There is no end to our night of union.

Saadi

O heart!
Be patient.
Worry not.
Eventually this night
will turn to day.

Hafez

Night
Poetry from the
Contemporary Persian Canon

Selected and adapted by
Abbas Kiarostami

Night.
All night.
Throughout.

Shamloo

Night,
in every direction,
as far as the eye can see.

Sayeh

Night.
Quiet.
Taverns silent.

Shafiei Kadkani

Alas, how dark is this night!

Sohrab Sepehri

Night long.
Desert dark.

Nima

Night
has no intention
of sleeping.

Shamloo

How heavy is night?

Hossein Monzavi

Night.
Eloquent, pure, open.

Sohrab Sepehri

There is truth in night.
Hidden truth.

Nader Naderpour

Night, it seems, is wet.

Sohrab Sepehri

Night seems to be stubborn.
The heart has an excuse.

Siavash Kasrai

Behind closed doors.
A night filled with daggers and enemies.

> Shamloo

We lived amid injury, night, flame.

> Shafiei Kadkani

In darkness of night
no one knows of the knife in my back.
In darkness of night
a dagger sticks in my shoulder.

> Hamid Mosadegh

What unseen dagger
on this moonless night
has caused me such pain?

> Ali Salehi

O gloomy night!
How suffocated I feel.

> Siavash Kasrai

I was born at the end of the day.
Because of this
my path crossed the city of night.

Shamloo

"This night never ends," I said.
"This wind never ends.
This strange torture never ends."

Ali Salehi

A calling invites me from afar.
My feet in tar of night.

Sohrab Sepehri

I am soaked in the smell of night.
Where have I come from?

Forough Farrokhzad

With a backpack filled with night,
a night of no remembrances,
with a backpack filled with night,
a night of fireballs,
I walk alone
down a wet road.

Manouchehr Atashi

I swear to God
that I am wracked with sorrow and anguish.
Night.
As always,
sorrow in my heart,
deeper than all other nights.

Hamid Mosadegh

In the hard night of ceaseless snow
I stopped at this caravansary.
Because of old age
I was tired from the start.

Shamloo

Night darkened and fell ill.
Wakefulness raided the eyes.

Forough Farrokhzad

I became night.
I became moon.
I came undone.

Nosrat Rahmani

If a bird sings deep into the night,
from my eyes
flow tears of sympathy.

Shamloo

The one who weeps
with the unrolling of night
is engaged in a secret dialogue with me.

Nima

Here am I
this night of sorrow and warm tears.

Fereidoon Tavallali

I have drunk the night.
I weep for broken branches.

Sohrab Sepehri

Like tears have I dropped
from the blind eyes of night.
I have lost my way this dark night.

Nader Naderpour

Evil lurks within this night.
It makes me weep.
Morning envies my honesty.

Hamid Mosadegh

At night
is the enchanting moon
drowned in water.
Weeping stars all around.

Shahriar

From depths of night
a star arrived breathlessly,
fell into the waves of my tears,
and died.

Manouchehr Atashi

O night!
O snowy night!
O winter night!
Tears choke me,
like dark clouds in the sky.

Nader Naderpour

O night!
O night of solitude!
I ask you:
In which house burns that shining star?

Hossein Monzavi

Alas!
Here am I,
starless night.

Manouchehr Atashi

We,
witnesses of history,
found history by digging into dark night.

Reza Baraheni

At night
are trees like motionless graves
and valleys like our abandoned sanctuary.

Yadollah Royaee

On this night of separation
love tortures us.
Such pain,
like the confines of a grave.

Shahriar

Night paints me the colour of oblivion.
There is no one to bring me a lantern
deep in my grave.

Fereidoon Tavallali

My father talked about light.
Night became filled with night.
"Another day gone," I said to myself.

Sayeh

Feverishly and with patience
I have built a home
on the other side of night.

Sohrab Sepehri

Night arrived.
My melancholic heart
longed for home.

Sayeh

At what moment of night
did that comet pass over our roof?

Hossein Monzavi

An ancestral home is night.
I love it out of habit.

Javad Mojabi

It was night and me.
It was sorrow and me.
It was sorrow and night.
Sorrow was drunk.
Me, drunk.

Nosrat Rahmani

Cold drops of rain
keep falling upon my ashes
this wet night.

Reza Baraheni

Now,
every night in this sorrowful abyss,
I bury empty coffins.

Shamloo

A night of exile made colourful by crystals,
by light and decoration.
Nothing to do with me.
I am unhappy here.

Simin Behbahani

O empress of night and poetry!
Tell me,
who has clipped the harp's hair?

Nosrat Rahmani

Light.
A bat...
Light.
A bat...
Light.
A bat...
Light.
A bat...

Shamloo

Without your breath
I cannot recall night's scent.

Yadollah Royaee

My heart,
trapped in your love,
has been weeping night after night.

Rahi Mo'ayyeri

O you!
Without you I am destroyed.
Without you night is exhausted.

Nosrat Rahmani

O lantern of sorrow!
Be a companion on my path,
this night of misery,
this narrow path.

Siavash Kasrai

Without your name
my day is like night,
as if fever has taken hold.

Nima

In the middle of the path,
between us and the night of existence,
our lantern is dead.
No light.

Sohrab Sepehri

Your face is like the moon.
Without it my night wears black.
But I dress even blacker than my night.

Shahriar

O shining star!
Remember my dark night.
I am like a new moon
with sorrowful head upon my knees.

Shafiei Kadkani

Open the window.
I can no longer suffer the confines of night.

Sayeh

This night smells of winter.
I am unable to believe in spring.

Nader Naderpour

I see neither night and stars
nor morning and its beautiful dawn.

Siavash Kasrai

All night
I worry about what my day will be.

Nima

Fearful am I
of both day and night.

Nima

Night filled my eyes with darkness.
Every spring dried up.

Nader Naderpour

This is me,
held captive by dark night.
All night I wait to hear the caravan bell.

Nima

Night.
No time for festivities of angels.
No world of secrets within its delicate silence.

Manouchehr Atashi

How ugly you must be
to blame the darkness
on this bright night.

Sepanlou

In my dreams
I still see unknown gifts of night.

Sohrab Sepehri

I bowed down before
the mystery of night's secretive night.

Reza Baraheni

Night.
Filled with profiles of objects and wind.

Yadollah Royaee

O night!
You, evil and frightening.
For how long will you let my soul burn?

Nima

A night of callousness is here.
Let us avoid it.

Sohrab Sepehri

Never look upon night as safe.

Sepanlou

Night needs no sun.

Yadollah Royaee

Night or day?
Time undecided.

Hamid Mosadegh

No difference between
night's beginning and morning's end.

Rahi Mo'ayyeri

Strange days.
Dawn, prophet of sorrow.
Night, interpreter of disappointment.

Nader Naderpour

For centuries perhaps
will come no dawn of words
on this all-consuming night.

Shafiei Kadkani

This is no night for agreement.
Turmoil this night.
The key to morning
lies in the depths of the lagoon.
This rotten night.

Nosrat Rahmani

Some do not know
how many birds return to their nest,
night after night,
thirsty and with no place in the sky.

Ali Salehi

I was like a bridge over the river of night.
This side a bank of emotions,
the other a meadow of wisdom.

Reza Baraheni

Night.
Barren cloud.
No moon in the sky.
It was night...
night...
night...
night.

Nosrat Rahmani

Through my eyes
life seems like night
without moonlight.

Fereydoon Moshiri

Silent sea.
Realm of silent moonlit night.

Shafiei Kadkani

All night
heartache dripped
from dark branches.

Forough Farrokhzad

Night spread its shadow.
Crows with tired wings
arrived thirsty.

Sayeh

In heart of night,
in silence of valley and moonlight,
is the silent body of a partridge
with a ripped heart.

Fereydoon Moshiri

Tonight.
A night of turmoil.
Night of turmoil.
It is a night of turmoil.

Hossein Monzavi

Night
has stolen the flowerpot
from our window.

Sohrab Sepehri

Suddenly
the window filled with night,
a night full
of many empty sounds.

Forough Farrokhzad

If there is no good reason
for night to be beautiful,
then why is it so?
For whom is it beautiful?

Shamloo

Because of your presence,
night is beautiful.
O night!
Let them call you
a metaphor for darkness.

Shams Langroudi

How decorative must be
the frost flower
in the bedroom of a man
dreaming of a flame
in coldness of night.

Sepanlou

Is inner heaviness a delusion
in night's darkness,
or some cumbersome dream?

Nima

Symphony of night
drips slowly
upon sunset's silent melancholy.

Shamloo

Night turns pavements into brides
wearing counterfeit jewelry.
Row upon row of jewelry.

Sepanlou

Sleep, my little angel.
Sleep, my little son.
Close your eyes.
Night is here.
Close your eyes.
This dark demon has arrived
with bloody hand
and smiling lips.

Forough Farrokhzad

No longer is the night
studded with pearls.
No longer is the night sky
brightly lit as before.

Shamloo

Glimmers from a feeble lantern
tell the tale of dark night.

Sayeh

No light across the night.
No bellowing across the meadow.

Shamloo

Even if every star becomes a moon,
night is still night.

Akhavan

Night.
Filled with stars.
Breeze blowing.
Lips silent.

Manouchehr Atashi

O night!
You are like a hyena.
I wish you would die
with no sequins and no stars.
I wish you would die
with no light and no morning glory.

Ali Salehi

Talking only about night and stars.
Arising.
Choosing.
Departing.

Ali Salehi

Pitiful that man,
talking to himself that night,
under the ceiling of night.

Shafiei Kadkani

Sorrow has blinded us this dark night.
Where is the cluster of stars?

Siavash Kasrai

All those people
who talk all night
of stars and moon
as the moon passes by.

Shams Langroudi

Crickets all night.
Crickets until dawn.

Shamloo

In its solitude
the stork of sorrow
confided to itself.
 "O night, how cruel are you!
You scoundrel!"

Akhavan

Night,
silent and indigo.
Me,
burning and patient.

Simin Behbahani

It is said
that the sun's redemption
is an ancient secret,
a sign of night's disappointment.

Ali Salehi

Every night
a rush of thunder.
Every night
a rush of lightning.
Every night
a rush of growth and movement.

Shafiei Kadkani

Like a dark flower
night has spread its petals.
Rain,
drop by drop.
Scent of acacia.

Nader Naderpour

Night.
Settling slowly
on gloomy windowpanes
like feverish ash.

Forough Farrokhzad

Nights of poets in captivity.
Indigo nights.
Dark nights I know nothing of.

Shafiei Kadkani

Night, endless night.
Gardens filled with flowers.
Sounds of poems
sung by night walkers.

Hamid Mosadegh

Night.
Aged night.
Homelessness makes it worse still.
Masks behind masks.
Torture behind windows.

Nosrat Rahmani

No light through the night.
No cries of protest through the day.

Shamloo

From the sea comes every sound.
Night lost amid crashing waves.

Sohrab Sepehri

Night.
Shadow of everything upside down.
Restless sea enveloped by its own waves.

Nima

From glorious ruins of night
rose a song
of neither bird nor ocean.

Shamloo

Painful night it was.
Silence and madness.
Air filled with powdered metal.
Stars like bloodspots.

Nosrat Rahmani

Within night
treasures retain their value.
Beyond night
suffering maintains its value.

Nima

Night is a long confession.
It is a long confession.
Night.
Freedom's shout.

Shamloo

Here is night.
Trees awake.
Birds trembling.

Shams Langroudi

From inside an oven
the burnt oak branch
sends sparkling stars into the night,
amid indigo smoke.

Fereydoun Tavallali

Night fire burning.
Through the smoke
is the outline of faraway ruins.

Sohrab Sepehri

A quiet forest path.
All that remains is a string of stones
forming an oven,
full of cold ashes,
from nights long ago.

Nima

It seems that all nights have been one night
and all days have been one day.
I have lived for just one day and one night.

Bijan Jalali

Neither light of day
nor darkness of night.

Ali Salehi

All days are one day,
piece by piece,
amid endless night.

Shams Langroudi

Day, feet in mud.
Night, bewildered and dull.
Day, no.
Night, no.
Neither.

Yadollah Royaee

O companion!
Go light the flame of wine.
Night and day are one.

Akhavan

Night
A wonderful metaphor.
Night.
Forced to drink
from the breasts of a broken lantern.

Ali Salehi

Like a guard with torch in hand,
night ambles across the sleepy city.

Forough Farrokhzad

The mouth of a blossom
stayed closed
in the night of the garden.

Sayeh

Night landed.
It slipped on the mountain.

Fereydoun Tavallali

Stars are white bees
on night's moist blossoms.

Shams Langroudi

Night was arriving.
Sad,
starless,
joyless,
moonless.

Fereydoon Moshiri

Let us not be overwhelmed
by the hardship of this
burdensome night.

Sayeh

Night.
Empty of moonlight.
Night.
Empty of stars.
Rainless gray clouds across the sky.

Hamid Mosaddegh

Now the tired night
passes by box trees.

Shamloo

Like struck matches,
one by one are lightning strikes extinguished.
Night remains night.

Shafiei Kadkani

Dark nights.
Melancholic nights.
Silent nights.

Fereydoon Moshiri

Flowing river
pulls in darkness of night,
then washes it away.

Bijan Jalali

My tired body burns.
Such severe fever.
This is night.
Yes.
Night.

Nima

Every night
my ardour and ecstasy
grow stronger.
Alas, my night!
Alas, my night!

Rahi Mo'ayyeri

On these nights
when flower is fearful of leaf,
leaf of wind,
and wind of cloud.
On these nights…

Shafiei Kadkani

Alas!
I am dead.
Night,
it seems,
is the continuation
of the same futile night.

Forough Farrokhzad

The plectrum of night
is broken
by the weeping of my flute.

Ali Salehi

My ship on ocean of night.
Hopeful morning light,
from port of salvation,
glimmers not.

Shamloo

Night.
Here are all those benighted
whose eyes have never seen morning.

Siavash Kasrai

Here,
at night,
all light extinguished.
No daytime turmoil.

Shafiei Kadkani

In clenched darkness of frightful night
a drop of blood dripped
from the throat of the night bird.

Nosrat Rahmani

Night.
Evil and dark like night.
Filled with pain.

Hamid Mosadegh

What is darkness of night?
Of whose dark soul
is night the shadow?

Forough Farrokhzad

Grass
on night's path.
Disheveled.

Sayeh

Night
wearing armour of rain
races on its horse.

Shafiei Kadkani

May curses from the star
be upon confounded night.

Ali Salehi

Roofs.
Bent under weight of night.

Shamloo

I need an escape
from the trap of night.

Siavash Kasrai

Night attacked.
It plundered.
Hot blood of evening twilight.

Sayeh

Night.
Overrun by cold moon.

Sepanlou

A colour
beside this infinite night
has expired.

Sohrab Sepehri

One can see the night of my autumn
from springtime morning.

Shafiei Kadkani

Bird of night,
weeping,
departed her nest.

Sayeh

Night creeps down
from indigo sky.

Sayeh

Night, dark and cold.
Dawn, hidden.
Path, wandering.
A passerby.
Lonely.

Shamloo

Night landed too heavy.
No survivors.

Nader Naderpour

Night knows
that its companions
will keep going.

Sepanlou

Darker than night,
riding atop
wandering wind.

Shamloo

Night,
like a black snake,
crawling on delicate, colourful curtains.

Forough Farrokhzad

Night.
Darkness is overly friendly
with this night.

Nima

Night.
Silent,
without moonlight.

Yadollah Royaee

Night.
Too heavy, too dark.
Like a nightmare.

Sayeh

My heart asks me to weep.
I do so until
the last bird of night is silent.

Nader Naderpour

I have closed every door.
Night is with me.
My night, dark as a grave.

Nima

Night's magical hand
closes the door
on me and sorrow.

Sohrab Sepehri

I raced through the plain of night.
I am silent.
I am a wave.
I have lost myself.
I am unconscious.

Nosrat Rahmani

Dark night.
I took root and grew.
Thirsty,
on the riverbank.

Forough Farrokhzad

My feeble cries.
I am like a bird of night.

Rahi Mo'ayyeri

Day is not my companion.
Night is not my confidant.

Nima

Tears because of this night.
Such a night.
No dawn.

Shafiei Kadkani

Night.
Fever and anguish are my companions.

Rahi Mo'ayyeri

Look how we burnt
on this dark night.

Sayeh

From inside dark night
my instinct is to look
in an unseen direction.

Nima

Cold winter night.
Even the sun's furnace
burns weaker than
the warm furnace
of my heart.

Nima

To me,
night and day seem to last a year,
although to my eyes is life
but an instant.

Shamloo

In dark desert of night
where is the path to ambition?
Where is the path to the day of deliverance?

Nima

Night again.
Another story of insomnia.
Night, halfway through.
I passed into unconsciousness.

Hamid Mosadegh

Unseen seashore.
Hope is strong.
Awake am I,
bringing night
towards moonlit meadow.

Manouchehr Atashi

Like a dream
I passed by in regret.
Night slept.
No one intends to sleep.

Shamloo

Fortunate is the one
in this frightful night of life
carried away to sleep's magical city
by peacefulness of heart.

Siavash Kasrai

If one night you achieve sleep,
remember those frustrated by night.

Simin Behbahani

Sleeping pill.
Sleeping pill.
Sleeping pill.
Night again.
Where then is the sun?

Shafiei Kadkani

From night until dawn
I sit awake in my cold grave.
Sleep stirs not in my eyes.

Shamloo

O so many dawnless nights!
Me, exhausted,
in my bed of insomnia.

Shamloo

Night.
Heavy with fear.
A world immersed in sleep.
I am awake in my delusion.

Sohrab Sepehri

My awakened eyes,
contemplating skies
and night's pleasing secrets.
This sleeping world.

Akhavan

Here are we,
my eyes and night,
sleepless both.
No moonlight.

Hossein Monzavi

You opened your eyes.
Night descended upon me.

Sohrab Sepehri

I did not sleep at night.
Nightly turmoil.

Akhavan

Night departed.
Such a fever in my body.

Nima

From night until dawn
I cannot sleep
because of tears
in my heart.

Rahi Mo'ayyeri

O friend!
Ask me how long
is the night of sorrows.

Nosrat Rahmani

It began with the first star,
with the first cup of wine.
Our night.

Hamid Mosaddegh

Night passes through.
Do not pass up wine.

Rahi Mo'ayyeri

Pour the wine drop by drop.
I worry that this night will outlast our wine.

Nosrat Rahmani

Night,
tired of its dark hesitation.
I took my shadow to the tavern.

Akhavan

Night runs from me.
I run from night.
Where are you?
Where are you?
Come, pour the wine.

Nosrat Rahmani

Night arrived.
My nightly companion did not.

Nader Naderpour

The night bird's weeping was silenced.
There is no one to bring us a cup of wine.

Nosrat Rahmani

Call the drunkards of midnight,
those thirsty rogues.
Shout down the alleyways again.

Shafiei Kadkani

Moon.
Night.
Companion.
Cup of wine.

Nima

Silence.
Complete stillness.
All hands and feet
in tar of night.

Sohrab Sepehri

When?
Where?
O I know not!
O you cupbearer!
O you night!
I wait here.

Fereydoon Moshiri

Cold night.
Unhappy am I.
Too far to go.
My tired feet.

Sohrab Sepehri

Night is all joy.
No sorrow here.
Pour a cup of wine, another cup, and yet another cup.
Me, blowing freely in the wind.

Nosrat Rahmani

It is not night.
There is no moon.
Neither day nor sun.
We stand outside time.

Shamloo

When one hundred stars,
from farthest distance of night,
rained down upon the sheltering sky,
you closed your door
and chose not to look.

Shafiei Kadkani

I have become a rabid wolf,
a gluttonous stray,
on this wintry, barren plain.
Night.

Akhavan

Perpetual grief.
Accumulated sorrow.
The night I see.

Nosrat Rahmani

Day or night?
O friend!
Neither.
Eternal dusk.

Forough Farrokhzad

All is silent.
A fragile wall between night and day
which you fail to recognise.

Shafiei Kadkani

Transformation and flight
from darkness
made morning preferable to night.

Nima

Weather, cold.
A heart in pain.
Night, silent.
Me, lonely.

Fereydoun Tavallali

Why this fear of darkness?
Night filled with diamond droplets.

Forough Farrokhzad

Tears of night settled upon ash.
Dawn.
The eyes of stars are astonished.

Yadollah Royaee

Fear of destruction
in the small city
of my night.

Forough Farrokhzad

Desert nights
are for the
silent solitude
of wind.

Siavash Kasrai

Sorrow and I
in this nostalgic night
of barren desert.
Much has happened to me.

Nosrat Rahmani

Let us pass through this hard night.

Sayeh

I have broken the final star of night.

Manouchehr Atashi

You.
Night made colourful through dreams of you.

Forough Farrokhzad

A pen
the colour of night
writes brightly.

Nima

Friday night.
Palpitations.

Sohrab Sepehri

Night has built a fence around me.
I contemplate you.

Shamloo

Shine like moonlight,
every night,
upon my bed.

Shahriar

I kiss the night.
It searches for you in the distance.

Javad Mojabi

You run away.
All night my mind is restless.

Yadollah Royaee

O moon!
The night bird sang continuously
in the heart of night.
Alas, a lover's night!

Rahi Mo'ayyeri

Night.
Sea.
Me
and meeting you
on this path.

Nima

If night arrives without you
it is not night.

Javad Mojabi

Rest not
for even a moment
upon the skirt of night.
Shine in darkness
like a glowworm.

Nosrat Rahmani

Although morning will come,
shine down upon my prison one night.
Although there are candles,
I will burn for you.

Shahriar

Night blossomed
in the eyes of Leila.
In mine,
the fiery flower of love.

Forough Farrokhzad

The freshness of your hair caressed the night.

Hamid Mosadegh

Your body white as snow.
Its scent runs
through the darkness
of my night.

Nosrat Rahmani

Make me dark,
as dark as possible.
Pour into me
the night of your body.

Sohrab Sepehri

Night.
When autumn attacked
I was separated from my tree.

Yadollah Royaee

Why so fearful?
Let me travel
through the night of your arms.

Sohrab Sepehri

I wish the moon
could watch me dance
like an autumn leaf
at midnight.

Forough Farrokhzad

Let wind twist with night.
Let willows dance in wind.

Shamloo

In this darkness,
on this dark and evil night,
I make a pilgrimage to your dark hair.

Hamid Mosadegh

Let your hair spill out.
Scatter night into the night.

Nosrat Rahmani

I wish my hand
could find a way
through the night maze
of your hair.

Hamid Mosadegh

Our hands,
in love,
have built a bridge across the night,
bearing words of perfume,
of light and soft winds.
People are talking.

Forough Farrokhzad

A bitter and tired night.
Play the game.
Fear not failure.

Nosrat Rahmani

Night.
Desire for flesh.
Making love.
Night.
Sleeping.
Arousal.
Satisfaction.

Sepanlou

I will not allow my night
to be freed from
a warm and delicate body.

Manouchehr Atashi

Dark is the night.
Everyone but me has a beloved by their side.
Morning arrived.
But not my beloved.

Nima

Night of melancholy.
The patience of a lonely man,
like a mirror with no reflection.
A house of solitude.
Emptiness.

Sayeh

Transparent night.
Sound of a cup
of solitude.

Sohrab Sepehri

Night.
Sorrow surrounds me.
O friend!
Come sit before me.

Akhavan

Sorrow of separation darkens my bright day.
You, moon, belong to dark night.

Shahriar

Far from you.
Nights of sorrow.
Life spent in darkness.
This is death.
We call it life.

Shafiei Kadkani

It seems that from the start of night
tomorrow's sorrow hides behind the door.

Shamloo

With hands did I caress the night.
Whispered prayers creep through
my awakened fingers.

Sohrab Sepehri

Tonight I escape sweet sleep.
More joyful is to dream of you.

Forough Farrokhzad

This long night kills lovers,
unless I am promised union with you.

Sayeh

Whispers of night made me drunk.
The window of dreams was open.

Sohrab Sepehri

Her dream departed through my window.
Night continued.
I continued.

Yadollah Royaee

At night
every word forms in me
a star.

Ali Salehi

Blood splashed on western horizon.
Nearby night.

Shafiei Kadkani

Night sang its anthem.
Now the window's turn.

Sohrab Sepehri

Night.
Full of cruelty.
Watch moon and water.
Break your prayers.
Break your fast.
Break the cup.
Put an end to failure.

Nosrat Rahmani

Night.
Home to stars.
Let us spend all night beside the fireplace
and listen until dawn to a story.

Ali Salehi

Night.
Poplar trees in line, held captive.
From their highest branches they send messages.
Their shadows whisper.

Yadollah Royaee

Night entered the moon's bridal chamber
as musicians of Venus played.

Shahriar

Midnight.
Swaying fruit
made strange the shape of trees.

Sohrab Sepehri

Time passed.
Night descended on bare branches.

Forough Farrokhzad

When Venus is a window to bright night,
you are the window to the suns in my heart.

Shafiei Kadkani

You arrive.
Night departs every face.
No more secrets in life.

Sohrab Sepehri

Put aside your excuses.
Sit down.
Of night there remains but a moment.

Nosrat Rahmani

Long night.
Listening to companions.

Nima

How far did I travel with you last night?

Akhavan

Night.
Yes, a wakeful night.
Thief and police both asleep.

Nosrat Rahmani

Empty house.
Ecstatic guard.
In the heart of night
no worries about being
or not being.

Nima

Night.
All paths seem the same.

Javad Mojabi

Night halfway done.
The guest went home.

Sepanlou

Night.
A journey through poetry.

Nosrat Rahmani

Night.
Pregnant with a poem.

Hossein Monzavi

I write poetry.
My words:
night, river, seashore.

Shafiei Kadkani

Night.
Let us smell the scent of melody
and hide our faces.

Sohrab Sepehri

The god of light fills the cup of night with his song.

Sohrab Sepehri

Many nights
did dreams steer my boat
close to moonlight's boat.

Shafiei Kadkani

Endless spring night.
I am happy for no reason.

Shams Langroudi

Since my heart learned the language of night
it has understood the reasons for many things.

Nima

Last night at midnight
we saw a new moon attended by servants.

Akhavan

How wonderful. ·
Spring's first night
was born after
winter's final day.

Nader Naderpour

Gravity of night's beauty
brings the distant dream
of reaching you
that much closer.

Forough Farrokhzad

Which shall remain:
Night,
with its intricate shelter,
or bright day?

Akhavan

I long to wash the hands and faces of stars
in the spring of night
and so shed light upon the path.

Ali Salehi

I am the firebird,
gathering up night
under my red feathers.

Siavash Kasrai

In mild autumn sunset
I stand
and salute night.

Sepanlou

O night!
Greetings.
You are the night which turns
desert wolf eyes
into sockets of faith and trust.

Forough Farrokhzad

Night whispers faded.
The dance of angels ended.

Sohrab Sepehri

Pitch your tent near night.
As the moon emerges
unsheathe your sword
and place it beside you.

Shamloo

Shadow of doubt
scattered on threshold of magical night.

Sohrab Sepehri

Such a night.
Moon, smiling.
Grass, soft.

Nima

Night.
Nightly gardens.

Akhavan

For how long must I deal with this night and silence?
Time to arise.

Sayeh

Night was the sky's black tulip.
It blossomed.

Simin Behbahani

Tonight
the path of ascension to Heaven
is clear.

Sohrab Sepehri

Keyvan became a bright star
and showed those blinded by night
in which direction to move.

Sayeh

No conversation about the sun
with those accustomed to night.

Hamid Mosadegh

No advantage to those who inhabit the night
from good news of morning.

Sayeh

Day passes.
Night comes.
It delivers up the dawn.

Simin Behbahani

One cold night,
in the garden of red roses,
I sang the song of light to water.
I gave good news of flower and bud to dawn.

Sayeh

In the tedium of night
from a distance is heard
the sound of footsteps.

Shamloo

Sudden lightning
from unknown far horizons
split the night
and shook the earth.

Reza Baraheni

Like a fireball, escaping night.
Always ready for union,
like the morning.

Siavash Kasrai

Flowers of colour
blossomed
in dust of night.

Sohrab Sepehri

Use the power of heart and hope.
Arise!
Make your night bright as day.

Nima

Arise!
The illusion of a flower
brought night to earth.

Sohrab Sepehri

Return from the path
and begin again
old stories of alleys and nights.

Yadollah Royaee

How majestic is our night
when darkness unites the city.

Siavash Kasrai

No light
at the end of this land's eternal night.
O morning!
Help us.
Nights everywhere.

Nosrat Rahmani

O young man!
Your patience has run out
this anguished dark night.
Where is your sunshine intelligence?

Shafiei Kadkani

Like me, you have fallen to the ground.
Arise!
Night has been here for a long time.
Arise!

Akhavan

Come,
let us remove the thorn of night
from the foot upon the path.

Nosrat Rahmani

I am that beautiful monster
who has stood
upon the equator of night.

Shamloo

I will open
the prison of the longest night
and escape.

Sayeh

Dogs have conquered the night,
yet our vines still creep towards the grape.

Hossein Monzavi

The sludge of night
settled at the bottom of the sun.

Nosrat Rahmani

In silence
night hears
what we see
in our dreams.

Javad Mojabi

Smell of nightly sleep.
Scent of morning awakening.

Yadollah Royaee

Nights awaiting dawn.
Fire in my heart.

Sayeh

Look not upon night as mere darkness.
Morning is born of darkness.

Nima

Silence of night, broken.
A spark lit up my melancholic heart.

Hamid Mosadegh

No.
I never believed in night.
I longed for a window beyond its confines.

Shamloo

All night, awake,
longing for morning,
longing to meet the morning sun.

Shafiei Kadkani

Redemption will come.
Dark night will turn into bright morning.

Nima

Roots of brightness split rocks of night.

Sohrab Sepehri

Night splits.
Smiles blossom.
The earth awakens.

Sohrab Sepehri

I shall not turn my back on conquering this night.

Ali Salehi

The poem everyone knows:
At dark night's end is dawn.

Nosrat Rahmani

The path began at night and reached the sun.
Now it passes the border of darkness.

Sohrab Sepehri

Worry not if night is dark and quiet.
The morning is ours.

Shafiei Kadkani

Place night between me and moon.
Awake with the caravan's early morning star.

Ali Salehi

Pure is the tree,
living on faith through the night,
awaiting morning.

Shafiei Kadkani

In this desert
rain makes night bright.
Wondrous is the chandelier
hanging from the sky.

Sepanlou

I read an unread poem.
Night was ripped to pieces.

Nosrat Rahmani

If night is dark,
believe in your heart.
Dawn closes in.

Hamid Mosadegh

Every night they bury a star on this earth.
Yet this sorrowful sky is filled with stars.

Siavash Kasrai

The kindly old sun
will remove nightly tears
from our cheeks.

Ziya Movahed

Night.
The mirror sees dawn in its dream.

Sayeh

A big white flower trembled in the water of night.

Manouchehr Atashi

O God!
Bright light everywhere.
How nightly is this night!
It has blossomed on the horizons,
like trustworthy mornings.

Reza Baraheni

Dawn uprooted night.
Night fled like a snake.

Yadollah Royaee

Desert, ready for brightness.
Night's persistence wanes.

Shamloo

How wonderful!
In the prison of darkness,
during longest nights,
you asked the sun for light.
And it rose.

Sayeh

Cherish the moment.
Watch as the sun flies into night sky.

Shamloo

On night's seashore,
where eyes of lemons were bright,
we too switched on the light.

Sepanlou

Sing in the name of red roses
in the desert of night,
and gardens will awaken
and bear fruit.

Shafiei Kadkani

Night.
When even the star is sleeping
the garden's white flowers are awake.

Siavash Kasrai

I found my hope in disappointment,
my moonlight at night,
my love in a bad year.

Shamloo

Beside this candle,
which we extinguished like this,
let night be blessed.
Congratulations to us.

Zia Movahed

On the breast of night is a white flower
with one thousand secrets of love.

Nosrat Rahmani

Night.
Breeze.
Garden.
Moonlight.
Me.
Creek.
Awakening of water.

Shafiei Kadkani

O God!
Look not upon me as cold ash.
Tonight I am the joy of water
and warmth of fire.

Nader Naderpour

I will make a path of purity
from the bazaar of dark night
to the bright city of your eyes.

Reza Baraheni

Stories should be told of this miracle.
Wind brought the song of waterfalls
into silence of night.

Nader Naderpour

Trunks of light grow in wetland darkness.
Magical night drained of colour.

Sohrab Sepehri

On helpless nights one sees good days only in dreams.

Sayeh

Night will arrive.
Does it know that this ailing person
may not live until morning?
God forbid.

Fereydoun Moshiri

Neverending sound of alarm.
All lights off.
Night.
A city unconscious, consumed by darkness.

Hamid Mosadegh

Again, another night.
A long cold night.
A night of blizzards.

Akhavan

There is nothing at the end of this night
but the light of a bright day.

Nima

This day is like night.
No one knows how it will end.
So be it.

Reza Baraheni

Night is what it was.
Darkness is what is was.
The lantern remains a symbol of hope.

Shamloo

645

Published by Sticking Place Books

Lessons with Kiarostami
Edited by Paul Cronin

A Wolf on Watch (dual-language)
Poems by Abbas Kiarostami

With the Wind (dual-language)
Poems by Abbas Kiarostami

Wind and Leaf (dual-language)
Poems by Abbas Kiarostami

Wine (dual-language)
Poetry by Hafez
Selected and adapted by Abbas Kiarostami

Tears (two volumes) (dual-language)
Poetry by Saadi
Selected and adapted by Abbas Kiarostami

Water (dual-language)
Poetry by Nima
Selected and adapted by Abbas Kiarostami

Fire (four volumes) (dual-language)
Poetry by Rumi
Selected and adapted by Abbas Kiarostami

Night (two volumes) (dual-language)
Poetry from the Classical Persian Canon
Selected and adapted by Abbas Kiarostami

Night (two volumes) (dual-language)
Poetry from the Contemporary Persian Canon
Selected and adapted by Abbas Kiarostami

In the Shadow of Trees
The Collected Poetry of Abbas Kiarostami

9 781942 782438